SO-AAA-876

T·h·e
Stay-at-Home
Parent
Survival Guide

Real-Life Advice from
Moms, Dads, and Other Experts

Christina Baglivi Tinglof

CB
CONTEMPORARY BOOKS

Library of Congress Cataloging-in-Publication Data

Tinglof, Christina Baglivi.
    The stay-at-home parent survival guide : real-life advice from moms, dads,
and other experts A to Z / Christina Baglivi Tinglof.
       p.   cm.
    Includes bibliographical references.
    ISBN 0-8092-2676-6
    1. Parents—Life skills guides.   2. Parenting.   3. Child rearing.
I. Title.
HQ755.8.T57   2000
649'.1—dc21   99-87522
                                                               CIP

Cover design by Jeanette Wojtyla
Interior design by Susan H. Hartman
Interior illustrations by Kevin Tinglof

Published by Contemporary Books
A division of NTC/Contemporary Publishing Group, Inc.
4255 West Touhy Avenue, Lincolnwood (Chicago), Illinois 60712-1975 U.S.A.
Copyright © 2000 by Christina Baglivi Tinglof
All rights reserved. No part of this book may be reproduced, stored in a retrieval
system, or transmitted in any form or by any means, electronic, mechanical,
photocopying, recording, or otherwise, without the prior written permission of
NTC/Contemporary Publishing Group, Inc.
Printed in the United States of America
International Standard Book Number: 0-8092-2676-6
00 01 02 03 04 05 CU 18 17 16 15 14 13 12 11 10 9 8 7 6 5 4 3 2 1

To Kevin, for his love, wisdom, and enormous support

Contents

Acknowledgments

A special thanks to my agent Betsy Amster, to my editor Kara Leverte, and to the staff at Contemporary Books, especially Julia Anderson. To the parenting experts and to the parents themselves who gave their time to be interviewed for this book, my deepest thank-you. To my sister, Mary Ella Donleavy, for her enormous help with researching romantic retreats. And to my husband, Kevin, and my sons, Joseph, Michael, and Matthew, for allowing me the time that I needed to write this book.

Introduction

Although the decision for me to stay home with our three young boys was an easy one, my husband, Kevin, and I knew that we would both have to make some sacrifices. He would have to become the sole breadwinner of the family and with it accept an increased sense of responsibility. I, on the other hand, would have to temporarily give up a career and part of my sanity.

I loved my job as an editorial assistant, but it didn't make sense to continue working outside the home. First, we considered the cost of day care and the extra taxes we were paying to Uncle Sam each week. (A second paycheck is often eaten up by a disproportionate amount of taxes because the wages usually push a two-income family into a higher tax bracket.) After those two large bites, my salary seemed more like a morsel than a meal. Score one for pulling the professional plug.

Next, neither one of us was comfortable leaving our kids at day care. Shortly after the birth of my twin sons, Joseph and Michael, I investigated several facilities close to my job, thinking I could rush over and nurse the twins during my lunch hour. What I found was discouraging, to say the least. Although most of the day-care providers seemed like warm, caring people, the facilities left me cold. Furthermore, I thought, I can hardly give my twins the individual attention that they crave and deserve, so how can another woman with several other children to contend with give my kids equal time? She couldn't.

Yet the most compelling reason for my staying home was rather a simplistic one—I'm their mother, and no one in this world (with the exception of their father) could care for them and love them the way I do. From recent research we now know how important the first three years of a child's life truly are, and I want to be the one who makes a positive impact. Childhood is so fleeting, such a small blip of time, and I want to play an active part. I want to be there. I want to see it all, not hear about it from someone else. My kids are funny, personable little people, and I feel so lucky (most of the time) to be able to spend my days with them.

When my kids look back on their childhoods, I want them to remember the fun they had with their mom—the trips to the zoo, planting a spring garden, baking muffins on rainy afternoons—not the day little Johnny bit them in day care. Granted, many of their memories will also include the day Mom lost it in the supermarket and gave them a time-out in the bread aisle or the night when their father walked through the door and found Mom locked in the bathroom crying, "I can't take it anymore!" as they jumped from a table onto the couch in the living room; but, hopefully, even those fiascoes will become cherished memories, or at least humorous ones.

Financially, it's been a stretch but not much. Once we did the calculations (my salary minus job-related expenses) we realized that it would be easy to make up the financial shortfall by cutting back. We can't go out to eat as often, or buy the latest computer software and CDs, but the kids don't notice. And frankly, we don't mind either. The joy of being together far outweighs a house full of stuff.

The Survival Guide

With three boys under the age of four, and all within two and a half years of each other, I know a thing or two about surviving at home full-time. I know the rewards as well as the stress. Over the years, however, I've learned to minimize the loneliness and chaos and capitalize on the freedom and sheer fun of being with my kids and watching them grow. I gather support wherever I can find it, I keep the day going with scheduled events, and I have reinvented myself more times than Madonna.

Whoever said that being a full-time parent is easier than working outside the home has obviously never done it. Yet each year thousands of parents, yearning for more time with their kids, put away their briefcases in favor of staying home. Moms and dads of the '90s are quickly learning that they can't do it all—raise a family and pursue a profession—and still truly enjoy their lives. Each is a full-time job, and there simply aren't enough hours in the day to do both equally well. Something's got to give. Like you, more and more parents are choosing to temporarily give up their careers to stay home with their kids.

Geared toward parents with toddlers and preschool children, the time when most choose to remain home (but full-time parents of older children can also pick up a tip or two on what to do with the kids after school, or how to better manage their busy lives), *The Stay-at-Home Parent Survival Guide* helps these former career go-getters successfully transition from full-time employees to full-time parents.

When they've spent the last decade or so building a successful profession, it's difficult for some to give it up and stay home, no matter how strong the desire. It is an emotional sacrifice that few realize when they're saying good-bye to their office cohorts but quickly figure out once they're in the midst of a domestic free-for-all. Their once-structured lives have now become unstructured play time without direction. Most quickly take control of their new vocations and reinvent themselves by focusing on enriching their children's lives and in the process enhancing their own, but others have difficulty, feeling a loss of identity and isolation. They need support, advice, and organization. Whether you're a new full-time parent who needs assistance in making the transition a success or a seasoned veteran just looking to pick up a tip or two, this book can help.

Advice from the Trenches

The Survival Guide offers practical tips and plenty of concrete suggestions to get you through the tough days and ways to enhance the fun ones—from quiet indoor activities to set up on a rainy day to how to make it on just one salary. Written in a practical *A*-to-*Z* format, the book's chapters address specific issues on at-home parenting and most contain advice from an expert on the subject. Keep *The Survival Guide* nearby and refer to it again and again when new questions and concerns arise. Look to the field trip chapter for suggestions on places to take the kids and ways to make the journey fun and stress free; or turn to the television chapter when you feel guilty for leaving the set on a bit too long and want to know if you'll ruin the kids for life. *The Survival Guide* offers advice on disciplining the kids; how to exercise, make dinner, or clean the house *with* the kids; tips on keeping the marriage on track now that you and your spouse have new roles; ways to manage your family's time; ideas to beat the stay-at-home blues and gain support through parenting organizations; how to start an at-home business; and, when the time is right, how to successfully return to your career—thirty-two topics in all.

Although the book is written from the female perspective, the more than two million at-home fathers will benefit from *The Survival Guide*, too. And though it is my belief that full-time parenting is a better lifestyle choice than putting the kids in day care, the purpose of this book is not to judge or condemn working parents but rather to encourage those considering leaving the workforce to believe that they can in fact do it.

Throughout the book I refer to moms and dads who have left the workforce (or who have never entered it) to care solely for their children as full-time or at-home parents. Neither term is precise enough, and both may offend some readers. Although *full-time parent* best describes the job (Question: "What do you do?" Answer: "I care for the kids full time."), isn't every parent a full-time parent? Can you be a part-time parent? And what about the "full-time parent" who sends her kids off to school every morning? Isn't she really a full-time parent working part-time hours? The term *at-home parent* isn't much better because most moms and dads who care for their kids all day rarely stay home, and the phrase connotes (to me, anyway) an image of a mom or dad in sweats lounging on the couch watching television. Nothing could be further from the truth. Conversely, *working parent* is a bit of a misnomer, too. After all, I "work" pretty darn hard from the moment my kids get up (6 A.M. these days, thank you very much) to the time they finally go to sleep (8 P.M.). I just don't get paid or promoted for my efforts. Still, full-time and at-home parent are the best the dictionary has to offer. But, hey, I'm open to suggestions.

The Art of Staying Home

The next time you find yourself questioning your decision to stay home, as most of us at some time do, remember three things: (1) look for the humor even during the worst tantrums; (2) childhood goes by quickly, so cherish the little moments; (3) pick up this book.

The sacrifice in full-time parenting can be great but so are the rewards and the profound sense of satisfaction in nurturing your own children.

Activities

Indoor

In my house territorial toy wars break out between my boys usually once a day. My job is to bring both warring factions to the table in hopes of bringing about a peaceful solution. Fortunately, we live in Southern California; and on most days all I need to do is open the back door, escort them outside, and the war is over. But on rainy days, I need to be quick on my feet with lots of indoor, creative play.

You don't have to be Merlin to whip up fun stuff for kids to do. In fact, the simplest activities are often the most exciting. The key to a good time is to offer direction and know when to step out of their way. When the kids get bored with one activity, move on to the next. And don't forget to mix up your playtime repertoire. Try some group reading, coloring, block building, educational TV show or video, cooking or craft project, and quiet-time activity. Kids don't need to be entertained by adults all the time; in fact, given the opportunity, they'll create elaborate games all on their own.

I look at rainy days as nice downtime. I don't feel like it has to have the same kind of energy as a sunny day. I think giving the kids a break and letting them enjoy the quiet time with movies and TV is fine because we don't do that on nice days.

7

The Basics: Coloring, Painting, and Block Building

You can never have too many crayons, colored pencils, markers, or pastels around the house. Children as young as eighteen months can learn to scribble. In fact, you should encourage your young Picasso to master the art of holding a crayon. Coloring not only helps in developing a child's fine motor skills, but builds his concentration and creativity, too. Painting, whether it's watercolor or finger paint, is another artistic medium to add to your artist's palate, although most children won't be able to hold a paintbrush until two years.

Use your imagination when choosing the medium on which to let the kids express themselves. Spread butcher paper across the entire length of your kitchen table, or tape a sheet on the hallway wall or floor and let the kids go. Have everyone hop into the bathtub and do some body painting, or let them paint the windows with holiday scenes. Don't worry about creating a mess or staining the furniture—most paints and crayons are washable, but check the labels just in case.

Broken Crayon Blues

Ever wonder what to do with all those broken crayons? Create crayon muffins, a fun rainy-day project that not only creates new crayons, but also teaches kids about recycling and classifying. Here's what you'll need:

> Muffin tins
> Foil muffin holders
> Broken crayons

1. Preheat oven to 275°.
2. Place foil muffin holders in muffin tins.
3. Remove crayon wrappers from all broken crayons. Break crayons into one-inch pieces.

I try to be judicious about what I do with them. I find that if I'm the one who's directing all the play, then they rely on me the whole day. I love to do things with them, but I also want to encourage them to do things on their own so they'll be more creative and come up with their own ideas; and, frankly, sometimes I just want them to leave me alone.

I keep paints, markers, and modeling clay in a kitchen cabinet. When I'm trying to get something done in the kitchen, I just pull them out, and the kids sit at the table and do a craft project.

4. Have the kids divide the crayons according to color—all green crayons in one pile, red in another. Fill muffin holders halfway with broken crayons of the same color. Use extra or odd crayons to make one colorful, abstract muffin.

5. Place muffin tins in preheated oven for 3 to 5 minutes until crayons melt.

6. Cool completely; then remove from holders.

A toy-box staple for generations, blocks are not only fun, but experts say block building is an important educational tool second only to reading. Kids cultivate their social skills as they trade shapes and sizes and learn cooperation when building a tower with other kids. Physically, block building helps form fine muscle control in fingers and establishes hand-eye coordination. It teaches balance, symmetry, gravity, and other abstract principles, the cornerstones in understanding math and science. Most importantly, block building encourages creative play. Blocks act as symbols for kids' ideas as simple forms suddenly become castles or cities.

Building Tips

- **Use age-appropriate blocks.** Large blocks in simple geometric shapes work best for toddlers; smaller blocks in a wide range of shapes and sizes are great for preschoolers.

- **Encourage children to describe their designs.** "What kind of tower are you building?" "Where is the kitchen? Is that a window?"

- **Let your children knock down their creations.** Ignore the noise and let them knock away. It gives them a sense of control and power.

- **Leave ribbon and other craft materials near blocks.** Decorating their block projects inspires kids further.

For a set of truly original building blocks, collect empty cereal and pasta boxes, oatmeal and cracker containers, and even milk cartons. The kids will have a ball constructing all kinds of forts and towers. The best part is, these blocks don't make noise when they come crashing down!

In the Kitchen

Want a little exercise but it's too cold to go outside? Try a game of balloon volleyball. Simply inflate a balloon and hit it back and forth. Don't let it touch the ground or your opponent gets the point.

I have vivid memories of growing up and spending lots of time by my mother's side in the kitchen as she baked some sweet delicacy or an elaborate Italian dinner for our family. Those one-on-one cooking lessons brought me closer to my mom and gave me a deep appreciation for good food and cooking. Elaine Magee, mother of two and author of *Someone's in the Kitchen with Mommy* and *Alphabet Cooking*, encourages parents to use cooking as a daily project with kids. "One of the benefits of doing a cooking activity is instant gratification," she says. "When you make something, you see it, you eat it. You don't have to figure out where to store it." (To read more on cooking with kids, see the chapter entitled "Mealtime.")

Peruse your cookbooks for some simple recipes that can withstand some abuse just in case you all don't follow them exactly. I try to choose something with a sweet payoff—cookies or fruit-filled muffins are always winners with my boys. Here are three of their favorites.

Olivia and Catherine do a lot of water play inside. One of their favorites is when I give them squirt bottles filled with water and old rags, and they clean the windows. They don't do a fabulous job, but they love it and it gets the fingerprints off.

Chocolate-Chip Peanut-Butter Cookies

½ cup butter, softened
1½ cups flour
½ cup sugar
1 tsp. baking soda
¼ tsp. salt
½ cup firmly packed brown sugar
¾ cup crunchy peanut butter
2 tbsp. milk
1 egg
1 12-oz. package semisweet chocolate chips

1. Preheat oven to 375°.

2. In mixer, cream butter until smooth, then add flour, sugar, baking soda, salt, brown sugar, and peanut butter. Mix well.

3. Add milk and egg. Blend until smooth.

4. Stir in chocolate chips.

5. Form one-inch balls and place on ungreased cookie sheet.

6. Flatten balls using a crisscross pattern with tines of fork first dipped in sugar.

7. Bake until edges are just brown, about 10 to 12 minutes.

8. Immediately remove from cookie sheet to cool on wire rack.

Makes about 40 cookies.

Raspberry Muffins

    1¾ cups flour
    ¼ cup uncooked whole oats
    ¼ cup sugar
    3 tsp. baking powder
    ¼ cup melted butter
    1 cup milk
    1 egg (beaten)
    ¼ tsp. salt
    1 cup frozen raspberries (thawed)

1. Preheat oven to 400°.

2. In large mixing bowl, stir in all ingredients—except raspberries—until just smooth.

3. Stir in raspberries.

4. Spoon batter into greased muffin tins, about ⅔ of the way full.

5. Bake for 20 minutes. Makes about 12 muffins.

Guacamole and Chips

    2 ripe avocados
    1 tbsp. mild salsa
    1 tsp. fresh lime juice
    dash of salt
    Tortilla chips

1. Slice avocados in half, carefully navigating around the large pit.

We do a lot of cooking. Stuff that's easy. It's quick gratification.

2. Remove the pits from the centers, and scoop the meat from the shells with a spoon. Place in a large mixing bowl.

3. With a fork or wooden spoon mash the avocados against the side of the bowl.

4. Add the salsa, lime juice, and salt. Mix well.

5. Serve with your favorite tortilla chips.

Crafts

Before I throw out old magazines, I flip through them and cut out pictures of cars, people, animals, food—you name it—and save them for my two-year-old son. He loves to glue them onto paper. I've even laminated two of his collages, creating his own personalized place mats.

One day during a craft project immediately following library story time, I noticed a mom eagerly coloring, cutting, and gluing her son's project while he sat by passively. Although the hand puppet that she created looked great, her son didn't look that happy. She missed the point—it's not the end result that counts, but rather the journey getting there.

Crafts provide a great vehicle for a child's self-expression. As she grows and develops, so will her creativity. It's also a wonderful sensory experience as she touches different textures, identifies colors, and distinguishes new smells.

Art Supply Checklist

Fill an old shoe or cigar box or, better yet, an entire kitchen drawer (if you have the room) with a variety of interesting art supplies, so when bad weather comes to call, you'll be ready. Here's a list to get you started.

- Safety scissors (for children three and older), colored paper, nontoxic paste or glue, crayons and colored pencils

- Backyard items: acorns, leaves, feathers, seashells, pinecones, small stones

- Kitchen items: empty boxes, coffee cans, corks, egg cartons, sponges, paper doilies

- Household items: buttons, ribbon, bows, old magazines (have them cut out pictures)

- Craft items: glitter, confetti, beads
- Art smocks (protect clothes and put kids in the mood)

Here's a Crafty Idea

Have a few budding da Vincis on your hands? Break out the craft box and clear off the kitchen table. The following are just a few ideas for the kids to try.

NATURE COLLAGE *Ages Two and Older*

Items needed: glue, paper plate, twelve-inch piece of string or yarn, hole punch, and leaves, sticks, seeds, and anything else found outside that's colorful or has an interesting texture *(Parents should check all items to make sure they're safe to use or don't present a choking hazard.)*

Directions: Glue various nature items to the front of a paper plate. Punch a hole in the top of the plate, and loop string through; then, tie a knot. Display your collage from a doorknob.

FOOTPRINT TREE *Ages Two and Older*

Items needed: large piece of green construction paper, 8½-by-11-inch paper, scissors, glue, crayons

Directions: Draw a large tree on the green construction paper. Trace foot on 8½-by-11-inch paper, and carefully cut it out. *(Adult supervision is required for children under three.)* Decorate foot with crayon, and write child's name and date on it. Glue the foot onto the personalized tree. Update tree every few months, and watch how the feet grow!

PAPER BUTTERFLY *Ages Two and Older*

Items needed: Paper cutout of butterfly (see illustration), crayons, plastic straw, stapler

My girls are heavily into crafts. They love to color and glue paper. My husband, Matt, calls them "paper intensive."

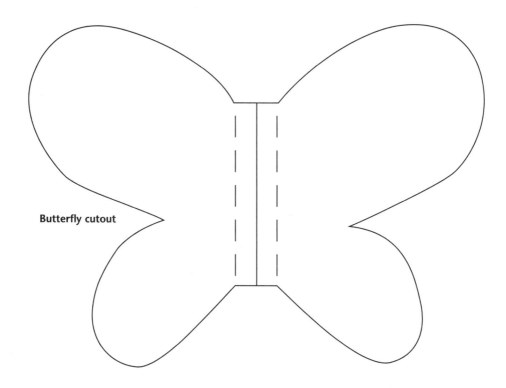

Butterfly cutout

Directions: Using the butterfly illustration as a guide, draw a butterfly on a piece of 8½-by-11-inch paper, and carefully cut it out. Color the wings with crayon. Place straw down the center of the front of butterfly, and fold paper over it. Carefully staple the straw in place from the back. Fold open. Hold end of straw, and gently wave to watch the butterfly flutter away.

PASTA NECKLACE, HOLIDAY GARLAND
Ages Three and Older

Items needed: food coloring, rubbing alcohol, plastic containers, slotted spoon, cooling rack, dry pasta (uncooked, preferably hollow shapes), twenty-inch pieces of string or yarn *(Warning: rubbing alcohol is harmful if swallowed; adult supervision is required.)*

I have a box that I just throw in old cards, pieces of a broken radio, bits of other things that have broken, buttons, beads, and stuff like that. When we have some snowy days, I take the box out, and the girls just go through it all and make all sorts of crafts.

Directions: Dye the dry pasta by mixing 1 teaspoon of food coloring with 7 teaspoons of rubbing alcohol in a plastic container. Use one color for each container. Add pasta to container; close lid and shake gently to evenly coat pasta. Open the lid and remove pasta with slotted spoon, and place on cooling rack to dry completely. String pasta to create necklace or colorful Christmas garland. *(Small pieces of pasta are a choking hazard to small children; adult supervision is required.)*

WRAPPING PAPER *Ages Three and Older*

Items needed: a variety of blank paper—bags, butcher paper, construction paper—washable paint, paper plates, painting sponges or unused household sponges cut into stars, circles, and squares

Directions: Pour a small amount of paint onto paper plates, a separate plate for each color. Next, spread out paper. Gently dip a sponge into paint and then press it carefully onto paper. Continue dipping and pressing until the paper has the desired design. Let paper dry completely before wrapping presents.

> Periodically recycle toys by hiding a box of unpopular or out-of-favor playthings in your closet. Two months down the road, when the kids complain that they're bored, pull the box out. The kids will think it's Christmas all over again.

SILHOUETTE PORTRAITS *Ages Five and Older*

Items needed: 8½-by-11-inch piece of white drawing paper, masking tape, pencil, desk lamp with movable neck

Directions: Have a friend or sibling sit in a chair with her profile parallel and about a foot away from the wall. Tape the drawing paper to the wall at the height of your subject's head. Darken the room and angle the lamp's beam at her head until a strong shadow appears on the paper. (You may have to move the lamp a bit until a sharp outline appears.) Tell your subject to hold still as you trace her outline onto the paper.

Variation: Use colored paper (black is a good choice), then cut out the silhouette and glue onto white paper.

Reading

When you're indoors, you have to be flexible and have more than one thing planned. I move the kids around, too. For instance, they'll play with their toys in the basement, then they'll play on the computer for a while.

Reading to young children instills a lifelong love of books and aids in language development. When a parent reads to a child, it creates a loving bond, too. It's a great transitional activity, instantly quieting and calming even the fussiest of toddlers. When you read together, allow your child to interrupt at will to ask questions about the story or the pictures he sees. Reading is an activity kids can do on their own, too, by simply turning the pages of a sturdy board book. Make books accessible by placing them on the lower bookshelves in your child's room.

Indoor Garden

Even if it's twenty degrees outside, you can still plant a garden. All it takes are a sunny windowsill and an interested toddler.

- **Potato vine.** Insert several toothpicks around a medium-size sweet potato and suspend two-thirds of the body into a water-filled jar. Place on a sunny windowsill. Refill the water periodically. Within two weeks, roots and leaves will sprout.

- **Bean sprouts.** Soak a few lima beans in water overnight. In the morning, sandwich the beans between moist paper towels and a glass. Place glass on windowsill. Dampen the paper towels several times a day. Within a week you'll see the beans sprout.

- **Seed tree.** Dry the seed/pit from a lemon, lime, or avocado overnight. Place seed one-inch deep in a pot filled with planting soil (with avocado, plant pit two-thirds in soil). Water well, and place on a sunny windowsill. Keep the soil damp, but not soaking wet. Within two weeks (longer for avocado), you'll see your tree begin to grow.

- **Indoor lawn.** Punch a few small holes in the bottom of a shallow, disposable aluminum roasting pan, and fill with potting soil one inch from the top. Pat the dirt firmly to eliminate air in the soil. Sprinkle grass seed on top, and then cover with an ⅛-inch layer of potting soil. Place on sunny windowsill. Mist with water twice a day until grass sprouts, then once a day thereafter. Cut "the lawn" as needed.

Imaginary Play

Experts say children who are encouraged to use their imaginations during play become better problem solvers and have better self-esteem. So how can you inspire your young thespians? Just gather some props (most can be found in the typical house) and set the stage for them; they'll know what to do next.

Each scenario takes two people, either two children or one child and one parent. Most children ages two and up can participate. Obviously, the older they are, the more elaborate the scene will become.

Dressed for Success

Just like vaudeville actors of long ago, create a "trunk" of old costumes for the kids to use for dress-up play. Keep a box in your closet, and fill it with a variety of unwanted hats and caps, high-heel shoes and loafers, worn-out suit jackets, shawls, large costume jewelry (small pieces are a choking hazard to young children), belts, and handbags. On the next rainy day, pull out the box and call the kids. They'll love dressing up like Mom and Dad.

Camp Out

    Props. Big blankets, pillows, flashlights

    The actors. Campers

    Set the stage. Drape blankets over a table creating a cozy "tent" underneath. Tell ghost stories, sing songs by the "campfire," and snuggle down for the night only to hear strange noises outside your tent. Could it be a bear?

When they were little, they got antsy being inside all day. Tension would build, but it was too ugly to go outside. Yet they wanted to be physically active. Often I took them downstairs to the basement, and I'd let them ride their trikes. We'd play music and dance and act crazy. It was a good release for them.

We'd sit in a circle and "call" grandmas and grandpas, then pass the phone around. Everyone's always anxious to hear what everyone else has to say.

Radio Days

As a kid my favorite rainy-day game was creating an old-fashioned soap opera. I'd gather up my girl-friends, a tape recorder, and a variety of props—rotary telephone, windup alarm clock or timer, shoes, a squeaky door, a noisy candy wrapper. We'd each take on a variety of charac-ters and make up the plot as we went along (we were always pressing the pause button); and we frequently took commercial breaks, imitating our favorites. We called our show *To Live or Die* and began with this introduction: "Welcome to *To Live or Die* [loud slap, followed by a scream]. Tonight's thrilling episode is [fill in the blank] . . ." The best part was listening to our play on tape when we were finished. We never made it on the air, but we sure had hours of fun.

STORE

Props. Empty cereal boxes and plastic bottles, calculator, apron for the clerk, play money, basket, small paper bags

The actors. Store clerk, customer

Set the stage. Let the kids take turns being the store clerk or customer. Have the clerk help the customer pick the best cereal to buy. Have him ring up the groceries, bag them, and collect the money.

POST OFFICE

Props. Discarded junk mail, stickers, ink pad with stamp (for older kids who hopefully won't label the furniture), satchel or basket, play money, small boxes

The actors. Post office clerk, customer

Set the stage. Have children take turns being the clerk and the customer. The customer wants to send her letters to Miami and her packages to Hong Kong. The clerk stamps and weighs each and collects the fee.

OFFICE

Props. Old rotary or push-button telephone, scrap paper, pencils, old typewriter, calculator, stapler (for children three and up), folders

The actors. Office manager, high-powered fashion executive

Set the stage. Have kids take turns being office man-ager and executive. A call has just come in from Milan, Italy. The designer didn't receive the latest designs and needs them ASAP!

SAFARI

Props. Toy binoculars, lightweight rope, compass, toy camera

The actors. Two wildlife photographers or one photographer and one wild animal.

Set the stage. You're on safari in Africa. Suddenly, you spot a wild lion, and the chase is on to photograph him before he attacks.

RESTAURANT

Props. Table, chairs, play menus (create them from old folders or scrap paper), plastic plates, cups and silverware, apron for waiter, pen and pad of paper

The actors. The customer, the waiter

Set the stage. Have the kids take turns being the waiter and the customer. Many different scenarios can occur, including "The Absentminded Waiter" or "The Cynical Food Critic."

We light candles in the bathroom and get into the tub. We sing or play classical music CDs. It's so much fun.

Science Experiments

Children are naturally curious about the world around them (just count how many times the typical three-year-old asks the question, "But why?"). Help them become creative problem solvers in the future by encouraging their curiosity today. Although most three-year-olds can master the following experiments, they're better suited for four-year-olds and older kids. Yet the more you do the experiments, the clearer they'll become. Gather up the materials, but let the kids do the experiments as you guide them.

HOW PLANTS DRINK

What you'll need. Celery stalk, red food coloring, tall drinking glass, water, blunt knife

Procedure. Fill glass with water and add several drops of red food coloring. With a blunt knife, cut off bottom of celery stalk, and place the stalk in the colored water. Several hours later, cut open the celery to see the red stripes. The experiment shows how plants drink water.

Variation. Fill two glasses with water and put red food coloring in one and blue food coloring in the second. Cut off the bottoms of two celery stalks, but leave the leafy tops in place. Put a celery stalk in each glass. Let them sit for 48 hours away from the sun. In two days the plants will have changed color.

COLOR COMBINING

What you'll need. Six clear glasses; red, yellow, and blue food coloring; water

Procedure. Fill three of the glasses with water; leave the other three empty. In the first glass of water, mix a drop or two of red food coloring; in the second, blue; and in the third, yellow. Next, pour half of the red and then half of the yellow liquid into one empty glass to make orange. Now, pour the second half of the red and half of the blue into another empty glass to create purple, and finally, pour the remainder of the blue with the remaining yellow to make green. The experiment shows how three primary colors—red, yellow, and blue—create three secondary colors—orange, purple, and green.

SAND TIMER

What you'll need. Two glass canning jars with lids, hammer and nail, strong glue (something that will work on metal), one cup (or more) of fine sand, a watch with a second hand

Procedure. Glue jar lids together top to top using a strong glue like epoxy (be careful not to get the glue on your fingers or clothes). Once the glue is dry, punch several holes in the lids using hammer and nail. *(Adult supervision is needed for these two steps.)* Fill one jar halfway with sand and screw double lid on, then turn the empty jar over and screw to the top. Turn the jars over and watch sand pour into empty jar. Using a second hand, time how long it takes for sand to move from one jar to the other. Add or subtract grains of sand until it measures the amount of time you want.

CHEMICALLY REACTIVE PENNIES

What you'll need. A glass jar with lid, vinegar, salt, old pennies

Procedure. Fill a clean glass jar halfway with vinegar. Add some old, dirty pennies, then a teaspoon of salt. Put the lid on the jar and shake vigorously. The chlorine in the salt eats at the copper on the pennies and shines them up. Rinse the pennies in water to stop the chemical reaction.

Rainy Day Relief

Being stuck in the house on a rainy day can be an enriching experience allowing your kids a chance to flex their creative muscles. Remember—what works one day probably won't work the next. And not all kids like doing the same things. For instance, my guys can spend a good thirty minutes engrossed in imaginary play or fussing in the kitchen, but if I pull out a craft project, I can count on five minutes, tops. (Unless, of course, there's glue involved, but that's a different story!)

RESOURCES

Books

Barron's Science Wizardry for Kids: Authentic, Safe Scientific Experiments Kids Can Perform! by Margaret Kenda; Hauppauge, NY: Barron's Juveniles, 1995.

Block Adventures: Building Creativity and Concepts Through Block Play, by Karen Stephens; Weston, MA: First Teacher Press, 1991.

Child's Play: 200 Instant Crafts and Activities for Preschoolers, by Leslie Hamilton; New York: Crown Publishing, 1989.

Cosmic Science: Over 40 Gravity-Defying, Earth-Orbiting, Space-Cruising Activities for Kids, by Jim Wiese; New York: John Wiley and Sons, 1997.

The Little Hands, Big Fun Craft Book: Creative Fun for 2- to 6-Year-Olds, by Judy Press; Charlotte, NC: Williamson Publishing, 1995.

175 Easy-to-Do Thanksgiving Crafts (and other holiday-themed books), by Sharon Dunn Umnik; Honesdale, PA: Boyds Mills Press, 1996.

365 Days of Creative Play: For Children 2 Years and Up, by Judith Gray and Sheila Ellison; Naperville, IL: Source-books, 1995.

Internet Sites

www.familyfun.com—Official website of *FamilyFun* magazine. Offers a variety of indoor (and outdoor) activities and loads of craft ideas.

www.crayola.com—Loads of games and crafts (with an emphasis on coloring, of course) from this crayon giant.

www.elmers.com—Craft ideas as well as woodworking projects for the older kids.

www.nickjr.com—Fun and games with Blue's Clues, Maisy, Franklin, and other Nickelodeon characters.

www.pbs.org—Visit the "Kids' neighborhood" for some interactive learning with Arthur, the Teletubbies, Mr. Rogers, and other PBS favorite kid characters.

Activities

Outdoor

Most kids love the great outdoors. If your backyard is brimming with lots of state-of-the-art toys, you've won half the battle in keeping the kids happily occupied. But most kids eventually tire of sandboxes and bicycles—they want to be entertained. Then what?

Water holds such incredible fascination for young children. On warm, sunny afternoons, break out the garden hose and have the kids wash the car. Children as young as eighteen months can get the hang of it. They may not do a great job, but who cares? Or how about washing the dog? I give each of my kids a small bucket of water and an old paintbrush and watch as they "paint" the house. My son Michael can spend a good hour just wandering the yard with the hose, stopping periodically to water a plant or bush. He gets soaked from head to toe, but he's had a grand time in the process.

What were your favorite games as a kid? Kick the can? Hide and go seek? Red light, green light? Follow the leader? They're still favorites today. Just ask your kids.

When the girls were little, I'd let them have flour and they would play with it outside. They would measure it, mix it; they'd pour it; they'd put their hands in it. We'd put the flour on a tray or plate, and they would draw pictures. Of course it would spill all over the place and they'd want more! But that's why I'd only let them play with it outside. On occasion, I'd let them mix it with water. Now that's really messy.

Sports (of Sorts)

Okay, so these games may not build strong muscles or instill the concept of teamwork, but they're fun and easy to set up.

MINIATURE GOLF *Ages 2½ and Older*

Not for the parent who prizes a green lawn!

Directions. Set up your own golf course by digging holes and inserting empty cans throughout your lawn every fifteen feet or so (save the turf and dirt to reapply when the game is over), making sure the cans are flush to the surface. Tie colorful ribbon to the top of garden stakes and implant them next to the holes. Using plastic clubs (or putters if the kids are old enough) and lightweight plastic balls, play a round or two. Don't forget the scorecard. When the game is over, remove the cans and flags, and replace the turf. Water the lawn well. Hope for the best.

BROOM BALL *Ages 2½ and Older*

Directions. Give each kid a pint-size broom (available at most toy stores for less than $5) and a large rubber ball at least five inches in diameter. Set up two cardboard boxes at either end of the driveway or patio. The object of the game is to sweep the ball into the box, or goal.

WATER SOCCER *Ages 3 and Older*

Save this one for a hot afternoon when you have a bunch of bored kids on your hands. Bathing suits are the uniform of choice.

Directions. Set up two goals about twenty feet apart (if orange cones aren't available, two lawn chairs will do). You'll need two teams (a minimum of two kids per side), two garden hoses (about twenty feet in length each), and a soccer ball.

The object of the game is to get the ball across the goal using only a stream of water—no kicking allowed.

LAWN BOWLING *Ages 2½ and Older*

Directions. Collect ten aluminum cans and rinse out with water. Set up at the edge of patio or driveway in *V* formation. Give your child a ball and have her or him stand several feet away. Bowl away.

SNOWBALL BULL'S-EYE *Ages 3½ and Older*

If it's not snowing outside, mud will do but, oh, what a mess!

    Directions. Take an old sheet (one ready for the rag pile) and cut several holes about a foot in diameter each. Hang the sheet from a clothesline or between two tree branches. Stand your child ten feet back and have her try to throw snowballs through the holes. Each "hit" is worth a point.

LAWN OLYMPICS

Directions. Set up a miniobstacle course in your backyard using lawn furniture, large terra-cotta pots, and anything else hanging around your yard. The object of the game is for your child to navigate under, over, and around the maze you've created within the allotted time, say, five minutes. You can increase the difficulty by adding more obstacles or have her hold something in her hands.

Gardening Galore

What kid can resist sticking his hands in soil, whether digging a hole to plant some vegetables or searching for some earthworms? Kids are fascinated with how things grow. As they watch a plant flourish and produce fruit, they begin to

Nature Hunt

Encourage kids to explore and respect the environment by making up a nature kit for them. An old muffin tin or egg carton works great for sorting backyard treasures like rocks, wood chips, twigs, leaves, and anything else they can find (be sure to remind them not to put anything in their mouths). Give them a small beach rake and shovel for below-the-surface prospecting, a plastic magnifying glass to examine plant life up close, a compass for a sense of adventure, and, of course, a glass jar filled with a few blades of grass and air holes punched in the lid for bug collecting.

make the connection between food and where it comes from. Gardening teaches children to care for something, to take responsibility. It's also a great way to casually introduce science. More importantly, though, gardening is an inexpensive way for parents to spend time with their kids. And, truth be told, kids who cultivate their own vegetables are more likely to eat them!

Children as young as three can start their own gardens, but kids as young as eighteen months can help out by throwing leaves and grass into the compost pile. My own sons started making the daily pilgrimage out to the compost bin at the ripe old age of twelve months. Each would take a turn holding the food-scrap bucket and dumping it on top of the warm soil. We'd make the rounds of our three raised-bed gardens each day to see what was ready for harvesting, pick off the bugs from the plants, and water the crops (another favorite for kids).

> Attract butterflies to your garden by choosing plants that provide nectar for them to drink. Look in field guides to find out which butterflies live in your area and the type of plants they feed on.

GARDENING START-UP TIPS

- **Keep their interest.** Plant vegetables that grow quickly, like radishes (mature in less than four weeks) and lettuce (germinates quickly), or vegetables that give a huge payback, like pumpkins and sunflowers.

- **Start small.** No need to dig up half the backyard to expose your kids to the joys of gardening. A four-foot-by-four-foot raised bed will produce more than enough produce all summer long. If space is at a premium, try container planting—several large pots on the patio or terrace filled with flowers, herbs, and small crops like lettuce or strawberries.

- **Keep it simple.** A kid's attention span will rarely last more than twenty minutes, so plan short activities each day. Do the grunt work like preparing the soil yourself, and call the kids when you're ready to scatter the seeds.

- **Make it accessible.** Designate a "kids only" area where they have total control over what's planted and what's not (brussels sprouts? No way!). Let your kids wander to the garden at will to check on the progress of their plants.

- **Teach the basics.** Practice proper watering (give the plants a good drink only when they need it; don't overwater), weeding (pull from the root, not the top), and feeding (a nontoxic organic fertilizer rather than a synthetic brand).

- **Visit every day.** Make it a part of your daily ritual. Note each plant's progress, perhaps with a measuring stick. Draw pictures.

- **Give your garden variety.** The more assortment of plants, the merrier. Different plants grow at different rates and offer an array of colors, textures, and heights for inquisitive little gardeners to ponder.

> To make picking up tiny seeds easier for little hands, mix seeds with a tablespoon of sand before spreading.

Flower Pressing

Once your garden is in full bloom, you'll want to preserve some of your most colorful plants by drying and pressing them. Go out to the garden early in the morning (many flowers close in the afternoon) and carefully cut off both the blossom and a few inches of the stem from several flowers. On a sheet of eight-by-ten-inch corrugated cardboard, place several sheets of newspaper and, on top of that, a piece of white paper or blotting paper. Next, carefully lay your freshly cut specimens on the paper, giving each flower lots of space. Cover with another sheet of white paper and more newspaper, then a second sheet of corrugated cardboard. Place a stack of large, heavy books on top to weigh down your herbarium. In several weeks, your flowers should be dry and ready for mounting. Glue to white note cards for some colorful thank-you notes.

- **Make it fun.** Add small ceramic animals to their garden, colorful streamers to gardening stakes (which scare off hungry birds, I might add), and other garden ornaments. Encourage older kids to keep a gardening journal filled with pictures, diagrams, cuttings, and tasting notes of favorite vegetables. Although the garden is an ideal outdoor classroom, don't force the science lessons—they get it.

Loving the Great Outdoors

Even if you don't have a backyard for the kids to romp around in, create your own tropical jungle on your patio or terrace, or go exploring in your neighborhood park. Sunlight and fresh air are important for all of us.

RESOURCES

Books

Gardening with Children, by Beth Richardson; Newton, CT: The Taunton Press, 1998.

Gardens from Garbage: How to Grow Indoor Plants from Recycled Kitchen Scraps, by Judith Handelsman; Brookfield, CT: The Millbrook Press, 1993.

The Little Hands Nature Book, by Nancy Fusco Castaldo; Charlotte, NC: Williamson Publishing Company, 1997.

355 Outdoor Activities You Can Do with Your Child, by Steven Bennett and Ruth Bennett; Holbrook, MA: Adams Media Corporation, 1993.

Catalog

Gardens for Growing People catalog: P.O. Box 630, Point Reyes, CA 94956; E-mail: growpepl@sun.net.

Earthworm Habitat

Light-sensitive earthworms burrow deep in the ground, swallowing dirt and excreting castings against the walls of their tunnels, or to the earth's surface. Collect several worms and put them in a dirt-filled glass jar. Mist the dirt with some water and add a few fresh leaves to the top. Cover the jar with cheesecloth and secure with a rubber band. Place the jar inside a paper bag and staple shut. Keep the jar at room temperature away from direct sun. Every few days, remove the jar from the bag and take note of how the earthworms have tunneled through the soil.

Baby-Sitters

A Stay-at-Home Parent's Best Friend

After more than two years, Betsy, my beloved baby-sitter, is leaving our family. I've tried all sorts of incentives to entice her to stay, but she just graduated from college and wants a full-time job. Go figure.

Over the months, I've grown to rely on her. On designated mornings, she'd show up to happy greetings from my sons, "Betsy's here!" Once she was in the house, my sons could not have cared less where I went or when I'd be back. All they knew was that their buddy Betsy had arrived, and all was right with the world. And I thoroughly agreed.

Being a stay-at-home parent doesn't necessarily mean that you must *stay at home* every day, every minute. On the contrary, full-time caregivers need to get out of the house regularly, even if it's just a few hours a week, to renew their spirits and clear their heads. Some parents choose to put their kids in preschool, but others prefer to have a sitter come to the house a few days a week for several hours while the kids are small.

The most important quality I look for in a baby-sitter is someone who wants to play with my kids.

Having a regular, reliable baby-sitter is a gift. Finding her and keeping her happily employed, however, take some effort and a bit of ingenuity.

Seek and Ye Shall Find

So where do all the good baby-sitters hang out? Actually, good sitters can be found just about anywhere. The best source for finding one, however, is through word-of-mouth. Spread the word that you're looking for a baby-sitter to everyone you think can help—friends, former coworkers, family, neighbors. A personal referral from someone you know and trust is usually better than hiring one cold. If you can't find a sitter by networking, advertise in the local high-school paper, or ask a teacher to recommend a responsible student. If you live in a college town, call the campus employment office and ask to put an ad up on their job board. (That's how I found Betsy.) Your local church or synagogue is also a good place to look. Another source is your local day-care center—often day-care providers moonlight as evening or afternoon sitters. You never know where a good one will turn up. I once found a great baby-sitter through a referral from my supermarket checker!

I like to hire a baby-sitter where I have some kind of connection. For instance, we had the daughter of the secretary at Emily's preschool sit for us.

Make a List

Before you interview prospective sitters, you must first decide what your needs are. In addition to being reliable, prompt, and responsible, what other qualities must your future sitter possess? What will her responsibilities be? Must the sitter be female? Or is a male sitter also acceptable? Teenager or senior citizen? Do you want someone to do light housekeeping, or is watching the kids her only responsibility? Can she bring her schoolwork during the day, or must she pay attention solely to the kids? Is it okay for the sitter to take the kids in her car for a jaunt to the local park? And, most importantly, what are you willing to pay? Find out from other families or child-care agencies what the going rate is for your area. Once you have the job description narrowed down, and the salary, jot everything down on paper and use it during the interview so that you are clear about what the job will entail.

The Interview

The interview process begins on the telephone as you explain the job to (hopefully) several prospective sitters. Although you shouldn't make a decision based on one conversation, get a feel for the type of person he or she is. If your radar tells you it's time to meet, set up an appointment. Try to meet with at least three candidates.

First impressions go a long way. When I first met Betsy, after I greeted her at the door, she came into the room and immediately sat on the floor with my boys (they were seven months old at the time). They crawled all over her as we talked. By the time she left I knew that she was the sitter for me.

Qualifications are also important. Has your prospective sitter actually been around kids, or does she simply think that being with kids all day would be fun? A good sitter should have a least two years of experience to properly take care of infants less than six months in age. Does she have emergency training, and if not, would she be willing to attend a class at your expense? And finally, does she have recent references? Always check with her former employers (preferably families with children close in age to yours) no matter how wonderful she may seem or who recommended her.

Although you may have specific questions to ask the sitter during the interview, the following will help you get started.

It's very important for stay-at-home parents to have a regular baby-sitter. They need time for themselves, and the kids need another adult around so that they can get used to someone else other than Mom.

- Tell me about yourself. What's your job history?

- What kind of training do you have in child care? Do you know how to change a diaper? Bottle feed and burp?

- What's your general health? Any physical problems that would restrict you from taking care of the children? Have you had a tuberculosis (TB) test within the past five years?

- How do you relate to children? What's your discipline philosophy?

- What would you do if . . . the phone rang while you were bathing the children? . . . the carbon monoxide monitor in the kitchen went off? . . . someone came to the door at 10 P.M.?

Baby-Sitters' Pet Peeves

You thought she was happily employed, but then one day she calls to say she won't be returning. What went wrong? Didn't you pay a good wage? Aren't your kids well behaved? Take a look at these baby-sitters' pet peeves and see if you're guilty of any.

Pet Peeve	Prevention
"A mom once asked if I would bathe her daughter before bed, but I couldn't find a bath towel, or even her pajamas."	Always lay everything out for the sitter, from extra diapers and clothes to favorite toys, juice cups, important phone numbers, and snacks.
"Their house was a mess. Dirty dishes everywhere, clothes on the sofa, dog hair on the rug. I was afraid to even have a glass of water!"	Take a half hour before the sitter arrives to straighten up: clear the counter of dishes, pick up toys and clothes, do a quick check of the bathroom, and vacuum.

Pet Peeve	Prevention
"They told me they'd be home by midnight, but it wasn't until 2:30 in the morning when I finally heard the car pull up. Not only was I upset because I had to get up early, but I was worried that something had happened to them."	Be realistic in the time you expect to come home so that the sitter can schedule her evening accordingly. If you're running late, always call, even if it's at night.
"We had agreed on $6 per hour, but if they arrived home at half past the hour, they'd round off backward, gypping me of money that I had clearly earned."	Always round up the hour, giving the sitter a few extra dollars. And if you really want to please her (in hopes of keeping her happily employed), round dollar amounts up in five-dollar increments. For instance, if she sat three hours, at $6 an hour, her fee would be $18. Throw in the extra two and round up to $20.
"Once in a while, they'd ask me to watch a relative's kid, too, yet they'd never pay for the extra kid. When we agreed on how much I would be paid, it was for two kids—their two kids."	If you need your sitter to look after an additional child, tell her so in advance and together decide on how much the addition will cost per hour. Looking after three kids is a lot more work than looking after two.
"They paid me by check! I was 16 years old. I didn't have a checking account."	If you're short on cash, stop by the ATM and withdraw some money, or ask in advance if a check is okay.

Baby-Sitters' Information Sheet

Tack it on the fridge or leave it by the phone, but wherever you decide to post this information sheet, make sure your sitter sees it. (And don't forget to leave the telephone number of where you'll be.)

A. Names of parents _____
   Address _____
   Nearest cross street _____
   Phone number _____
   Names of children _____
   _____

B. Spouse's office number _____
   Cell phone number _____
   Pager number _____
   Neighbor's name _____
   Phone number _____
   Nearest relative's name _____
   Phone number _____

C. Poison control _____
   Height of children _____
   _____
   Weight of children _____
   _____

D. Pediatrician's name _____
   Phone number _____
   Nearest hospital _____
   _____
   Insurance _____

E. Local police _____
   Fire department _____
   Emergency 911

A: She may have written down your address to find your home the first time, but she probably won't remember it, especially in an emergency. Also, be sure to write down a major cross street so that the police or fire department can find you.

B: When I leave the sitter during the day, I can't be reached, but my husband can. Always leave the names and numbers of other people that the sitter can contact in case of an emergency.

C: Leaving the number of poison control might seem obvious, but the height and weight of each child is equally important because the dispatcher will need to know it in case of an accidental poisoning.

D: It's a good idea to leave the name of your health insurance in case the sitter needs to go to the emergency room.

E: Although 911 is the quickest way to get help, many towns rely on local fire and police departments for assistance.

There's Always a First Time

Finding a great sitter is only half the battle. Now you have to convince the kids that's she great, too. Building trusting relationships between you and the sitter and the sitter and the kids will take time. These trusting relationships can't be rushed. Although it's tempting to run out the door the first day she arrives, plan on a few visits before everyone feels comfortable.

On the sitter's first day, give her a thorough tour of the house. Show her all the little idiosyncracies that you take for granted. For instance, does the side of the baby's crib stick when you unfasten it? Do the kids nap in only T-shirts and socks? Show her how the stove and microwave work. Show her how to operate the heating and air-conditioning. Do you keep your extra toilet paper in an unusual spot? Show her.

Next, have an activity planned—like coloring or finger painting—for the sitter and kids to do together. Introducing the sitter in a playful, nonthreatening way will help to build trust. Once the sitter begins to build a rapport with your children, leave the play area and go do something else, but remain nearby.

On the sitter's next visit, remain at home still, but go about your business of making phone calls, fixing dinner, and so forth. By her third visit, you should be ready to head out the door. Be sure to tell the kids that you're leaving, and tell them when you'll return. Don't just quietly slip out the door; they'll think that you've abandoned them.

Bye-Bye Baby

Although it may seem like you're spending more time home in the beginning than you'd like, remember your sitter is a stranger to your kids and to you, and a period of adjustment is part of the process of developing a happy relationship.

Resource

Book

In-Home Child Care: A Step-by-Step Guide to Quality, Affordable Care, by Debra K. Shatoff; St. Louis: Family Careware, 1998.

Budgeting Basics

- -

You Can Afford to
Stay Home Full Time

I f you think full-time parenting is just for families with lots of money, while middle-income families need two paychecks to stay afloat, think again. In every neighborhood, in all socioeconomic groups, you'll find households where one parent works while the other stays home with the kids. So how can they do it and you can't? For some families it requires lots of sacrificing and creative budgeting, but for the rest, the decision to stay home was easy. It was simply a matter of running the numbers—two paychecks don't always add up to more money.

"There's an all too common belief or assumption that most families have to have a second income to make ends meet," says Linda Kelley, home economist and author of *Two Incomes and Still Broke? It's Not How Much You Make, but How Much You Keep.* "The second income often disappears with all the assorted job expenses that crop up when you add a second income to your budget."

What a Tax Racket

What kind of expenses? Taxes for one—federal, state, and social security (a whopping 7.65 percent of your gross income).

When both incomes are mixed together on a joint federal tax return, the second income (usually the spouse who earns the least amount of money is deemed the second income earner, and because women, on average, still make less than men, most couples count the wife's paycheck as the second paycheck) ends up paying a higher tax rate in two ways: first, two paychecks often push couples into higher tax brackets, say, from 15 percent to 28 percent. Second, although there are two incomes, deductions can only be taken once.

Exemptions, deductions, and other credits can cut a one-paycheck family's taxable income by half, thus reducing the tax rate by half. If, for example, a one-income family has an adjusted gross income of $40,000, they would fall within the 15 percent tax bracket, but with deductions and exemptions their taxable income is reduced to $20,000, paying an effective tax rate of only 7.5 percent.

If you want to know what the true tax rate is on your second paycheck, Kelley suggests refiguring last year's joint tax return by substituting the two-income entries with just the

IRS Tax Table (for 1998)

Bracket	Married, filing jointly (taxable income)
15%	$0–$42,350
28%	$42,351–102,300
31%	$102,301–155,950
36%	$155,951–278,450
39.6%	$278,451 and up

Source: Internal Revenue Service

first income (the higher income). Then, subtract the *total tax* paid by the first income from the *total tax* paid by the combined incomes (the difference from line 54 on Form 1040, line 28 on Form 1040A, or line 10 on Form 1040EZ). Be forewarned: the result could make you faint.

To illustrate, let's say John and Gina are a working couple with two kids. John makes $42,000 a year, while Gina earns $30,000, making their joint income $72,000 a year. With deductions and exemptions ($20,600) their taxable income is $51,400, making their federal tax bill for last year $14,392. If Gina leaves her job, their income would drop to $42,000. Because their deductions would stay the same, their taxable income would be reduced to $21,400, making their tax bill only $3,210. So while Gina earns less than her husband, she pays three quarters of their total tax bill.

$$\begin{array}{r} \$14{,}392 \text{ (combined tax)} \\ - \quad \$3{,}210 \text{ (tax on first income)} \\ \hline \$11{,}182 \text{ (tax on second income)} \end{array}$$

The Incredible Shrinking Paycheck

Okay, so taxes are a bite, but everyone pays them, right? And what if you don't mind paying higher taxes for the extra cash that a second income brings in and the lifestyle that it affords your family? Kelley stresses that there are many more expenses that eat into a second paycheck, fooling many into believing that their lives are much richer for their troubles.

Let's start with child care—clearly the most visible cost for two-income households. "Everyone recognizes their cost for child care," Kelley notes. "That's the one thing that's blamed for everything. Couples often say, 'Once the kids get a little older and that cost disappears, that money is going to be ours to spend and life's going to be good.' What they don't realize is that there are so many other expenses that can dwindle away that second paycheck. In fact, they may be prone to spend more money on these other expenses once that babysitter bill disappears."

The cost of a corporate wardrobe (including dry cleaning and the unending expense of pantyhose), commuting daily, and lunches out with colleagues, as well as time-saver items (like quick-to-fix meals, housekeepers, cell phones) and rush shopping (buying something in a hurry without comparison shopping in the hope of getting home faster) all quickly devour a second paycheck.

There are hidden costs, too, items that families often overlook. The biggest culprit? Reward-guilt buying—those little gifts that parents give as payment to the kids and to each other out of guilt for their hectic schedules and not spending as much time with the family as they would like, or gifts they give to themselves because they've "earned it" for working so hard.

Crunching Your Own Numbers

To tabulate second-income expenses, go through last year's date book or calendar, checkbook, and credit-card statements to help ensure your figures are as accurate as possible. Better yet, have the second incomer carry a notebook to work daily for a month so that he or she can jot down and keep track of all the little extras like midmorning coffee and donuts, office pools, coworker gifts, nail salon visits, and the like.

"After they identify what they're clearing from that second paycheck, most people know what to do next," Kelley says. "If that second check is netting, for example, only 10 or 20 percent, couples need to decide if that small sum is worth it. Now if you're spending that money on groceries, eating is a hard habit to break. But if the money is being spent on a new car payment, maybe a slightly older car is the answer."

When figuring your own true take-home pay, benefits like health coverage, retirement pensions, and life insurance policies are worth their weight in gold and should be carefully considered in your final tally. A family caring for a child with major medical problems, for instance, might need the extra health benefits of a second income and may choose to continue working solely for that reason. It's worth noting, too, that before pulling the plug you should consider other long-term ramifications such as loss of 401(k) contributions and possibly jeopardizing future career advancement.

Even after tabulating your true take-home pay, you may still be torn between working and staying home. You may feel that you need the extra income, however small, to keep your household bookkeeping in the black. Now is the time to make a choice. Keep in mind, though, that with very little effort, most people can shave thousands of dollars off the family budget without giving up such creature comforts as food and housing—some financial experts say the average family can cut 20 percent from their current budgets without feeling the pinch. If you're determined to make full-time parenting a reality, your next step is to create an effective budget, one that makes up for the second-income shortfall and, most importantly, one that you can stick to.

We've made a lot of adjustments. We stay in a small house in a neighborhood that's good but not where we'd freely choose to be. We don't take as many vacations; we don't go out to eat as much. There are a lot of sacrifices, but it's worth it.

Before the Budget

Whether your dream is to have enough money saved so that one parent can stay home with the kids or you want to retire by age 55, before you sit down to draft a budget you'll need to think about both your short- and long-term goals. "Money is a means to an end. And before you go after the means, you should know what the end is," says Kathy Kristof, syndicated financial columnist and author of *Kathy Kristof's Complete*

Fact

More than 80 percent
of America's self-made
millionaires consider
themselves "frugal."

*I think husbands and
wives have to be in it
together. Both parents
have to agree that this is
what they want for their
children. I've witnessed
other couples who have
children, but it's almost
like they haven't made
the commitment together.
Yeah, the mom may stay
home, but the dad still
drives the nice sports car
while the mom is penny-
pinching. That's not
sacrificing. The parents
have to recognize that
each one has to give a
little bit.*

Book of Dollars and Sense. "If you don't have a plan, there really is no point in accumulating money. When you set goals, you tend to get them."

Kristof suggests that husbands and wives first make separate wish lists, each thinking about what it is that they truly want—say, within five years, and then again in twenty—then discuss their goals together.

Husbands and wives often have different aspirations. While one spouse may be thrifty, saving for a European vacation, the other may be a spender, bringing home a new household toy weekly. A couple will quickly blow their budget as the saver becomes frustrated with the spender: "For every dollar I save, he spends. Why bother?" Instead, according to Kristof, discuss individual goals and then let each person get a portion of his or her dream.

But can setting goals actually help curb spending? Absolutely, insists Kristof. "If more people actually sat down and set their goals, they would have less trouble reining in their spending. Then if they impulsively buy some luxury item, they would see the things they really cared about slipping away." And this, she says, will stop most people from spending further.

Creating a Budget

Okay, so your goals are set. Both you and your spouse are on the same page. Now what?

First, never plan a budget on what you think you *should* be spending. (I'd like to spend $100 a week on groceries, but that's just a dream. Our actual tab is closer to $130, so I work around that.) Instead, take a financial history by writing down everything that you spent last year. Although a notepad for documenting your spending will do, almost all personal finance books (including Kristof's) include work sheets listing many expenditures that may be overlooked (like school supplies, magazine subscriptions, and baby-sitters). Several computer programs like Quicken can also help. It will take several hours to log in last year's expenses as you comb through old credit card statements, checking account ledgers, business receipts, and any other documents that might be helpful. For those who spend cash, rarely using credit cards, Kristof suggests carrying around a notebook (in the same way that Kelley recommends second incomers do) notating each expense, large or small. This way, she says, you can take a good look at your spending habits.

Once it's all down on paper, the next step is to put limits on things. Kristof notes that you never truly think about your spending repercussions until you see it all in black and white. "When my husband and I were first married, we used to go out to dinner all the time," she recalls. "We never thought about what it was costing because we didn't go to expensive places. Then we actually sat down and figured out it was costing us $400 to $500 a month! One glance at that and I said we can cook at home more often."

We've always been very judicious on how we spend money. We've never been into material things, conspicuous consumption, so it wasn't a huge change to give up my paycheck. It doesn't make us better or worse; it's just who we are. We had a lot of money in savings so we felt in pretty good shape when I quit my job. That's one of the advantages of waiting to have kids.

Budgeting Basics

- **Make sure your budget is realistic.** Don't give up every little pleasure like an occasional dinner out, a weekend trip to the beach, or a bouquet of roses just to meet long-term goals. Reduce, don't eliminate.

- **If you need something, buy it.** Money is for spending. If you truly need something, don't deprive yourself of it. Plan for it, then buy it.

- **Live within your means.** Lay off credit cards and spend only what you have. Ignore peer pressure to keep up with the Joneses.

- **Create healthy habits.** Don't binge shop to fight depression. Don't project your needs onto your kids. (Do they really need designer clothes and elaborate birthday parties?) Give up smoking and fast-food snacking. Ask for receipts. (It's easier to keep track of spending.)

- **Go easy on yourself.** If you fall off the wagon and buy that big-screen television, don't imagine that one digression will ruin you for life—it doesn't. Try again.

- **Beware of incidental spending.** Benjamin Franklin once said, "Beware of little expenses; a small leak will sink a great ship."

I don't think we sacrificed; it didn't seem like a big deal. But I was good at making ends meet on one salary. We had a lot of hand-me-down furniture. I gardened and canned. I made all my own baby food. I used cloth diapers. I shopped at bread thrift stores. It made a big difference. We never lived beyond our means.

BUDGET TRIMMING AND OTHER HEALTHY TIPS

Enough talk. What about some serious slashing? Or at least some painless ways to save some big money.

■ **Get rid of credit-card debt.** Having a nest egg of several thousand dollars in a 3 percent passbook account amounts to nothing when you're paying the minimum each month off a $4,000 credit-card bill at 18 percent. Start paying off credit-card debt by canceling all but one account (to use only in emergencies), and try these suggestions.

1. **Move high-interest credit-card debt to a lower-interest card.** Look in business newspapers and magazines for a list of competitive companies. Many offer low "teaser rates," some as low as zero percent, that can last from six months to a year, plenty of time to make a serious dent in your debt.

2. **Liquidate your lower-interest bank accounts to pay off bills.** Then start fresh by saving regularly.

3. **Look for a no-fee, no-point, home-equity line of credit to pay off debt.** The interest is usually tax deductible.

■ **Pay yourself first.** Out of the red and into the black. The most painless way to sock some money away is to enroll in an automatic savings plan through the working spouse's employer. You can have money siphoned off your biweekly paycheck and automatically deposited into a designated account. After the first few weeks, you'll adjust and forget you ever had that extra dough. Many mutual-fund companies, for instance, will tap your checking account monthly for small deposits of $50 or $75. And you'd be amazed at how quickly your money will grow. If you invest $50 a month in a conservative stock-oriented mutual fund (assuming an 8 percent return), for example, in five years you'll have nearly $3,700. Up it to $75, and it rises to more than $5,500. With those figures, short-term goals don't seem so nebulous, do they?

One more word of advice when it comes to saving money. Experts warn that if your nest egg is accessible (say, in a savings account at your local bank), you're more likely to tap into the account and spend it. Instead, keep your savings in an out-of-town credit union or brokerage account.

■ **Save money on big-ticket items.** Insurance, whether for your car, home, or life, is often the largest household expense and one that many people neglect to consider when trying to reduce spending. Because insurance rates change frequently, shop your policies around every few years to see if there's a better deal out there. Also, think about raising your deductibles. For instance, if you increase your home-owner's insurance deductible from $250 to $1,000, you could save more than 10 percent a year on your premiums. If your health insurance is a preferred provider organization (PPO), think about switching to a health maintenance organization (HMO).

If your car is more than five years old, you may want to drop your comprehensive and collision coverage because these two expenses cover the cost of repairing or replacing your vehicle (and after five years, your car may not be worth much). In his book, *The Consumer Bible*, author Mark Green advises that you wait until your premium is more than 10 percent of your car's current value before dropping the coverage. For example, if your car is worth $6,000 and your yearly comprehensive and collision premium is $750, you might want to eliminate it (10 percent of $6,000 is $600, $150 less than your premium). But be sure to put away the money you save in premiums so you'll have an adequate cushion to buy a new car in case you do get into a major accident. He also suggests dropping your medical coverage if you can get on your spouse's medical plan through his or her job.

■ **And speaking of cars . . .** Did you know that cars depreciate dramatically in the first few years off the showroom lot? That means that you can buy a two- or three-year-old car for only 60 percent of its original value. If you're worried about running into mechanical trouble, most new-car warranties are transferable to second owners. In addition, pre-owned cars cost less to insure.

You Are What You Drive?

Take a look at how much it costs to own and operate some of the top-selling cars and sport utility vehicles (SUVs) of 1999 in the United States (costs include operating expenses: gas, oil, maintenance, and tires; and fixed expenses: insurance, depreciation, taxes, and licensing). All four-door models are similarly equipped.

Vehicle	Annual Cost
Cadillac DeVille	$14,834
Oldsmobile Aurora	$13,943
Buick Riviera	$12,947
Buick LeSabre Limited	$10,603
Nissan Maxima GXE	$9,793
Ford Explorer XL	$9,713
Chevy Blazer	$9,408
Dodge Intrepid	$9,328
Ford Taurus SE	$9,060
Jeep Cherokee SE	$9,009

Vehicle	Annual Cost
Chevy Lumina	$8,845
Dodge Caravan Passenger	$8,442
Toyota Camry CE	$7,729
Honda Accord DX	$7,461
Saturn SL2 Sedan	$6,756

Source: Runzheimer International

■ **Your home.** When it comes to refinancing your home, the old 2 percent rule (to make refinancing profitable, home owners should refinance only when market rates are 2 percent lower than their current rate) is a thing of the past. These days, thanks in part to no-cost loans, home owners can still save thousands of dollars by refinancing their homes even if the difference is a percentage point or less. Whether you should take advantage depends on two things: refinancing fees (yes, even no-cost loans cost *something*) and how long you plan on staying in your home. Obviously, the longer you stay in your home the better chance you'll have of making up the closing costs and reaping the financial rewards.

Shopping for a new loan on the Internet can save you lots of time. In addition, most home-loan websites (like e-loan.com) spell out the fees associated with refinancing. To get a rough idea of how long it will take you to begin saving money, subtract the monthly payment of the new loan amount from the old loan amount, then divide that figure into the cost of refinancing. The answer will tell you how many months it will take to break even. For example, let's say your current monthly payment is $1,200, but if you refinance, the amount will drop to $900. Take the $300 difference ($1,200 − $900 = $300) and divide it into the cost of the refinance. For instance, if it costs $3,670 to refinance your loan, it will take 12.23 months to break even (3,670 ÷ 300 = 12.23), roughly one year. Is it worth it? That all depends on whether you plan on staying in your home for more than a year.

Another point to consider: when you refinance, your loan is reamoritized and begins as a new loan. So if you've been paying on your current loan for fifteen years, you need to apply for a fifteen-year loan for the two to properly compare; otherwise, you'll be starting a new, thirty-year loan all over again.

When you plan, you don't waste money.

If the thought of going through all the refinance paperwork sends your head in a tailspin, there might be another way to save money on your mortgage. Many banks will *reconfigure* your current loan for a small, one-time fee. I recently called my lender to ask if they had such a program. For $500, I converted the interest rate from my existing loan from a variable to a lower fixed-rate. No escrow, no paperwork, and the loan adjusted the following month. I shaved $90 off my monthly payments with a single phone call.

But what if your home has decreased in value from when you bought it, making a refinance out of the question? You might want to consider having your home reassessed in the hope of lowering your property tax bill. Call your county tax assessor's office for an application. You may be stuck with your current mortgage, but at least you could save hundreds of dollars annually in property taxes.

■ **Groceries.** In our house, we love good food, and my grocery bill reflects it. Fortunately, I have learned a few tricks to keep the costs under control.

1. **Beware of the warehouse.** Although you can usually save big bucks by stocking up on canned items and paper goods at warehouse stores, that's not always the case, and it pays to know prices. In addition, you have to be aware of waste and extreme excess when you buy in bulk. When there's a thirty-ounce box of cereal on your table, you're bound to pour yourself a heaping bowl that you may not finish.

With three small kids, we use a lot of antibacterial soap in our house. I bought a gallon of the liquid germ fighter and saved big, but that was more than eighteen months ago! I still have half a bottle left. And I don't think I'll ever use up the three pounds of baking powder I bought, no matter how many cookies I bake for the kids. Solution? Cancel my membership ($30 a year) and stock up on grocery-store specials instead.

2. **Keep a price notebook.** Because most people tend to buy the same products week after week, a notebook documenting the cost of products and their sale prices in various stores will cue you in on a money-saving sale.

3. **Clip coupons on only those items you use regularly, and when you see them on sale, buy them, even if you don't need them at the moment.** You'll save twice as much.

4. **Know which day your local supermarket changes its specials, then shop the day before for incredible "manager's special" deals on meat and poultry.** (My supermarket butcher told me they need to clear out the inventory to make way for the new items.)

5. **Eat smart.** Start a vegetable garden. The kids will love picking vegetables for dinner; eat meatless meals more often; and cook from scratch whenever possible (convenience items cost much more).

■ **Energize me.** Energy costs—electric, water, and gas—are another big household expense but one that can be tamed.

1. **Switch to compact fluorescent lighting.** It's the word on the street—fluorescent bulbs are much more efficient than regular incandescent bulbs. For the same lighting output, fluorescent bulbs use 75 percent

I've always been frugal, but now I've just stepped up my level of frugality! When I buy clothes on sale—I only buy clothes when they're on sale—I keep my receipt and go back two weeks later and see if it's been marked further down. If it has, the store gives me the difference. I keep meticulous records. I mark on the calendar when the fourteen days are up. There isn't a piece of clothing that I take back that I don't get at least half of my money back. It's part of my weekly routine with Francesca, "OK, Mommy has to go to the store to see if this has gone on sale."

Converting Incandescent Bulbs to Fluorescent Bulbs

If your incandescent bulb is . . .	Fluorescent bulb equivalent is . . .
25 watts	4 watts
40	11
60	15
75	20
90	23
100	27

less electricity. And although they initially cost more, they last ten times longer than regular bulbs.

2. **Be appliance savvy.** Wash clothes in cold water only. Not only will you save on natural gas, but your clothes will last longer, too. Use the air-dry setting on the clothes dryer rather than the heat-dry setting. Turn up the air conditioner a degree or two. Run the dishwasher late at night when water costs are down.

3. **Insulate around doors and windows and up in your attic.** More than half of the energy used to heat or cool your home escapes because of poor insulation.

■ **Save on traveling.** Just because you're cutting costs doesn't mean you must deprive yourself of life's fun stuff. On the contrary, once you get your spending and saving under control, you should be able to have the money to travel with your family. The secret is not spending a fortune to do it. Before you book airline tickets or make hotel reservations, check out *consolidators*, companies that buy tickets or hotel rooms in bulk, then pass some of the savings on to you.

On a recent trip to New York City, we stayed in a large one-bedroom suite with a kitchen at the very nice Beekman Towers near the United Nations. The *rack rate* (regular listed price) was $329 per night, but by booking through Express Reservations (800-356-1123), we paid only $220 per night. We saved even more by taking advantage of the fully equipped kitchen and cooking many of our meals right in our room.

■ **Bargain.** As I was scrutinizing our family budget a few years back, one glaring expense was drinking water that we have delivered to our door in five-gallon jugs. (Here in Southern California, few dare to drink the tap water.) At a cost of $8 per five-gallon jug ($1.60 a gallon), our monthly bill ran about $40, or $480 a year. I decided a better alternative was to buy the water from the supermarket at 99 cents per gallon. When I called the water company to cancel my account, they immediately transferred me to a supervisor. Without any hesitation, she said, "How about if we lower the cost from $8 to $6?" Her comment startled me. You mean you can actually negotiate these things? The answer is a resounding yes!

Next time a long-distance phone carrier representative calls, try your hand at bargaining. The offer they first present may not be the best. Ask about waiving certain fees or tossing in some frequent flyer miles. Even mortgage loans can be negotiated. It never hurts to ask.

■ **Massive consumerism.** Have you ever wondered why many of our parents were able to successfully live on one income and still have money for a yearly vacation and a nice house in the suburbs? The answer might be right in front of your eyes. Today's families are afflicted with "affluenza," the need to buy excessively. If you need more proof, consider this: personal bankruptcies are on the rise. More than one million Americans filed in 1997 alone. As of October 1997, outstanding consumer debt had reached $1.23 trillion, according to Federal Reserve figures.

Just take a look at all the little extras that many households take for granted and that our parents never even heard of:
- Health-club memberships
- Cell phones and pagers

- VCRs, video rentals, satellite dishes, cable television
- Call waiting, three-way calling, message centers, call forwarding
- Faxes, computers, Internet services
- Microwave ovens, dishwashers, clothes dryers
- Magazine and newspaper subscriptions
- Fruit-of-the-month, wine-of-the-month, flower-of-the-month

To be sure, many of these items are so mainstream, we'd be lost without them, but all of them cost money—in many instances, lots of money (not to mention time away from family). If you're trying to conserve on cash, you might want to think about cutting back or cutting a few out of your life completely.

Start Slashing

This has been a mere sampling of ways to cut expenses. There is a plethora of great personal finance books out there that can help you get your spending under control, making your dream of full-time parenting tangible indeed.

RESOURCES

Books

The Consumer Bible: 1001 Ways to Shop Smart, revised edition, by Mark Green; New York: Workman Publishing, 1998.

Kathy Kristof's Complete Guide to Dollars and Sense, by Kathy Kristof; New York: Macmillan, 1997.

Miserly Moms, by Jonni McCoy; Elkton, MD: Holly Hall Publications, 1996.

Shattering the Two-Income Myth: Daily Secrets for Living Well on One Income, by Andrew Dappen; Mountlake Terrace, WA: Brier Books, 1997.

The Tightwad Gazette and *The Tightwad Gazette II,* by Amy Dacyczyn; New York: Villard Books, 1993, 1995.

Two Incomes and Still Broke? It's Not How Much You Make, but How Much You Keep, by Linda Kelley; New York: Times Books, 1996.

Unbelievably Good Deals That You Absolutely Can't Get Unless You're a Parent, 2nd ed., by Cary O. Yager; Chicago: Contemporary Books, 1997.

Consolidators

Express Reservations
(800) 356-1123
Room Finders USA
(800) 473-7829
Room Exchange
(800) 846-7000

Internet Sites

loanworks.com or e-loan.com—Refinance your home on-line.

Childproofing

Creating a Safe At-Home Environment

When you're at home all day with the kids and you haven't taken the time to childproof, not only are you putting your children's well-being at risk, but you're also setting yourself up for a stressful day, as you must now monitor their every move to keep them from harm.

When you create a suitable home atmosphere, however, free of harmful boundaries, everyone benefits. The kids are able to roam on their own inside the house and out, exploring at will. Childproofing offers parents peace of mind, too. No more hovering by children's sides all day, fearful that they may hurt themselves on the fireplace hearth or wrap themselves in the floor-lamp cord.

But how do you create such an environment without rubberizing the walls or hermetically sealing your house for the next ten years? "If you can deal with a problem without childproofing it, do it," says Christina Elston, editor of *LA Par-*

ent magazine and author of *Safe and Secure: A Loving Parent's Guide to Child Safety*. Instead of installing a cabinet latch (a somewhat misleading safety gadget that most kids learn to operate anyway), move the kitchen cleaners from underneath the sink to a shelf where your child can't reach them. When it comes to childproofing your home, Elston says, always choose the least complicated solution.

> Home may be where the heart is, but it's also where the most injuries occur to infants and young children.

A Childproofing Philosophy to Live By

We all know how important it is to childproof to protect our little ones from injury. But how much is enough? And is there such a thing as too much? Although parents should take the time to meticulously eliminate danger zones throughout their home, there is a hidden drawback to going overboard. "If you childproof to a point where you never say no, or you start to limit your child's experience, you're missing an opportunity to teach them about things that are unsafe," Elston says.

If you put all knickknacks away, making your whole home accessible, for instance, then your kids are bound to go through life thinking that they can touch anything that's within their reach. There has to be balance when safeguarding your home. Instead of removing all breakables, place a few expendable ones throughout your house and use them as a teaching device.

In our house, we have an antique lamp with colored glass panels in the living room. Although they know that it's off limits, my boys love to tug at the pull chain. They did pull it to the floor once, breaking one of the panels to the tune of $150, but they haven't touched it since. They learned their lesson, albeit an expensive one!

Putting baby gates up all around your house is another childproofing technique that parents should reconsider. Not only is it inconvenient to continually hurdle across them, but corralling your child in one room and cutting off his access to others—especially the kitchen—may keep him safe, but Elston warns that it does little in teaching him about how to act responsibly when in that room. Instead of never letting him near the kitchen, take him in with you when you cook. "The greatest childproofing device for the kitchen is to have your child cook with you," Elston notes. "A young child can wash vegetables in a bowl of water placed on the floor. She'll wash a zucchini for an hour!"

Teaching children about danger and how to act accordingly is often harder to do than simply eliminating the danger, but parents will reap the rewards of a responsible child in the future.

Boo-Boos, Myths, and Other Common Misconceptions

To avoid the two most common bathroom accidents—scalding and accidental drowning—lower the temperature of your hot water heater to at least 120 degrees, and *never* leave a child under the age of three unattended in the bathtub.

When it comes to parenting, we often repeat what we heard as kids, regardless of its effectiveness. One such example is thinking that scaring children will teach them about safety. "When you scare kids you close up their little minds," Elston says. "If you explain, they become receptive."

When in the kitchen, instead of yelling, "Don't touch the stove. It will burn you!" calmly explain what will happen if they touch it while it's in use. "See this frying pan? I'm going to put some food in it. See what happens when I do? That's what will happen if you touch it."

"It's almost like a science experiment," Elston notes. "If you explain in a very calm way, it's not scaring them, and that's going to get you a lot further."

You've installed safety latches in all the cabinets, drawers, and all other hinged apparatus that you could think of. The kids are safe, right? Not necessarily. Another childproofing misconception is assuming that your child can't learn how to operate a safety device. "The business of children is to learn how the whole world works," Elston says. "Their minds are built to look at something and figure it out. They will watch you operate things and they will learn how to do it, too." With that in mind, you might want to rethink where and how you store the household cleaners—they may not be safe in the cabinet under the sink, even with a childproof latch.

Remember, too, that childproofing is an ongoing process. You can't take a tour of your house when your baby is six months old, appropriately childproof, and then never do it again. Parents often forget that with each new developmental step, their child is capable of getting into new mischief. Make an inspection of your home every time your child reaches a new stage of development, and update accordingly. "Parents are used to their kids not being able to do something, like rolling over, or sitting up, and then one day they can," Elston says. And often parents find out when it's too late, like when a once-sedentary baby suddenly rolls off the bed and onto the floor.

"If parents just pause a bit and go slowly, they know all they need to know about childproofing," observes Elston. "They can tell when something is unsafe."

Childproofing Room by Room

KITCHEN

- Keep all knives and other sharp utensils in top cabinets or latched drawers. Avoid storing on countertops.
- Make a habit of using back instead of front burners when cooking. Keep pot handles turned in.

- Keep all cleaners in original containers, and store them well out of reach of kids.
- Keep a small fire extinguisher handy, and know how to operate it.
- Keep counter appliances unplugged and out of reach.

BATHROOM

- Use a nonskid rubber mat or decals on the tub bottom to prevent slipping.
- Keep all small appliances like hair dryers and curling irons unplugged and out of sight.
- Keep all medication and cosmetics (especially nail polish) in original containers and hidden away in a high cabinet.
- Keep the toilet seat closed and install a child-proof latch.
- Close the bathroom door to discourage kids from exploring inside.
- Use plastic cups and accessories—no glass.

CHILDREN'S BEDROOM

- Keep crib away from miniblinds to avoid accidental cord strangulation.
- Make sure crib slats are no more than 2⅜ inches apart.
- Bolt all bookshelves to the wall to prevent them from falling over if a child climbs up to reach a toy.

LIVING AREAS

- Install child safety outlets on all electrical outlets (plug protectors can choke a small child if they dislodge).

- Identify and dispose of any houseplants that are poisonous.

- Install smoke detectors on every floor of your home and especially in each bedroom.

Daily Safety Check

Regularly cruise around your house baby-style—on all fours—to look for potential danger zones.

- Remove all small toys from the floor—a choking hazard for children under three.

- Make sure window screens are secure, especially on second-floor windows.

- Keep drapery and miniblind cords out of grabbing distance.

- Discard plastic grocery bags and broken balloons.

- Check for frayed electrical cords.

Outdoor Obstacles

It never occurs to most of us that we should pay as much attention to the landscaping surrounding our homes as we do to the potential dangers inside our homes. Many plants, shrubs, and trees—like oleanders—growing right in our backyards are dangerous and sometimes fatal if eaten. Parents should take the time to identify each plant in their yards and teach their kids not to put any plant life in their mouths.

"Most people don't even know what's growing in their own yards," Elston says. "Ask someone what the name of the plant is that's growing right next to the sandbox and I bet most can't tell you." Although it may be an arduous job to identify all your plants from a botanical book or taking a cutting to your local nursery, it could save a life.

Make sure there's adequate fall space surrounding outdoor play equipment (a minimum of six feet on all sides). And while grass may seem like it's soft enough to break a child's fall, it isn't. Wood or rubber chips or sand are better alternatives.

Where I live, in California, accidental drowning is the leading cause of death for children under five. With that sobering thought in mind, backyard pool safety should top every parent's childproofing list. Install several layers of protection around your pool by using fences, safety covers, alarms, or infrared detection.

Safely Situated

By taking the time to root out potential dangers in the home, family members and friends can enjoy their time together. But remember, no matter how well you childproof, or how often you repeat safety instructions to your kids, nothing takes the place of adult supervision. Always know where your kids are and what they're doing.

RESOURCES

Books

At Home (Safety), by Kyle Carter; Vero Beach, FL: The Rourke Book Co., 1994.

On the Safe Side: Your Complete Reference to Childproofing for Infants and Toddlers, by Cindy Wolf; Wichita, KS: Whirlwind Publishing Co., 1998.

Safe and Secure: A Loving Parent's Guide to Child Safety, by Christina Elston; New York: Berkley Publishing Group, 1998.

Baby Equipment Manufacturers' Phone Numbers (for Recall Information)

Century: (800) 837-4040
Cosco: (800) 544-1108
Evenflo: (800) 962-7730

Fisher-Price: (800) 432-5437
Graco: (800) 345-4109
Kolcraft: (800) 453-7673

Organization

U.S. Consumer Product Safety Commission hot line
(800) 638-2772

Commitment

- -

Are You Ready to Stay Home Full Time?

I'm not just here to baby-sit them. I'm here to interact with them, read to them—and even if they're watching TV, I sit and watch with them. I'm here to teach them. My staying home gives them a sense of security and stability during their early years that will make a difference later in their lives. Even as Rachel gets into elementary school, I want to be the one who helps her with her homework in the afternoon. I don't want someone else doing it, and I don't want to have to do it after work at eight o'clock at night either.

Whether it's the realization that parent care is better than day care, a longing to spend more time with your kids, or the desire to minimize the stress of your dual career as full-time professional *and* full-time parent, it's OK to want to stay home. In case you haven't noticed, being home with the kids full time is no longer frowned upon by our neighbors, friends, and relatives. Although you may still hear the occasional "What do you *do* all day?" from clueless observers, most applaud parents who choose to drop out of the workforce to nurture their own kids. What a change from the career-driven '80s.

Raising a family full time is enormously rewarding and enriching to both kids and their parents. On the other hand, it's difficult for many who have given up successful careers to be at home. It takes a huge commitment from both parents to make the transition successful.

Can You Have It All?

- -

In her book, *Sequencing*, Arlene Rossen Cardozo explores a rebirth in full-time mothering. No longer buying into the feminist teachings of the '60s and '70s that full-time mother-hood plus full-time career lead to fulfillment, more and more women are realizing that their dual roles don't provide them with happiness. Instead, trying to be all things at all times to all people leads to feelings of guilt, frustration, exhaustion, and conflict.

Yet, Cardozo writes, today's women can have it all—marriage, family, and career—but not all at the same time. *Sequencers*, as she calls them, mix modern feminism with tra-ditional mothering. The idea is simplistic but a sound solu-tion to an often difficult problem. First, complete an education and pursue a career. Next, when it's time to marry and have kids, leave the workforce to raise them full time. Finally, once the children are either in school or grown, incorporate your profession back into your life by either working from home, working part time, or any number of other innovative solutions that won't conflict with family.

Although the more than 300 sequencers that Cardozo interviewed for her book had similarities—all set out to dis-pute the myth that men and women must act similarly in all ways at all times; and as mothers, they could best take care of their own children—the group couldn't have been more dif-ferent. "I can't say that sequencers fit any kind of personal-ity type, because they don't. I can't say it's people from one kind of occupation group, or one part of the country, or one income group either, because it isn't," Cardozo says. "You can't characterize or generalize sequencers. It would be nice. Then people could say, well, I'm that kind of person so I know that's what I should be doing."

Reinventing the Wheel

Gone are the days when full-time moms referred to them-selves as housewives. Today's at-home moms have reinvented themselves, learning from the problems of the past.

We should have had the talk about our philosophy on raising chil-dren long before we got married, but it never occurred to me that I wouldn't stay home with Francesca and it never occurred to Dan that I wouldn't stay home with her. We were lucky that we both felt the same way.

I always assumed I'd go back to work after having kids. Then I had a kid and handed her over when she was seven weeks old to a woman I had met once. It came home to me very quickly. To me it seemed completely unnatural to hand over an infant to someone I thought was really nice but basically didn't know. While I was working, I just missed Jenna. It was like a physical need to be with her. It didn't feel right to be away from her.

I couldn't imagine going back to work. My six-week maternity leave had come and gone, and I had negotiated for three more months. Then at the end of that there was no question in my mind that I couldn't go back.

Unlike women of today, women of the '50s and '60s didn't have many career options. After high school, most married, settled in suburbia, and started a family. It's what you did. But to say that all women of that generation didn't work isn't so, Cardozo notes. "Women have always had their careers. They were teachers, they were nurses, they were secretaries," she says. "They just didn't have the range of choice that women today have." And that's the key difference between now and then—today's at-home moms have been in the workforce for any number of years before embarking on full-time motherhood. They are the first generation of women to stay home completely by choice. It's where they want to be.

Portrait of a Housewife

For me, I just can't imagine not being with her. I'm enjoying this more than I've enjoyed anything in my life. And I can't imagine somebody else doing the things that I feel are my job, my responsibility.

Women have traveled a long road to get where they are today. "Back in the very old days, when everyone was a full-time mom and that was the expectation, there was a sense of contentment that life was good for the most part," Cardozo says. Women's lives revolved around family and home. "Women were enjoying their kids. There was comfort in being who you were." Then something happened—the '60s.

In 1963, Betty Friedan wrote *The Feminine Mystique*, giving a voice to the discontentment that many women felt being isolated in suburbia with the kids all day while their husbands toiled away in the city. She called it "the problem that had no name." Society, she said, had unrealistic and outdated expectations of women. Since women were having far fewer children than their grandmothers, and life expectancy had risen dramatically, Friedan wrote, by the time they hit forty many women would be home alone, children grown and husbands enjoying the pinnacle of their careers. With more than half their lives left, these women faced a boring and dismal future. The answer was clear—get an education that would lead to a full-time career. Although the essence of Friedan's message was true, unfortunately she and other feminists who followed her maligned motherhood in the process.

"Feminists, in their wonderful equation, made it all make sense," Cardozo notes. "Except that they didn't have any room for children. They never thought about the children. Gloria Steinem didn't have any children. Betty Friedan's children were already grown." Cardozo points out that women who took Friedan's theory to heart threw the baby out with the bathwater. Although single women, married women without children, and married women with grown children all benefitted from Friedan's philosophy, married women with young children suffered.

"Everyone forgot the children," Cardozo continues. "And if you asked about it in a meek little voice, because all this noise was going on all around you, they'd say the lady down the street or Grandmother will take care of the kids." The problem with that scenario, says Cardozo, is that the lady down the street and Grandmother were listening to the feminists, too. "They had had their families young, their kids were grown, and they were back in the classrooms or offices. The feminist message was always great for women who had already raised their families. It still is."

Yet many listened. Women were suddenly out of the closet, out of the suburbs, Cardozo says, burning their bras and often their bridges. Not only were they working forty to sixty hours a week in the office, but when they came home at night, they began another job—mothering their children and running the household. The stress built. "Through the '70s and early '80s there was a sense of discomfort," Cardozo says. "Whatever I'm doing is wrong. I'm guilty if I'm home. I'm guilty if I'm at work. That sense that you should be doing something else contributed to the discontentment."

Stressed out and constantly racing to catch up, more and more moms said enough and began to reevaluate their lives

Everything that you didn't want to teach your kids about gender stereotypes they learn anyway through observation. So I say things like, "Mommy used to work in an office, and used to go to meetings, but Mommy's working at home and it's a lot harder!" I try to let them know that being at home is work, too.

I still don't see it as a sacrifice to stay home with Francesca. In terms of sacrificing a career, I feel like I have plenty of time. I was ready to shift gears to a new career anyway when I got pregnant.

I don't think it's so much a sacrifice as it is an adjustment to stay home. It was a sacrifice for me to go to work, to be physically separated from Jenna and Peter.

and roles as mothers and as women. During the '80s, when women were expected to pursue careers, some did decide to leave the corporate world and mother full time. Unfortunately, they were looked at as "dropping out" or following the "mommy track." It wasn't until the '90s that a cultural shift recognized full-time motherhood as a valid option. For women of this decade, family life and career have become more fluid. Over the course of their lives, women are now entering and exiting the workforce many times and to various degrees.

Is This a Trend?

I had major culture shock, and I honestly experienced major depression. I went from being responsible for the lives of six to twelve patients to having the biggest crisis of my day being no peanut butter for lunch.

When *Sequencing* was first published, in the mid-'80s, women who chose to once again stay home full time were an anomaly. By the early '90s, though, it was the beginning of a trend as more and more women were hanging up their briefcases (albeit temporarily). Yet it's still hard to pin down the numbers.

How many full-time mothers are out there? No one knows for sure. The problem lies squarely with statistics—it all depends on what you do with the numbers. "*The Bureau of Labor Statistics* counts you in the workforce if you work an hour a year," Cardozo emphasizes. "The people who want to make a case for keeping women in the workforce can show they have a critical mass of women out there by counting the part-timers." When you do this, she says, it puts the number of working mothers well into two-thirds of all mothers. "If you actually take the part-timers and segment them into how much they actually work—how many work from home, or how many work under ten hours a week—you come out with a much higher number of women who are at home."

One minute you say, what have I done with my life? But five minutes later you say, oh, they're so cute and I'm so glad that I'm here. But I'd never want to do it differently.

My life is such an example. I consider myself a full-time parent because that is my primary role, yet I generate income, causing the bureau to count me as a working mother.

Full-Time Benefits

For many women, including myself, the benefits of staying home far exceed the challenges. I know that my kids need me and that I make a huge difference in their young lives. Day care, no matter how cutting edge the play space or how educated and caring the provider, can never take the place of a parent loving and caring for her own kids.

Which brings us to another benefit: when you're an at-home parent, day care becomes a nonissue. No more frantic searches for a sitter when your child is too sick to attend school on the day you have a 10 A.M. meeting. In the day-care profession there's an enormous amount of employee turnover giving rise to inconsistency of care, while full-time parenting offers continuity of care. There are added health benefits, too. Kids who don't attend day care suffer from fewer colds and ear infections during the first three years of life since at-home kids are exposed to fewer germs.

When it comes to kids, quantity of time is as important as quality. The argument that an hour a day reserved just for one-on-one interaction with your child is enough to cement the parent-child bond doesn't hold water. Most male-female relationships couldn't survive on the quality-time theory, and kids are no different. Putting in the time is what matters most. Being there the moment your child needs you is what counts in her eyes.

Many families claim that when one parent stays home the amount of household stress drops dramatically. With dual-income families, time is at a premium. When both parents arrive home, dinner must be made, homework checked, baths taken, and bedtime stories read. By the time the kids are tucked away for the night, many parents feel robbed of any intimate time together, never mind any playtime with the kids. Weekends are spent catching up on the tasks that had to slide during the week—bill paying, household chores, grocery shopping. But when one parent stays home, much

At work, I was a real task-oriented person—I had a checklist of things that I had to accomplish every day. But during the first few months of staying home with Zach I was lucky if I got out of my pajamas. And I kept thinking, "Geez, I haven't done anything today." But the baby's alive, as comedienne Roseanne had said. Yes, it was an adjustment. I missed that sense of accomplishment that I got from my job. But as he got older and I learned how to juggle my time and work in things like gardening and canning, and fill our week with activities, it gave me that sense of accomplishment that I needed.

*I*t's a two-sided issue. Yes, I do believe that full-time motherhood can be a strain and a sacrifice. Everything to do with you gets put on the back burner. You tend to come last. You're always putting out energy, and by the time it comes to you, you're so exhausted there's nothing left. On the other hand, staying home with the children has allowed me to pursue other interests; it allows me to be a painter.

*T*here are some days when I feel like it would be so easy just to get up and go to work. Going to a job is so much easier because you can leave it when you come home. When you go to work, you do grown-up things—talk on the phone, send a fax—and you can go to lunch and talk to people. But those are fleeting feelings, and it's not close to anything that I really want.

more can be accomplished. (Admittedly, with a little organization and planning, but that's why you bought this book.)

But by far the most important reason that most stay home is to be an active part in their children's lives. They're young for such a short, short span of time, and parents don't want to miss it. They're there for all the firsts—good as well as bad. They get to participate in the most important years of their kids' lives.

"There's a value change," Cardozo observes. "Before you have a child, you don't know what it's all about. You're happy doing one thing—your job. But after you have a child, you see that you can't do both at once. You find that you have all sorts of responsibilities at home that you didn't have before."

Full-Time Challenges

There are many days (usually when the kids are hanging on my legs) when I wish I could escape to an office. I remember the time B.K. (before kids) when I went to work daily, had lunch with colleagues, and shared intelligent banter with other adults who didn't say things like, "Mommy, I have to take a poopey."

In addition to the demands of nurturing children full time (the whining, the fighting, never a free minute alone), there are personal challenges, too. To many, it's a huge emotional sacrifice. The feelings of isolation and loneliness that plagued some moms of the '50s and '60s still bother many mothers today. To combat those stay-at-home blues, you have to be proactive. You have to be a doer, an organizer. You have to seek out support, maintain relationships, and reinvent your life by redirecting and refocusing your goals. You have to be committed to your new role as a mom. Happiness comes from both external as well as internal motivation.

Another challenge is the loss of income. For many families, there's a substantial drop in salary when one parent pulls the professional plug. Belts have to be tightened and budgets carefully scrutinized to make one income do double duty. It can be a difficult adjustment to cut back on a lifestyle that was once comfortable, maybe even affluent. Yet many report barely feeling the pinch once they decided that family life is more important than having a new car every three years.

For women who had been very successful in their careers, it is an added difficulty to give up their jobs that they worked so hard to achieve. Some women report feeling cut off from the outside world (a.k.a. *coworkers*). A kitchen full of dirty breakfast dishes and the echoes of Barney singing in the background have taken the place of a structured office environment. When they leave their careers, they often feel like they leave their identities behind, too. It can be a blow to their self-image and self-esteem.

And let's face it: sometimes staying home can be downright boring compared to the constant stimulus of a busy, buzzing office setting.

Furthermore, when you're a full-time parent there's no recognition for a well-done job. No one says, "Hey, your kids are so well mannered. You've done a great job with them." In the corporate world, you're recognized for your accomplishments through promotions, awards, and bonuses. No such luck when you're at home.

Then there's the marriage. With one parent at home and one taking sole responsibility for the family's financial well-being, feelings of inadequacy from both can surface. The stay-at-home parent feels like she's not earning her own money or contributing to the family kitty, while the wage-earning spouse may feel an enormous amount of stress to produce and keep the family finances in the black.

Although women who stay home these days face challenges, they're not nearly as great as those of the early '80s, when few women were at home. Now role models abound.

It took me a year to fully adapt to staying home. I quit my job and immediately had a new baby, and it was hockey season, which meant Bob was on the road a lot, and it was winter in Northern Michigan. Those first two years, we were really isolated. I'm on the block and I'm alone. All day long, it was me and my kids. All my life I had either been in school or in work, where I didn't have to try to build a community; I had a ready-made community of people just like me, but now that was just gone. I realized I had been living in Big Rapids for five years and I hadn't made any friends there. I had to create a new community. Over the next four and a half years, I slowly built a lot of connections by doing community work.

I had times when I felt very isolated. In the mid-'80s, it seemed like I was the only mom who stayed home. There were no other full-time mothers in the neighborhood. But I'd say to myself, obviously, if I'm bored I haven't done enough to get out and meet other people. I needed to branch out. I took some child-development, mommy-and-me type classes offered at Michigan State University, where I met other interesting stay-at-home moms in similar situations.

When I first had Sam, I didn't recognize that it was a big commitment to stay home. It wasn't until a few years into it when I started to struggle with self-esteem issues—I thought I wasn't interesting enough or intriguing enough because I wasn't in the adult world—when I realized I was making a huge

You can't be in an office or corporation where there hasn't been someone before you who's either taken an extended maternity leave, phased out work, done some work from home, or left completely. Today, you're not alone, and there's comfort in numbers.

Make the Commitment

For some, the transition from full-time employee to full-time parent will take time. During the first months, many women feel elated to have the opportunity to stay home with their kids all day. They're filled with energy and pour their souls into mothering. But as the weeks slowly progress and they're on their one-hundredth round of "The Wheels on the Bus," their enthusiasm begins to wane. They start to feel antsy and unsure of their decision. Their careers, which once caused them stress, now seem like a heavenly proposition as they fantasize about staff meetings and power lunches. It's at this time that action is badly needed to regain that feeling of contentment and optimism.

- Focus on the real reason you decided to stay home—to love and nurture your kids and watch them grow into responsible and caring little people. Enjoy the present, think about the future, but don't dwell on the past.

- Take care of yourself so you'll have the energy and enthusiasm to take care of others. This means finding time alone to exercise and pursue other outside interests.

- Set realistic goals and boundaries. Apply your business skills at home—prioritize, organize, delegate.

- Have realistic expectations of your day. Caring for children in itself is an important achievement, but making "to do" lists gives you an even greater sense of accomplishment as you scratch off each task.

- Accept help when offered.
- Network with other full-time parents. Try to form a crew of other stay-at-homers and trade off baby-sitting.

"You have to be comfortable with yourself, and with your decision to be where you are," Cardozo advises. "If you're sitting around ambivalent, thinking 'I can be earning money,' or feeling demeaned because you're at home, it's going to detract from your general happiness."

RESOURCES

Books

Being There: The Benefits of a Stay-at-Home Parent, by Isabelle Fox, Ph.D.; Hauppauge, NY: Barron's, 1996.

The Feminine Mystique, by Betty Friedan; reprint edition; New York: Dell Publishing, 1997.

Reinventing Ourselves After Motherhood, by Susan Lewis; Chicago: Contemporary Books, 1999.

Sequencing, by Arlene Rossen Cardozo; Minneapolis, MN: Brownstone Books, 1996.

Staying Home: From Full-Time Professional to Full-Time Parent, by Darcie Sanders and Martha M. Bullen; New York: Little, Brown, 1993.

What's a Smart Woman Like You Doing at Home? by Linda Burton et al.; Vienna, VA: Mothers at Home, 1992.

personal sacrifice by staying home. I put an incredible amount of pressure on my husband to make me feel important, so the marriage went through a low. Finally, we pursued marriage therapy, and that led to individual therapy. It was a process of trying to figure out what's going on and how can I not put the pressure on my husband to make me feel pretty, important. And how can I find that within myself? I think that it was largely based on moving away from a career where my work was critiqued, and people would tell me how well I was doing, into a world where that wasn't going on anymore. Eventually, I realized that my work was my children and that they were moral, happy, and healthy. That was my positive feedback. It took me a while to recognize that that was a good thing.

Dad

- -

The Next Renaissance Man

They're not baby-sitters, substitute moms, or househusbands; and please don't call them "Mr. Mom" (an irritating moniker taken from the 1983 film starring Michael Keaton). They're stay-at-home dads who take their roles as full-time parents seriously. These days, it's common to see men romping around the playground or perusing the grocery aisles with their kids on weekdays, a time slot in the past dominated by the mom. Although women still make up the majority of full-time caregivers in this country, at-home fatherhood is a growing movement. Unfortunately, no one is exactly sure how big the movement actually is.

The Department of Labor Statistics says it's impossible to know exactly how many fathers are full-time parents because they don't have a category that exactly matches. It's estimated, however, that two million fathers take care of the kids and the house, nearly double the number from 1990. Obviously, stay-at-home parenting isn't just for moms.

"I wouldn't say that we're a movement or a revolution, but rather an evolution," notes Peter Baylies, publisher of a quarterly newsletter, *At-Home Dad*. "A dad with preschoolers at home has little time to reflect on putting together a *movement* as he is too busy wondering if he can do the laundry when the kids are napping."

After he was laid off from his software engineering job more than four years ago, Baylies and his wife, Susan, an elementary school teacher, decided he would stay home and take care of the couple's two children rather than send them back to day care. "As more women get into the workplace, receiving higher pay and breaking through the glass ceiling, more men are electing to stay home as they are making less than their wives," he says.

Through a survey of 368 readers of his newsletter, Baylies cites four main reason why dads stay home:

1. Couple didn't want to send the children to day care.

2. The wife made more money.

3. The wife wanted to work more.

4. The husband had a greater desire to stay home.

In these days of corporate downsizing and home-based businesses, many other full-time fathers are "telecommuters," corporate dads who work via the telephone, fax, and modem. By day they cart the kids around to playgroups and art lessons. But once the kids are in bed, either at nap time or nighttime, they shift gears and become entrepreneurs. Regardless of how they get there, though, stay-at-home dads are finally gaining attention.

> *Neither of us wanted our child to be brought up in a day-care–type situation. We discussed my doing this, as I have a more nurturing and patient character and would probably handle the onslaught of day-to-day stuff a bit better. My wife was also on a promising career path, and she made the larger salary of the two of us. It was no big deal for me. I'm not hung up on being the breadwinner.*

Tracking a Trend

The trend toward at-home fatherhood shouldn't surprise us. For years, American men overall have been trying to find more ways to spend time with their families. Gone are the days when Dad comes home from the office at six and disappears into his study to read the paper until dinner is ready. In fact, experts speculate that today's dads spend 33 percent more time with their kids than fathers of twenty years ago.

Most men pitch in with family responsibilities the minute they walk through the door. Whether it's to give the kids a bath, start cooking dinner, or simply sit down and play with their children, today's dad is right in there helping out. Yet few men have taken advantage of the Family and Medical Leave Act passed by Congress. The bill, designed to give working parents more time with their families, grants parents up to twelve weeks of unpaid leave to care for a sick family member or new baby. Many thought that dads would pounce on the opportunity to become more involved in their kids' lives by taking some time off from work. Few have. It's speculated that men are fearful that the time at home would hurt career advancement. Or maybe it's in their *jeans*. Culturally, especially in this country, most men are strongly connected to their professions and have a harder time being away from their jobs than women.

In other countries, especially in Western Europe, parental leave has been around for decades. Sweden, for instance, grants each parent a one-year leave of absence with 90 percent of pay in place. France, Germany, Finland, Italy, Canada, and Japan all have outstanding parental-leave policies, too.

The Benefits

Aside from the obvious benefits of full-time parenting in general, Baylies says that full-time fatherhood specifically offers children something more. "Because I am home, I know that my two boys will be less stereotypical, less biased," he says. "They will see that mommies stay at home and work,

At-Home Dad

Eager to connect with other full-time fathers, Peter Baylies launched *At-Home Dad*, a quarterly newsletter, in 1994 shortly after he was laid off from his job and decided to stay home to care for his two young children. Each issue contains six regular sections—Cover Story, Spotlight on Dad (interviews), Home Business, KidTips, Father Connections (resource list), and At-Home Dad Network (a national directory of dads interested in forming playgroups). The newsletter, which grew from E-mail conversations Baylies had with other stay-at-home dads, now has more than 600 subscribers.

and daddies do both, too. This will give them a realistic view of the outside world and they will be better prepared for it."

Dads relate differently to their children than moms do. Not better or worse, just differently. They're usually more physical with the kids, often seen wrestling on the living room rug. They drive the kids just a bit harder, asking them to meet higher expectations; and dads offer a distinctly male perspective on the world. Kids growing up in homes with Dad as primary caregiver tend to receive more parental nurturing than a household with Mom as primary caregiver because he gives his attention during the day; then, she steps in after work to lavish her love in the evening. In the past, society has often overlooked the positive influence and the vital role that men play in the lives of their children. Fortunately, we now know better.

WHAT FULL-TIME FATHERHOOD OFFERS

■ **A once-in-a-lifetime experience.** Dad gets a chance to step out of his traditional role as breadwinner and take on the important role of nurturer.

■ **A chance to develop closer bonds with children.** If you're working forty to sixty hours a week outside of the home, it's hard to be completely involved in your kids' lives. "Your job can wait," Baylies says. "Your kids can't." He adds that many of his subscribers remember their dads occupied with careers, with little time for family. Not wanting to follow in their fathers' footsteps, these fathers actively choose to break the cycle.

■ **An opportunity to cultivate new interests or investigate new careers.** During nap time and in the evenings, full-time dads are sometimes free to change career paths or pursue new interests. Many go back to school in the evening to get a degree or have started cottage industries with the help of a computer, fax, and modem.

Who says a role is defined by gender? I can kiss a boo-boo just as easily as my wife can. I think the problem is that in this society men have been brainwashed into believing that they must maintain the John Wayne image to be a man when in fact our emotions are just as strong and real as a woman's. We just don't express them as freely.

Think of the opportunity you will have to build a strong and firm relationship with your children that you most likely didn't have with your father. Our children need heroes again, and what better hero than their own dad?

The Challenges

It's hard being in the minority—fathers at home—of a minority—parents at home.

The first year as a full-time dad is usually the toughest as dads carve out their new roles at home. Although some moms find it difficult to adjust, too, dads have problems that are unique to their gender. For instance, when women encounter obstacles, they usually seek help. Men have a harder time admitting they are having a problem and therefore don't seek assistance as readily. "Dads tend to try to solve problems on their own," Baylies notes. "They don't reach out for support the way mothers do. That's why some at-home dads are isolated."

■ **Adjusting to a self-made schedule.** In the corporate world, many decisions are made for you—when to take lunch, office hours, appointments, meetings. When you're at home full time, you need to hammer out your own schedule, a difficult task for some men.

After Pam went back to work, I found myself taking on the same routine as Brett. I'd sleep when he'd sleep, eat when he'd eat. The house was not the neatest, and my own personal hygiene was not much better. Then I realized that this was not what being an at-home parent is all about. So I took a shower and cleaned the house on a regular basis. Brett and I started going places together.

■ **Societal labels.** Baby-sitter, unemployed dad—you name it, full-time dads have heard it all. Although society is slowly changing its perceptions of at-home fathers, they're still viewed by many as an anomaly. "I was talking to a friend and asked him what at-home dads have to do to get respect," Baylies remembers. "His knee-jerk reaction was, 'Get a job.' He meant it to be funny, but there was some truth to it. We are looked at as less than adequate by some who frown on us for spending so much time with our kids."

■ **Isolation.** While full-time moms complain of isolation and loneliness, too, full-time dads feel it more intensely because there aren't as many of them around.

■ **Loss of identity.** For most men, their identities revolve strongly around their careers. When you're an at-home dad, you need to reinvent yourself by changing your focus from corporate to community, something that many men find difficult.

DAD-to-DAD

After feeling left out from traditional female-run playgroups, Curtis Cooper put a small ad in an Atlanta-area newspaper looking for other stay-at-home dads. He got two calls. A small number, but Cooper was on his way. With his new friends and playgroup in place, Cooper began searching for other full-time fathers around the country. He wrote letters to other at-home dads, newspaper reporters, and TV and radio shows, spreading the word about his new organization, DAD-to-DAD. That was in January 1995. Since then, this national parenting group has grown to more than thirty chapters and provides other full-time fathers with the opportunity to form playgroups of their own, share fatherly information, and receive positive reinforcement. Each local chapter is different—some are small, some have a monthly newsletter, some have a monthly Dads-Only Night Out, but most meet for a weekly playgroup. Chapter members stay in touch with each other through the At-Home Dad Network, an extensive list of more than 300 other at-home fathers across the country. (The list is also featured in every issue of the At-Home Dad newsletter.)

Tips for Making At-Home Fatherhood a Success

- **Seek male support.** Whether you correspond with other at-home fathers across the country via E-mail or join a local support group, make an effort to find other men who stay home with their kids. If you can't find a fathers-and-kids playgroup, form one of your own. (Contact Curtis Cooper and DAD-to-DAD for additional help. *See* under "Support Group" at the chapter's end.)

Too many times folks get the idea that we're bumbling fools like Michael Keaton's "Mr. Mom" role, but we're far from that image. The press still hasn't figured out a way to put a positive spin on the story. They're always looking for a negative angle. But it is getting better.

I would go to playgroups with Brett, and the moms would be in the kitchen talking about whatever and I'd be in the other room playing with the kids. Actually, I think they felt as uncomfortable with me there as I did being there. I went to about five or six of these playgroups and then just stopped going. Of course, no one called to see why I stopped going. Now that I look back on it, I felt like a guy going to an all-girls school!

*M*ost people identify themselves as what their position is in their said careers, and they expect others to identify them in the same way. Even socially, people rarely step out of these identities. The first thing someone asks is, "What do you do?" When you stay home with your children, your identity falls more with what you think of yourself than what your job title is.

- **Schedule your time as if still at work.** Even small tasks like doing the grocery shopping on a certain day of the week give stay-at-home parents a sense of comfort. Schedule day trips with the kids, errands, phone calls, even household chores.
- **Get out of the house.** Make it a point to get out of the house on a daily basis. Everyone benefits from a change of scenery.
- **Find time for yourself.** Exercise is a wonderful stress reliever and confidence builder. Insist on making time for just you.

The New Suffragette

Although many at-home fathers feel like an oddity, Baylies urges perseverance. "We are pioneers," he says. "We are the first ones here and don't have a map yet. As more fathers are seen at the playground, that lost feeling will slowly go away. I know in my case people will eventually stop calling me Mr. Mom (we are fathers, not substitute for mothers), and they will eventually stop asking me at the supermarket if I am baby-sitting (how can you baby-sit your own kids?). In the meantime, while the rest of us are getting used to the new father, I don't take it personally. I just take it in stride."

Resources

Books

At-Home Dad Handbook, by Curtis Cooper; send a check for $12 per copy to ADDH/Curtis Cooper, 13925 Duluth Court, Apple Valley, MN 55124.

Trading Places, by Debbie Giggle (Georgian House, North Walsham Road, Hapisburgh, Norfolk, NR12 0QS, England).

Newsletter

At-Home Dad

> To subscribe, send $15 to Peter Baylies—*At-Home Dad*, 61 Brightwood Avenue, North Andover, MA 01845. E-mail: Athomedad@aol.com.

Support Group

DAD-to-DAD

> To find a DAD-to-DAD support group in your neighborhood, send an SASE to DAD-to-DAD, 13925 Duluth Court, Apple Valley, MN 55124. Telephone: (612) 423-3705; E-mail: Dadtodad@aol.com.

Internet Sites

www.slowlane.com—Offers a variety of newspaper and magazine articles on full-time fatherhood and links to fathering issues.

www.fathersworld.com/fulltimedad—The on-line magazine called *Full-Time Dads* offers advice and support through helpful articles, open forums, and a collection of Internet links.

America Online offers a weekly chat session for stay-at-home fathers on Monday evenings from 10 to 11 P.M. (EST). Find it in the "live events room" of Parents Soup.

Depression

Combating the Stay-at-Home Blues

ne winter when my twins were still small, we were stuck in the house for the third straight day because of the raging El Niño rainstorms here in Southern California. I was so desperate to get out of the house that I took a large sheet of thick clear plastic, an umbrella, and ushered the kids out to the car between downpours. My plan? Run some errands and then let the kids blow off some steam in the children's section at a local bookstore. When we arrived in downtown Pasadena, I put the kids in their stroller, wrapped some blankets around them, then covered the buggy with the plastic. My bubble boys were snug and dry, and I got out of the house. I was so elated to be moving that I hardly noticed the rain. As strange as my quest to be mobile might seem, that little two-hour journey saved my sanity that day.

Sure, I get the blues sometimes. It's hard to be with the kids all day, constantly giving directives ("Stop spitting water, or I'll have to take the glass away!") and answering the same question a dozen times in a single hour. Yet when I feel myself getting blue, I take action quickly. I know from experience that if I don't get up and get moving when I'm down, my blue mood unfairly affects the kids. I become more demanding of them, and they in turn act out for more attention.

Who Gets Blue?

Everybody at some point in his or her life feels down, blue, melancholy. It's a normal part of life. Although men experience the blues and battle clinical depression, too, women suffer from both more often. No one knows exactly why. "There's nothing documented as to why women get depressed more often," says Lisa Barnes, Ph.D., a clinical psychologist in private practice in Beverly Hills, California. Perhaps, she suggests, it's partly societal. "Generally, women are taught to be more self-reflective so that when they feel bad they turn it into themselves and it turns into depression. You could also say the opposite is true with men—they tend to look outward and get angry. Society doesn't teach them to look inward."

The Stay-at-Home Blues

The number-one complaint of stay-at-home parents is battling the occasional bout of the blues. For some, it's just a matter of getting out of the house for the afternoon or reconnecting with a friend, but for others, being with the kids all day without adult contact can be debilitating. This is especially true for parents who have recently left a career in which they interacted with fellow coworkers on a daily basis.

Barnes describes the stay-at-home blues as partly an identity issue, clearly affecting the way parents feel. "The full-time

It's worse here in the winter. In the spring and summer we're outside. We have friends that we meet, and we visit with lots of neighbors. That daily contact helps tremendously.

parent is someone who knew who she was in the working world and probably felt efficient, effective, and capable," Barnes says. A working parent closely identifies herself along career lines—a graphic designer, a doctor, a marketing researcher—whatever it may be, and takes comfort in that role. "Then all of a sudden, that identity is gone, and now she has a new identity. And if she's a new mom, it's a job she doesn't know how to do. She has to learn on the job, and it's a hard job to learn."

At the same time she's struggling to find a new identity, the stay-at-home mom is forced to face another problem: social isolation. Although some may argue that stay-at-home parents get depressed because they feel bored and unfulfilled with the new roles they've chosen, most full-time moms and dads would disagree. For newcomers it's the loneliness that sparks the stay-at-home blues. At the office, there was always someone to turn to for adult conversation, or even advice, but when you stay home all day, you quickly learn that your two-year-old has little to say about the rising stock market or the peace process in the Middle East.

When we were looking to move, we saw a lot of beautiful homes that were isolated, but we couldn't have that. So we bought a house in a new development where most residents are young. Because I stay at home and Matt works out of the house, we both needed the stimulation of neighbors.

"New stay-at-home moms don't get out there and join support groups or find places where they can meet other moms," Barnes explains. "They end up feeling trapped at home either because they've put their babies on very rigid schedules or they get overwhelmed about how hard it is to get out of the house. Certainly, it's hard for every new mom in the beginning, but there are people who get locked in and can't see their way out."

The Blues Versus Clinical Depression

Many people say they're depressed when actually they mean they're feeling a bit blue. So what's the difference? Good, old-fashioned *blues* occur when something negative has happened in a person's life: you experience a loss, you're particularly stressed out, things simply aren't going your way, or you've been treated unfairly. Although you might be feeling sad, or agitated, you can still *function* and are able to go about your day relatively in the same manner as when you're feeling good. *Clinical depression*, on the other hand, is an illness that affects not only how you feel, but how you think and how you act. Depressed people, no matter how hard they try, *simply can't function in normal day-to-day routines*. Often, there are biochemical changes in the brain as well. And while the blues usually disappear with little intervention, clinical depression requires the help of a doctor and possibly medication and/or hospitalization.

Symptoms of Clinical Depression

According to Barnes, clinical depression has the following signs:

- Change in appetite (significant weight gain or loss)
- Change in sleep pattern (insomnia or hypersomnia)
- Change in psychomotor agitation (quick to anger or complacent)
- Change in energy level (lethargic or restless)
- Subjective report of feeling sad, empty (may or may not be tearful)
- No longer taking pleasure in things that used to give pleasure
- Thoughts of hurting yourself or others

Determining whether you have the blues or depression—which is far more serious—depends on the severity of your feelings and the length of time that they exist. "We define clinical depression by having symptoms that last at least two weeks," Barnes explains. "A person must also

Postpartum Blues

Brought on by the dramatic and rapid change in hormones following the birth of a baby, *postpartum blues* (a.k.a. baby blues) are not much different from everyday blues. They can show up within a few days following the birth, or they can appear as late as eight to ten weeks following delivery. "Even if you're in good mental health, having a baby is a dramatic change," notes Barnes. "It's a hard transition." Postpartum blues can turn into *postpartum depression*, a serious condition similar to clinical depression, requiring a medical diagnosis and treatment.

identify the feelings as a significant change from previous functioning. It's not as though the person has always felt this way and now things are a little worse. The changes are notable."

Fixing the Blues

I'm the type of person who gets easily depressed. If I stayed inside a lot and didn't do anything physical, depression would hit. Getting out and exercising was imperative when I was a stay-at-home mom. I'd put the baby seat on the back of the bike and go for a ride with Zach. I'd find walking or running partners. Or I'd go to the Y and take some exercise classes with Zach.

Although clinical depression requires the help of a doctor, most people can fix the blues themselves. Usually there's an underlying problem that's causing someone to feel blue, and it's important to discover the cause and come up with solutions to the situation. Is the stress of living on one income making you feel blue? Or are you sad because you miss the stimulation of an office setting? For most people, an occasional bout of the blues can actually benefit them by giving them an opportunity to make positive changes in their lives. If money is tight, perhaps starting a small, home-based business is the answer. If you miss your former coworkers, try joining a support group and make new friends who are in a similar situation.

For the stay-at-home parent, the blues are usually associated with social isolation and loss of identity. Some report that it took close to a year to make the transition from full-time employee to full-time parent, and it was only through building new relationships and carving out a new role as a mother or father that they finally felt positive about their decision to stay home.

But regardless of what the cause of your sadness is or how you rectify the situation, there is one surefire way to quick fix the blues—exercising. "It's the whole idea of endorphins," Barnes explains. "When you exercise at some moderate level, your body creates and releases endorphins, the body's natural way of making itself feel better." Exercising gives immediate results.

Fortunately, it's not necessary to run a marathon to reap the benefits of endorphins. Barnes suggests that doing even simple things like taking a walk, visiting the park, or just leaving the house will help to keep the blues at bay. "Being sedentary begets a sedentary feeling," she stresses. "If you sleep too much, you feel sleepy all day. If you get moving, it's easier to stay moving."

BLUES BUSTERS

- **Make exercise a family affair.** Walking, hiking, biking, or just romping in the park—the benefits are plentiful, and the time spent together is bonding.

- **Get out of the house.** Although regular exercise is the perfect blues buster, simply getting out of the house daily will help. Keep the energy moving.

- **Set up a schedule.** Having a daily goal, even something as simple as grocery shopping every Monday morning, gives the stay-at-home parent feelings of self-worth and accomplishment. But don't let a regular schedule rule your life and keep you from meeting other stay-at-home parents and their kids. It's OK to deviate from a routine in favor of having a good time with your kids.

- **Develop a support system.** Find other stay-at-home parents by frequenting the same local park or library story time, join a support group like FEMALE (*see* Support System chapter), or enroll in Mommy-and-me-type classes.

- **Ask for help.** Don't wait until you're overwhelmed to ask for help from your spouse, other family members, or friends.

- **Keep in touch with former coworkers and friends.** Pick up the phone and call someone. Meet monthly for a night out or a leisurely lunch.

When I get that feeling, I know that means I need to surround myself with people my own age. I always call my friends to organize a coffee-and-bagel breakfast or pizza-and-wine dinner. It pulls me through it.

Singing Away the Blues

Music, too, has an enormous healing effect. When you feel yourself getting a bit melancholy, turn up the volume on one of these tunes, call the kids, and act a little crazy; or belt it out at the top of your lungs.

"Hold on I'm Coming," by Sam and Dave

"Pump It Up," by Elvis Costello

"What I Like About You," by The Romantics

"You Can Call Me Al," by Paul Simon

"Mustang Sally," by Wilson Pickett

"What'd I Say," by Ray Charles

"Respect," by Aretha Franklin

"I've Got You Under My Skin" and "New York, New York," by Frank Sinatra

"Honey, I'm Home," by Shania Twain

"In the Mood," by the Glenn Miller Orchestra

Is It OK to Tell the Kids?

You're having a bad day, and the kids sense there's something wrong. Should you tell them? Babies and small children pick up on the negative energy that surrounds them when parents are sad. Barnes suggest telling your children how you are feeling as a way of defining the tension that exists, but be careful not to trouble them with any kind of expectations. "It's OK to tell your kids that you're sad," Barnes explains. "But it's not OK to burden your children and to expect that they can understand what that means, or that they can somehow make you feel better."

Beyond the Blues

Remember, feeling blue is a normal part of everyday life, and it doesn't necessarily mean that something is wrong or that you've made a bad decision. Sometimes, feeling blue can actually be beneficial when you make positive changes in your life. "Ultimately, the hardest part of being a parent is that even when you feel bad you still have to go on," observes Barnes.

RESOURCES

Books

The Complete Idiot's Guide to Beating the Blues, by Ellen McGrath, Ph.D.; New York: Alpha Books, 1998.

Getting Un-Depressed, by Gary Emery; New York: Simon & Schuster, 1988.

Mind Over Mood: Change How You Feel by Changing the Way You Think, by Dennis Greenberger, Ph.D., and Christine A. Padesky, Ph.D.; New York: The Guilford Press, 1995.

Organizations

Depression After Delivery
P.O. Box 1282
Morrisville, PA 19067
(800) 944-4PPD

Depression Awareness, Recognition, and Treatment Program
National Institute of Mental Health
5600 Fishers Lane
Rockville, MD 20807
(800) 421-4211

National Mental Health Consumer Self-Help Clearinghouse
311 South Jupiter Street, Room 902
Philadelphia, PA 19107
(215) 751-1810
www.med.upenn.edu/~cmhpsr/mhlinks.html

Discipline

Keeping the Peace in an
All-for-One Household

"*The real menace in dealing with a five-year-old is that in
no time at all you begin to sound like a five-year-old.*"

—JEAN KERR

Open any parenting magazine on any given month, and you'll see it—an article on disciplining the kids. Follow the article's suggestions, and you'll be living life happily ever after. If truth be told, it's never quite that easy. In fact, most parents find disciplining their children daunting. A February 1998 *Parents* magazine reader's survey tells all: "Parents are most confused and insecure about handling discipline."

Whether you're home full-time or working full-time, teaching your child to listen to you and behave appropriately is an ongoing and time-consuming process. But unlike working parents, full-time parents must deal with temper tantrums, whining, and all the other naughtiness the kids can think of, on a much more frequent basis. For them, there's no escaping a child's misbehavior. Bad behavior is an in-your-face reality that must be dealt with quickly. There's no office to retreat to and often no spouse to immediately consult. They're on their own, and it can be very stressful.

If you've just pulled the plug on a full-time career to be at home with your kids, you (and your children) may be undergoing a huge adjustment. After all, at the office you had structure, a sense of rhythm that you created and could adhere to. The stapler and paper clips were always in the same spot, lunch was at the same time every day, and when you asked your assistant to do something, he actually did it.

Compounding your troubles are your kids' troubles! You thought they'd be more receptive and welcoming to your homecoming, but instead they're more demanding and downright defiant. But remember, they, too, are away from their routine of day care and probably miss the buddies that they've made.

But even if you've been home full time with your child from the day she was born, you're bound to experience discipline problems frequently and find yourself at times wondering if it would be better for all if you just returned to work full time. Don't hit the want ads just yet; there are ways to overcome the constant whining, nagging, and occasional temper tantrums. Getting into a peaceful, workable routine will happen, but it will take time.

It's harder to discipline them as the day progresses. Especially when Matt is away on business, we get to a point where the girls just won't listen to me anymore. After several days, I lose my clout. I tend to give in often, but I try to pick my fights. I'm not going to be a stickler over every little thing when my husband's not here, because I can't be.

A Discipline Philosophy

"Discipline is a positive approach to setting limits for children," says Sylvia Rimm, Ph.D., author of *Dr. Sylvia Rimm's Smart Parenting: How to Parent So Children Will Learn* and other parenting books, "NBC's Today Show"'s parenting expert, and founder of the Family Achievement Clinic in Cleveland, Ohio. "It's a positive structuring of the environment and your day so that children can know what to expect and are encouraged to meet those expectations."

Rimm suggests that, rather than focusing on punishment, parents should concentrate on teaching appropriate behavior, emphasizing what children are supposed to do instead of what they shouldn't do. "It's not enough to say, 'Don't hit Johnny.' It's important to add, 'If you want to share this toy, we take turns. This is the way we do it. You take five minutes, then Johnny takes five minutes,'" explains Rimm. Stay-at-home parents have the greatest opportunity to model correct behavior—in the supermarket, on a play date—because they spend the majority of the day with their children.

"If parents would think of themselves as proactive teachers [rather than disciplinarians], teaching the skills that kids need, they would have a lot fewer discipline problems," Rimm adds.

Parents can help promote positive behavior in their kids by creating a safe environment where children feel confident in exploring and following their natural curiosity without continually getting into trouble. "Parents need to understand that children feel more secure in a safe area where they can explore," Rimm states. She suggests early childproofing of your home, so that children can roam at will; limiting the amount of "Nos" and "Don't touch thats"; and scheduling your day with a clear rhythm. "You want your children to grow, learn, and feel secure, but also know that there are limits," Rimm stresses.

Alternate activities throughout the day with some outdoor, large-muscle activities; some quiet indoor projects, like reading; some restful activities; and some responsibilities and chores, like picking up toys. "That kind of rhythmic day is a disciplined day," says Rimm.

Time for a Time-Out

For my baby-boomer generation, spanking and yelling were the standard discipline techniques employed by our parents.

These days, however, more and more parenting experts are lecturing on their ineffectiveness and their dangers. Instead of swatting a bottom or engaging in a yelling match, they recommend using time-outs.

What is a time-out? It's a technique intended to stop a child's naughty behavior by providing a break in his dastardly doings. A parent (or caregiver) removes the offending child from the scene of the crime to a quiet location for a prescribed number of minutes. (Usually, time-outs last one minute per number of years of the child—although some say time-outs shouldn't exceed two minutes; otherwise, the child forgets why he was separated in the first place.)

"A time-out is simply an opportunity for a parent to set a limit without using any kind of physical action like hitting or spanking," Dr. Rimm explains. As an added bonus, time-outs also help parents by giving them a few minutes to regroup and refresh.

Rather than a form of punishment, parents should think of a time-out as a teaching tool. "It gives the child, theoretically, a chance to think about what he did wrong. What's clear to the child is a limit—you cannot continue to do this." Time-outs can be very effective if used properly. Yet Dr. Rimm cautions that parents should avoid giving time-outs for every infraction. "Too many doesn't make any sense to kids," she says. "Also, kids must be clear on why it's used." It's best to save time-outs for such transgressions as hitting, kicking, biting, and throwing toys. Dr. Rimm adds that time-outs are ineffective when protracted, that is, putting a child in a time-out for longer than a few minutes.

The experts vary slightly on when to first introduce your youngster to the time-out concept—anywhere from eighteen months to two years of age. Using a time-out on a child younger than eighteen months is useless, they say, because toddlers can't control their impulses at such an early age. And although time-outs are an effective device to add to your discipline arsenal, they're not a panacea. "It would be wrong for parents to assume that just by using time-outs, all bad behavior problems will be taken care of," Rimm concludes. "It just sets a limit. Children also need to learn appropriate behavior."

TIME-OUT TIPS

- Reserve time-outs for specific problems like hitting, biting, and so forth. For other infractions, like yelling and whining, it's better to ignore her, or distract her by refocusing her attention.

- For older children (preschool and beyond), use a timer to help keep track of the time. It also helps to make an impression on the wrongdoer.

- Don't rely on your little one to leave the room herself—escort her to her place of punishment yourself. If your child is younger than five, don't close the door—it could frighten her.

- Give one warning. Then, if the behavior continues, implement a time-out immediately. Never wait until the fifth or sixth time before stepping in.

- Explain the reason for the time-out. If, for instance, your son threw a tennis ball at your favorite lamp, say, "We never throw balls in the house. Time-out."

- Keep your cool. This, the experts say, is most important. Kids want you to react, regardless if it's negatively. For a time-out to be truly effective, you must respond without emotion. When the time-out is over, simply explain why they had a time-out: "No hitting the cat. Pet her softly, like this"; then, act as if nothing has happened. Never hug and "make up"; that's giving positive attention for a negative behavior, Rimm explains.

Concentrate on the Basics

Although some parenting experts vary in their opinions on controversial issues such as spanking, the majority believe that there are some basic discipline guidelines that all parents need to embrace. And remember, when you discipline your child during the early years, it goes a long way in curbing a teenage terror.

SETTING LIMITS

Although kids of all ages naturally push the limits to see if they can get away with a bit more, they need to know where they must stop. If there are no limits, children don't feel safe. Whether it's a physical limit, like playing only in the backyard, or an action limit, like not hitting, setting limits is the first step to a disciplined child.

BEING CONSISTENT

If it's not OK to stand on furniture in your house, then it isn't OK to stand on Grandma's sofa—don't forget to implement house rules once you leave the house. And if you decide that pulling the cat's tail warrants a time-out today, then tomorrow it also mandates a time-out. Parents must be consistent in enforcing guidelines. Yet no parent is consistent 100 percent of the time, explains Rimm. But if parents are reasonably consistent in maintaining limits, it helps children know what to expect. And remember, lighter, consistent punishment is more effective than waiting until anger builds and enacting an overwhelming penalty.

FOLLOWING THROUGH

At one time or another, we've all looked the other way when our child has broken a minor rule just to save ourselves from

We stopped at the bakery the other day for muffins. Tessa turned to me and said, "I want to eat my muffin in the car." She knows she's not allowed because those muffins are so messy. I told her, "No, you can't." So she started screaming, "I want my muffin in the car!" I said no again and added, "If you scream at me one more time, you're not going to get the muffin at all." Then she looked me right in the eye and hollered, "I want to eat my muffin in the car!" I said, "Get back in the car." I put her back in her car seat and drove away. She was screaming hysterically. Primordial screams all the way from the bakery to the house. I was literally just checking out in the front seat, Zenning. I just slowed my breathing down, determined not to let her get to me.

Sometimes I hear myself in their conversations, and often I don't like what I hear. For instance, the other day John was playing with his sister Emily, and he turned to her and said, "That makes me so angry when you do that! I'm going to give you a time-out and close the door!" When I hear him say things like that, I realize that I need to work on being more patient.

Kids learn very early that they can work off of their parents—if one says no, the other may say yes. The other day Robert asked me if he could have a cookie. Naturally, I said no because it was a few minutes before dinner. Without hesitating, he then turned to his father and asked the same question! Fortunately, Larry and I always back each other up. Parents have to stand together when it comes to discipline, or the kids will rule the roost.

the unpleasant task of disciplining him for his wrongdoing, but following through with the appropriate punishment, whether that's taking away the toy or giving your child a time-out, is crucial. If your youngster senses that your threat of punishment is idle, she's bound to ignore you and continue with the naughty behavior. When you say, "Don't throw toys or you'll get a time-out," you'd better give a time-out the next time she throws a toy.

"I encourage parents not to quickly give consequences and punishment," warns Rimm. "They must be thoughtful about what they're going to do to deal with a child's misbehavior. It's OK to take your time and say, 'We're going to set up a consequence, we'll get back to you.' Then parents are going to be able to follow through." But in the heat of the moment, she says, many parents quickly come up with an outrageous punishment they often can't follow through on. The child senses that the parent will ultimately change the punishment and quickly learns he can't count on any consistent behavior from his parents.

MODELING GOOD BEHAVIOR

"Kids unconsciously copy their parents, whether it's good or bad behavior," Rimm notes. Parents are very powerful in their kids' lives, more than they know, so it's important that parents become good role models for good kinds of copying. "What traps parents is what happens to all of us—we lose our tempers, and then we overpunish. We end up doing things that we feel bad about. Then we apologize to our child for doing something dumb to start with. The poor kid doesn't really have a role model to look at!"

If kids don't copy their parents, Rimm says, they'll copy other adults around them; or during adolescence, they'll copy their peers. "Parents should let their kids know that there are smart people, rational people, logical people," she says. And by the same token, explain that there are irrational people, inconsiderate people, and unpleasant people. Kids need to learn not all people are worth emulating. "When I talk to parents I tell them, 'You're a smart person; let your child know that, and respond as an intelligent person. Be thoughtful about your decisions.'"

PRAISING THE GOOD—IGNORING THE BAD

Some bad behaviors, like hitting, just shouldn't go ignored; but others, like constantly tapping the plate with a fork, if ignored, will most likely disappear. Moreover, according to Rimm, praising your kids' good behavior is an important element. "You don't have to get overly excited about every good behavior," she says. "Praise it casually and notice it around other adults. Children will feel like everybody expects them to be good. It's just part of the way they are." Praising also helps build a pro-social, positive self-image.

PARENTS PRESENTING A UNITED FRONT

Children are less likely to try and push and bend the rules when parents are united in their approach to discipline. Obviously one should never unite with an abusive parent. But if two reasonable parents have differences in how to raise their children, it's extremely important that they compromise and discuss their differences away from their children. "If a child believes that one parent takes his side against the other," Rimm warns, "it gives the child more power than the parent who didn't take his side." The child will often trap that parent into irrational acts and then align himself with the favorable parent against the other parent.

Furthermore, Rimm notes, parents who discipline from opposite corners inadvertently teach children that love is a relationship with a bad guy. They may grow up choosing relationships with partners who didn't like their parents either. Often the relationships build on what they are against, rather than what they like or have in common. "Unfortunately, they'll just continue the negative cycle," Rimm says.

Is It OK to Argue in Front of the Kids?

Although it's important to provide a united front, parents need not confine every argument out of earshot of their kids. "Children who never see their parents argue don't deal with conflict very well," explains Rimm. "They need to understand that people can have disagreements, but that they can solve them, too." Yet parents also need to offer some interpretation of how the argument was settled, Rimm notes. "Kids need reassurance that their parents aren't going to get a divorce because of that one particular fight." A simple explanation such as, "Yes, we were angry and we disagreed, but we talked it out because we love each other, and we came to an agreement," is enough.

Your Parenting Style

It's much easier to discipline the kids when Bob is around. I'm the constant presence in their lives so what I say doesn't impress them as much; it doesn't have as much impact anymore. Our disciplining styles follow along stereotypical lines, too. He's the firm, traditional dad. All summer long, he works with young kids, so he's a natural disciplinarian. I negotiate with them more. The boundaries are a lot softer, fuzzier with me partly because I'm with them all the time.

We all have our own brand of parenting—some of us are more submissive with our kids while others are a touch more strict. But how does your style affect your child and her behavior? Studies show that parenting style has a direct influence on children's conduct, self-esteem, and the kind of adults they will become.

Style	Description	Effect on Children
Authoritative/democratic	Reasonable strictness; allows flexibility	Children feel loved
	Parental guidance balanced between both mother and father; nurturing leadership	Able to make choices; self-disciplined
	Parents set limits and follow through with consequences when rules are broken	Feel trust and respect
	Parents teach responsibility by giving it	
Authoritarian/autocratic	Stern with many rigid rules; demands respect	Often feel afraid and guilty
	Maintains power over children; order over efficiency	Often distrust others, and distrust their own feelings
	Withholds information from children	To assert control, many run away, rebel, or withdraw
	Tendency to spank	

Style	Description	Effect on Children
Indulgent/ laissez-faire/ permissive	Wants to be a friend to child, yet offers little guidance	Children misbehave often; have difficulty with limits imposed
	Submissive, giving too much freedom	Lack self-discipline and social responsibility
	Inconsistent or nonexistent rules and limits	
	Afraid to anger the child	

Disciplining Boo-Boos

We all have good intentions when it comes to caring for and nurturing our children, but sometimes they just know how to push our buttons and we end up doing things we often later regret. By being aware of these discipline boo-boos, you can try to omit them from future interactions with your children.

CRITICIZING YOUR CHILD'S CHARACTER

It's OK to say, "I get very angry when you do that," but never add, "Don't be so stupid!"

GIVING LENGTHY LECTURES

Kids are notorious at tuning out their parents. Keep your explanations of the guidelines or why their behavior is unacceptable short, simple, and to the point.

Varying or Nonsensical Consequences

Connect the punishment to the behavior, and don't use a time-out for every infraction—not all naughty behavior has equal weight. Children need to learn that some inappropriate conduct is worse than others.

Pleading

"Please get dressed for me. It would really make my day," doesn't cut it. Keep the personal pronouns and your feelings out of your requests, "It's time to get dressed. When you're through, come downstairs for breakfast, please."

Mistaking an Accident for Deliberate Behavior

Sometimes kids inadvertently bump into other children or knock over a glass of milk by accident. Know the difference between an accident and aggressive behavior, and discipline only the latter.

Ignoring the Problem

We've all done it. And for minor infractions ignoring often works—a child gets bored and stops whatever naughtiness she is doing. But some parents ignore the problem while quietly building anger. And when Junior knocks into the end table with his Tonka truck for the tenth time, Mom or Dad explodes. Therefore, it's best to take action early by redirecting your child's play before you get angry.

Having Unreasonable Expectations

It's unfair to think that a two-year-old can sit quietly at the dinner table for an hour. Understanding your child's emotional development and what is developmentally appropriate will help you distinguish unbecoming behavior from a lack of social skills or simple curiosity.

Taming the Tantrum Tiger

Some parents call them "meltdowns"; others refer to them as "going ballistic." Regardless of what you label them, "tantrumming" is standard behavior to the typical two-year-old. It's a sign of independence—they want to make their opinions known but often lack the words to express themselves. Still, they're extremely unpleasant for parents and hard to take. To help ease your headaches, try these techniques for taming the tiger.

- **Ignore it.** Although it may be tempting to try to reason with your irate daughter, talking it out in the heat of the moment usually adds more fuel to the fire. It's best to ignore the tantrum until she calms down. Yet, if you think that your child might hurt herself during her fit of anger, pick her up and move her to a safe location.

- **Don't give in to the demand.** "I want to watch *Sesame Street*!" It seems like a harmless request, but if it's time to turn off the television, then so be it. Giving in to your child's demands only teaches him that yelling gets results.

- **Keep a sense of humor.** Take a few deep breaths and try not to overreact. Often, the worst tantrums seem funny when you tell your spouse two hours later over a glass of wine.

- **Be sensitive.** Know which situations set off your child, and prepare for them or try to avoid them. Know his moods and fatigue level. Always be prepared with diversions. It's best to head off tantrums before they start.

- **Talk it over.** Once the storm has passed, talk to your child about what happened and try to teach her words to help her express herself.

Sometimes when my son is tantrumming in the store and everyone is staring at me, I try to find the humor in it by stepping out of the situation and watching it as if we were on television. It becomes funny, like when he's flailing his arms against my legs; and sometimes I have to laugh at the absurdity of it all. It doesn't help my tantrumming son, but I'm able to take control of the situation with grace.

Daily Dilemmas

Not every misdeed requires a time-out. What about those little annoying habits like whining, refusing to share, constant interrupting? These daily dilemmas can wear even the most patient parent down.

Why the Whining?

Whining usually occurs when kids feel that their needs are secondary to their parents'. If you can, stop what you're doing and give your child your full attention. Get down to her level and say, "I can't understand you. Please use your big-girl voice and tell me what you want."

Share, Share, That's Fair

For the typical kid, sharing is a hard concept to master. And who can blame him? Adults rarely share their toys. (When was the last time you shared by letting a friend take your sports car for a joyride?) By the time children reach two or three, they can, however, understand the concept if Mom or Dad will patiently teach it to them. If two children continue to fight over a toy, for instance, give the *toy* a time-out. Or, pull out the kitchen timer and allow each child a few minutes with the toy.

Sibling Spats

My boys usually play very well together, but several times each day, territorial wars break out. The best plan of action? Never take sides. I tell them both if they can't share, stop hitting, whatever, I'll give them each a time-out, take away their toys, and so forth. Experts say that if both are punished, neither becomes the winner; therefore, both have a stake in behaving properly.

I Hate to Interrupt, But . . .

Get on the telephone and you can guarantee that your kids will want your attention. The best plan of action? Excuse yourself to the caller, cover the phone, and explain that when you are finished, you will get them a glass of milk, put on their shoes, and so forth. Explain yourself calmly but simply; then, return to your call.

The Trouble with Spanking

These days, spanking has become a politically incorrect form of discipline, yet according to a 1997 *Newsweek* poll more than 31 percent of parents admitted to spanking their children "sometimes or often." Still, parenting experts tell us it's not only ineffective but harmful to our kids. But why? Didn't millions of baby boomers a generation ago get hit by their parents? We turned out OK, didn't we?

Hitting Doesn't Work

Studies show that parents who hit their kids by age one are just as likely to hit them at age four, suggesting that their children aren't learning any lessons.

Hitting Makes It OK to Hit Others

Kids love to imitate their parents. When children see their parents hit, they quickly learn that if they don't want something to happen, they're supposed to hit. Parents who spank are inadvertently sending a message to their kids—it's OK to hit.

In our house, we use the kitchen timer often—the windup kind that ticks and then gives a loud "ding!" when the time is up. When I give a toy a time-out, my son used to cry and carry on; now, he quietly watches the timer and when it rings, he politely asks for the toy back. No whining, no crying. By watching the timer, he gains some self-control.

HITTING MAY LEAD TO AGGRESSIVE BEHAVIOR

Although there are no studies indicating that hitting has any positive value, numerous studies say that children who are hit are more likely to become aggressive adults, are more likely to abuse their own children, and, for boys, are more likely to become battering husbands.

Although an occasional smack on the hand will not destroy your child or turn him into a serial killer, it shouldn't be the typical approach to setting limits. Parents must find alternative ways to teach their children good behavior. And as Rimm points out, "In a society where there is way too much violence and aggressive behavior, we'd like children to learn how to resolve their conflicts in other ways."

Just Take a Deep Breath

There will be days (unfortunately, many) when you feel as though you've spent most of your time spewing directives— "Don't throw that! Sit down and drink your milk! Turn off the television!"—but remember, these are the golden days. Just wait until your kids become teenagers. So, enjoy your little ones now, and remember to keep a sense of humor.

RESOURCES

Books

Becoming the Parent You Want to Be: A Sourcebook of Strategies for the First Five Years, by Laura Davis; New York: Broadway Books, 1997.

Change Your Child's Behavior by Changing Yours: 13 New Tricks to Get Kids to Cooperate, by Barbara Chernofsky; New York: Crown, 1996.

The Discipline Book: Everything You Need to Know to Have a Better Behaved Child—From Birth to Age Ten, by William Sears; New York: Little, Brown, 1995.

Dr. Sylvia Rimm's Smart Parenting: How to Parent So Children Will Learn, by Sylvia Rimm; New York: Crown, 1997.

8 Weeks to a Well-Behaved Child: A Failsafe Program for Toddlers Through Teens, by James Windell; New York: Macmillan, 1995.

How to Talk So Kids Will Listen and Listen So Kids Will Talk, 2nd ed., by Adele Faber and Elaine Mazlish; New York: Avon Books, 1999.

Mom's Guide to Disciplining Your Child, by Ericka Lutz and Vicki Poretta; New York: Macmillan, 1997.

Win the Whining Wars and Other Skirmishes: A Family Peace Plan, by Cynthia Whitham; Glendale, CA: Perspective, 1995.

Emergencies

If your child suddenly stopped breathing, would you know what to do? Would you quickly pile everyone in the minivan and race off to the emergency room, hoping to get help sooner? Or would you begin to administer first aid for choking or cardiopulmonary resuscitation (CPR)?

No one likes to think about all the ways a young child can potentially hurt herself, but when you're home alone with the children all day, it's necessary to think of the what-ifs and prepare yourself and your home accordingly. Every parent should educate himself or herself on emergency procedures, but the stay-at-home parent needs to learn infant CPR and first aid for choking more than anyone.

A child's brain dies in four to six minutes, but the average paramedic response time is eight to ten minutes, explains John Tyler, head of Pediatric Training Division of CPR Prompt Training Services. "If no one is doing CPR before the paramedics

The first thing any parent should do in an emergency situation is to check for unresponsiveness in the child (see if he or she can wake up); then, immediately call 911.

arrive, chances of reviving the child are less than 3 percent with significant brain damage," he says.

Performing CPR on a young child keeps the body from entering brain death stages and gives paramedics a much greater chance of reviving him or her. "If you try CPR in the first few minutes, followed by paramedics, a child's or baby's chances go up to almost 85 percent with little or no brain damage," notes Tyler, a CPR instructor for more than eight years.

Unfortunately, parents often put off taking first-aid or CPR classes. Many don't know these startling statistics or don't want to think about their children falling victim to an accident. "If parents knew the statistics, they'd be packing emergency training classes," Tyler adds. "But they often think that the paramedics can handle it alone."

Once parents have been certified in first aid or CPR, Tyler suggests that they take additional classes every two years while children are young. And although it may seem unsettling and downright morbid to run through emergency situations in your mind, mentally rehearsing and thinking through what-if scenarios can actually help parents respond better. If you have a pool, for instance, think about what you would do if you found your son or daughter in the pool unconscious. "The more present in their minds parents can make it, the more effective they will be in an emergency," he says. Periodically practice your CPR and first aid for choking techniques on a doll, too, but not on your children.

Siblings should also educate themselves in first aid and CPR, especially if they baby-sit their younger brothers or sisters. Tyler feels most children would benefit from some kind of emergency training. "You can teach a child as young as eight," he says. "But as far as pushing on

> Infants and babies suffer most from choking and poisoning accidents, and toddlers and older children are more prone to biking accidents and accidental drownings.

> To avoid choking hazards, the Consumer Product Safety Commission recommends that small toys and balls be at least 1¾ inches in diameter. Toys any smaller should be thrown away or kept out of baby's reach.

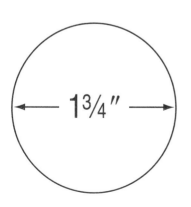

1¾″ **choke tube**

the mannequin and getting enough force, you need some strength." Therefore, children age twelve and older would most benefit from learning CPR.

Learn First Aid for Choking

The following is an introduction to emergency procedures for a choking infant, baby, or toddler, and is by no means meant to be used as a first-aid manual. To become fully qualified in first aid for choking, enroll in a certified program offered at many American Red Cross institutions or local hospitals.

FIRST-AID TECHNIQUE FOR CHOKING

Often, clearing the passageway of a choking baby or child is enough for him to begin breathing again on his own. If you suspect your child is choking, but he is able to cough, speak, or cry, it means that he is breathing. *Don't hit him on the back or begin CPR.* Be on stand-by alert, and allow his own gag reflex to dislodge the object. If, however, the child or baby cannot cough or his face is turning blue, it means that he cannot breathe and that an object is lodged in his throat.

FOR BABY UNDER AGE ONE

1. Hold baby face down along your forearm, hand supporting his upper chest. Rest your arm along your thigh, making sure baby's head is lower than his torso.
2. Using the heel of your other hand, give five quick blows to baby between shoulder blades.
3. If object still doesn't dislodge, turn baby over, supporting head and neck, and place on flat surface. Place your middle and ring fingers in center of breastbone, slightly below baby's nipples, and give five quick thrusts, pushing into chest.

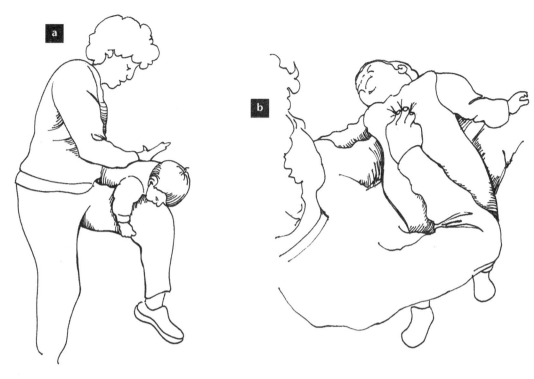

(a) Back blow and (b) chest thrust techniques for choking

4. Continue alternating with back blows and chest thrusts until object dislodges or you're able to see the object and gently remove it from his mouth.

FOR CHILD AGES ONE TO THREE

1. Place child on the floor on his back and straddle his body.
2. Place the heels of your hands, one on top of the other, on the child's abdomen, below the rib cage but above the navel, and give five upward thrusts. Check mouth for dislodged object and carefully remove it with your finger being careful not to push the object further down the throat. Repeat if necessary.

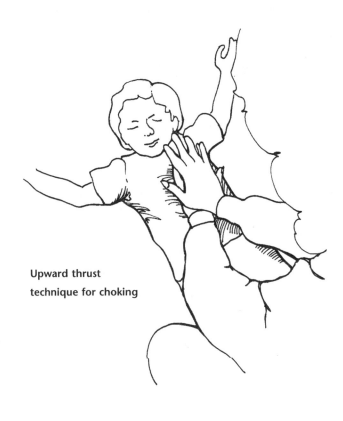

**Upward thrust
technique for choking**

For Child Over Three

1. Perform Heimlich maneuver by standing or kneeling behind the child, wrapping your arms around his middle.
2. Make a fist and cover with other hand. Give five, quick, upward thrusts to his abdomen being careful to avoid chest bones.
3. Check mouth for dislodged object. Repeat if necessary.

**Heimlich maneuver
technique for choking**

Common Choking Foods

Problem Food	Prevention Tip
Hot Dogs	Cut into small pieces, both lengthwise and crosswise, until the age of five.
Hard Candy	Not recommended for children under age five.
Grapes	For children under age four, serve only seedless grapes, cut up lengthwise and crosswise.
Raisins	Small pieces can easily get inhaled into airway; not recommended for children under age three.
Nuts	Pieces can easily get caught in airway; not recommended for children under age six.
Popcorn	Not recommended for children under age four. Always remove unpopped kernels before serving to children.

GENERAL SAFETY TIPS

- Kids do listen to their parents, so talk it up with safety instructions, like "Never put your toys in your mouth" or "Don't eat food that you find on the floor."

- Always blow up balloons for your children, and don't leave deflated balloons or balloon scraps on the ground where a child or baby can get to them.

- Remove seeds and pits from fruit. Avoid spreading too much peanut butter on sandwiches; never allow the kids to eat spoonfuls. For children under age three, serve only cooked carrots, apples, and pears, which are much easier to chew.

- Keep older children's toys, especially ones with small, removable parts, away from young babies and toddlers.

Conduct an inspection of your first-aid kit twice a year. Replace expired medicines, and replenish supplies that have been used up. Make sure your kit contains a flashlight and Ipecac syrup (two often-overlooked items) for accidental poisonings.

- Keep camera batteries, coins, and marbles out of young children's reach.

- Prepare yourself with a well-stocked first-aid kit and learn infant/child CPR and first aid by taking a certified course (call your local Red Cross for more information).

- Periodically practice first aid for choking on a doll, and discuss what-if emergency procedures with spouse and older children.

RESOURCES

Books

Baby and Child Emergency First-Aid Handbook, by Dr. Mitchell Einzig; Deaphaven, MN: Meadowbrook Press, 1995.

Children's Medical Emergency Handbook: Plus Over 150 Prevention Tips. Centax Books, 1997.

Emergency Childcare: A Pediatrician's Guide, by Peter Greenspan; New York: Avon, 1997.

A Parent's Guide to Medical Emergencies, by Janet Zand, Rachel Walton, and Bob Rountree; Garden City Park, NY: Avery Publishing Group, 1997.

Videos

CPR Prompt Home Learning System includes two practice mannequins (adult and child) and a video course for $59.95; (800) 464-6451; www.cprprompt.com.

How to Save Your Child or Baby, Loving Choice Baby Products, $19.95 plus shipping and handling; (800) 829-0080.

Exercise

- -

*"I've been on a constant diet for the last two decades.
I've lost a total of 789 pounds. By all accounts,
I should be hanging from a charm bracelet."*
—ERMA BOMBECK

Shortly after the birth of my son Matthew, I was in the supermarket with my three boys in tow. I was perusing the dairy aisle when I noticed another mom with her kids next to me. Her tailored white shirt was ironed and clean. (How did she manage that?) She wore leather loafers, no socks (the current "look"), and her hair was neatly pulled back with a decorative barrette. To make matters worse, her blue jeans *actually fit.* How could that be? She had an infant snoozing in a stain-free child carrier sack. She's a new mom! I had on my usual shopping attire— leggings, oversized sweatshirt, and sneakers. After two pregnancies, including a 65-pound gain for the twins, let's just say the last time I wore jeans I was at a rock concert.

"How old's your baby?" I asked, smiling at the cooing infant.

"Three months," the woman proudly answered. "And my son's eighteen months," indicating her little boy quietly

Exercising relieves a lot of the stress I feel as a full-time mom. All the bending down and picking up that you do with kids also helps strengthen your muscles, especially your back. It gives me time alone. I make the time early in the morning before Marty goes to work. I take the dogs for a walk, or I go for a run. Whatever I can do.

occupying himself with a toy in a nearby grocery cart. My twins had just knocked over several cartons of yogurt.

Suddenly, I felt depressed.

When I arrived home, I realized that my workout, or lack thereof, was in serious need of an overhaul. Before I started having kids, I was a slim woman who *never* had to worry about gaining weight. These days, however, my waist size is bigger than my bust size—not pretty.

Like most parents, I find it difficult to carve out a chunk of time where I can exercise, yet I know the benefits of a frequent workout routine. Not only does physical activity tone and strengthen muscles, and burn off calories, but exercising regularly also helps prevent cardiovascular disease, osteoporosis, and many types of cancer, including breast and colon. And what about the mental benefits? Exercising dramatically increases your energy level, builds self-esteem and a positive body image, and, most importantly, it wards off depression, a common malady of stay-at-home parents.

Working out alone is a little gift I give to myself when time permits (I swear I'm going to get back on that stair machine just as soon as I finish writing this book!), but on the whole it's not always practical. Recently though, with a little creative thinking, I've found ways to incorporate short bursts of exercise into my everyday routine. I stretch and tone in the morning, holding Matthew, for instance, and I get a cardiovascular workout when I'm romping with my older boys in the park or doing household tasks by wearing ankle/wrist weights. By making a concentrated effort to be more physical, I'm feeling and looking a lot better. But I still haven't pulled out those old blue jeans.

Exercising with Baby

It's easy to include your baby in your fitness routine. In fact, working out with your little one will give you some great bonding time and teach her that exercising is fun. Here are a few basic stretching and toning moves, but remember there are many other ways to keep fit with baby, like biking, hiking, and even walking together.

SADDLE STRETCH WITH BABY

Sit on exercise mat or carpeted floor with back straight and legs spread out 90 degrees.

Sit baby (she should be able to sit on her own) between your legs facing away from you.

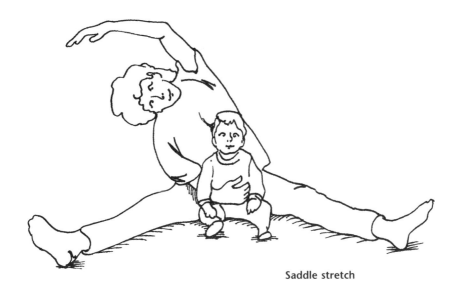

Saddle stretch

With your right hand wrapped around her waist, raise your left hand over your head and bend slowly to right until you feel a good stretch along your left side.

Then slowly rise. Switch sides. Wrap your left hand around baby's waist, raise your right hand over your head, and stretch to your left. Then slowly rise.

Repeat entire exercise twenty times.

Demi Plié and Relevé with Baby

Put baby in front child carrier or hold her facing away from you.

Stand with feet shoulder-width apart, toes slightly facing out at ten o'clock and two o'clock. Buttocks tucked in, back straight.

Slowly lower your body, bending your knees over your feet until your heels are just about to lift off the floor.

Then, slowly come up, squeezing your buttocks, and rise onto the balls of your feet, heels off the floor.

Hold position for five seconds. Return to standing position. Repeat ten times.

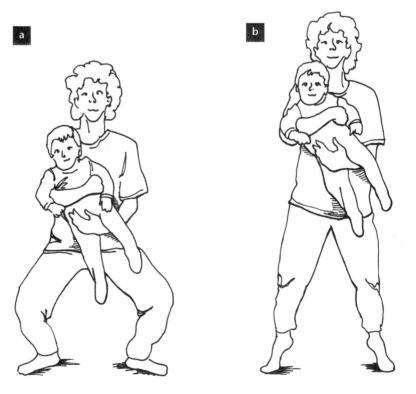

(a) Demi plié and (b) relevé

ABDOMINAL CURLS WITH BABY

With knees bent, lie on your back on exercise mat or carpeted floor.

Place your baby on your pelvis, her legs dangling over your waist. Hold her around her waist.

Slowly lift your shoulders off the floor, keeping your lower back on floor. Tighten abdominal muscles. Return shoulders to the floor.

Repeat ten times. Work up to twenty-five.

Abdominal curls

PUSH-UPS WITH BABY

Place baby on her back on an exercise mat or carpeted floor.

Place your hands on floor about shoulder-width apart on each side of her face, balancing on your knees.

Slowly bend your elbows and do a push-up. While you're down there, give the baby a kiss!

Push back up. Repeat five times. Rest. Do five more. Work up to twenty.

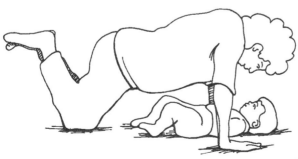

Push-ups

Sometimes I don't have time to exercise. In general, I take a walk every morning, but then the kids will get sick, or the world will come in on me, and I'll look up and it's been a month since I've gone. I do take the kids for walks, but I like to do my walk in the morning by myself. It's my time to focus and clear my head.

The Ten-Minute Workout

Think you don't have forty-five minutes to spare for a solid aerobic workout? Even small, ten-minute workouts can help tone muscles and burn calories. Try to fit in at least two a day and soon you'll be looking good. Her are a few energizing ideas to get you started.

- Put the baby in a backpack and vacuum the rug. Move faster than you normally do, but take twice as long to complete the task.
- Park the car far away from the store entrance. Put the baby in a stroller, backpack, or carrier, and briskly walk there and back. Or combine all errands within a few-block radius, park the car, and walk to each spot.
- Wear ankle and wrist weights while doing household chores, preparing lunch, or playing outside with the kids.
- Never take the elevator—always take the stairs.
- When standing at the sink doing dishes, do ten demi plié and ten relevé.

Exercising with Toddlers and Preschoolers

It's amazing that when given the chance the average preschooler will run like the Energizer Bunny—he'll keep going and going. Playgrounds are a great place to get exercise with your little athletes, but your own backyard offers ample opportunity for some outdoor fitness. Try these fun and fit games with your kids.

MOMMY MONSTER

This is my sons' favorite and a fabulous cardiovascular workout. Simply make some gruesome monster noises as you chase your child around the park or around your yard. (Don't forget to shout the occasional, "I'm gonna get you!") Let them choose the path to take and simply follow. When Matthew is awake, I put him in his baby carrier and take off after the boys. He loves the ride!

Follow the Leader

This childhood favorite is another wonderful exercise for muscle toning and strengthening. Have your kids follow you in a conga line, and shout out instructions, like, "Everybody raise your hands high over your head," "Walk on your tip-toes," or "Jump five times!"

Soccer Keepaway

The more balls and people, the merrier, but you can play the game with just you and your child and one ball. The object of the game is to keep the ball away from your opponent. Simply kick the ball away from your child, then have a race to see who can get to it first. Whoever succeeds in reaching the ball first kicks it away again. See if you can keep up the game for ten minutes.

Strollercise

Taking the baby for a stroll has added benefits when you think of it as an opportunity to get in shape. The stroller is a great piece of equipment for providing resistance, which only increases as the baby grows. Strap on ankle and wrist weights, and choose a hilly route to ensure a great cardio-vascular workout. Walk briskly, but don't run. Your stroller isn't designed for a fast-paced race, and constant bouncing could harm a young baby. At the end of your stroll, try some tummy toning by sitting at the edge of a park bench with stroller directly in front of you. Place your feet on the lower stabilizing bar of stroller, your hands gripping the park-bench edge on either side of you. Tighten your abdominal muscles and pull the stroller toward you with your feet, then push it away. Repeat twenty times. Work up to fifty.

Breathe In, Breathe Out

Commit to a few simple lifestyle changes and you'll be looking and feeling better in no time. If you haven't exercised in a while, however, remember to start out slowly and build up your workout time gradually.

RESOURCES

Books

Fifty Simple Things You Can Do to Raise a Child Who Is Physically Fit, by Joanne Landy and Keith Burridge; New York: Arco, 1997.

The 90-Day Fitness Walking Program, by Mark Fenton and Seth Bauer; New York: Perigee, 1995.

Primetime Pregnancy: The Proven Program for Staying in Shape Before and After Your Baby Is Born, by Kathy Kaehler and Cynthia Tivers; Chicago: Contemporary Books, 1998.

Videos

Fit Kids (for parents and kids ages three months to five years); HealthVision Inc., $20; (888) 609-3030.

Baby and You: Workout for Two (for parents and kids from birth to 33 pounds), $20; (888) 822-2968.

Mom-O-Rama: Workout with Baby/Mom-O-Rama: Workout with Toddler (for parents and kids from six weeks to twelve months/for parents and toddlers), $15 each; (888) 272-4671.

Exercise with Daddy and Me (for dads with baby less than one year old), $19.95; (888) 741-2229.

Field Trips

Age-Appropriate Destinations for Kids

When I was a kid, I made frequent pilgrimages into New York City with my mom. We'd hop the bus from our suburban New Jersey town and arrive just in time for the doors to open at the B. Altman department store. I can remember attending puppet shows at the FAO Schwartz toy store and story time at the New York City Public Library. At noon, we'd meet my aunt in Chinatown for dim sum, then hurry off to catch a Broadway show. In the winter, my mom always let me play hookey from school on the day they lit the enormous Christmas tree in Rockefeller Center. She once told me she stood in line for two hours at the Metropolitan Museum of Art with my two older sisters and me in a stroller, just to catch a twenty-second glimpse of da Vinci's *Mona Lisa* on loan from the Louvre, although I don't remember.

My mom loved the city, and her enthusiasm for the Big Apple was contagious. We share a love for adventure,

Field trips are very important. Aside from the obvious benefits of exposing kids to a variety of different sights, textures, sounds, people, and images, they also teach them to actually implement the skills you've been teaching them at home: politeness, how to mind you or stay with you, how to act around busy streets. The actual application of these things means much more than just telling them.

art, music, and good food, all things I'm trying to pass along to my boys. And although she made me walk *everywhere* (she hated spending money on taxis, and the subway frightened her), those day trips are some of my best childhood memories.

Get Up and Get Out

They find the wildest things on the smallest journeys.

Getting out of the house on a regular basis not only helps full-time parents feel refreshed and energized, but the kids benefit greatly, too. When children see and explore the world around them, they learn how society functions. And when parents see the world through the eyes of their children, they learn to appreciate life's subtleties, like the colors in a rainbow or the excitement of a racing fire truck. I've noticed that when I take my kids out on the town, no matter if it's to a museum or to the supermarket, when we arrive home they're calmer, more cooperative, and just plain happier. And I am, too. It's my theory that they get bored staying home every day, and going out gives all of us a much-needed change of pace.

When we're at home all day, my attention is often split between the kids and making phone calls, doing dishes, folding laundry, or paying bills—a perfect environment for whining. But when we're out of the house, my nagging stops and so does their whining. We have fun together. My attention is focused solely on them, and that's just how they like it. Although it takes effort to maneuver a baby and preschool twins out the door, I do it regularly because I find that in the long run, the payoff is well worth it. Field trips bring us closer together as a family.

You don't have to drop big bucks on children's theater tickets or travel an hour by car to a major metropolitan zoo to take the kids on an interesting field trip (although it is important to splurge every now and then). Just use your imagination and create fun and interesting outings right in your own neighborhood. How about a visit to a local farm? A tour of your neighborhood police or fire station?

Destination Derby

Children ages one or less are extremely portable and can travel just about anywhere without needing to be constantly entertained. (Take advantage of it by meeting friends for lunch at a restaurant or visit *your* favorite museum.) With kids eighteen months and older, however, parents need to come up with creative and fun places to go on a regular basis. Here are some suggestions to get you started.

Aquarium

Seals and sea lions, sharks and octopus—kids love to watch aquatic life up close and personal. Many aquariums have educational programs, and most offer interactive areas where the kids can touch live sea animals.

   Tip: call ahead to see if any special events are planned for kids. Also, indoor aquatic exhibits tend to be dark, so dress the kids in brightly colored clothes to easily keep track of them.

Airports

Pack a picnic lunch and head for your local airport. Find a grassy area nearby, spread a blanket, and tell the kids to lie on their backs for a fascinating free air show.

   Tip: small municipal airports are usually a better choice than larger metropolitan airports—small planes are less threatening to young children.

Sometimes, after preschool I take Emily to the Parenting Center at the local Jewish Community Center. It's just a room with couches, tables and chairs, and toys. I pack a little lunch for her. We spend an hour or two there instead of coming home and being stuck here. It's just a change of scenery. She thinks it's great.

Botanical Gardens and Nature Preserves

Great places to picnic, botanical gardens and nature preserves provide an excellent opportunity to introduce kids to native flora and fauna.

Tip: time your visit around special events such as when the tulips/roses/poppies are blooming. Be sure to bring tools for nature exploration: binoculars, magnifying glass, and so forth.

Children's Theater

Look in your local parenting newspaper to find out the latest on puppet shows, children's musicals, and concerts. Not only are theater performances fun, but experts say music may help develop a child's math and reasoning skills.

Tip: some performances, like afternoon matinees, cost less. Some children's theaters sell subscriptions, too, so you can save up to 50 percent by buying a group of shows.

Children's Museums

Science and technology, art and natural history—kid-friendly museums are a great place to let the little ones explore and learn at their own pace.

Tip: consider becoming a member at your local museum. When you spend $20 on admission, you often feel like you have to cram everything into one visit. When you're a member, however, you can make shorter, more frequent visits.

Museum Musings

There are more than 300 children's museums nationwide. Rather than limiting kids to looking instead of touching, these family-friendly places actually encourage active participation. Here's a list of some of the finest.

Etiquette Smetiquette

Once during a children's theater performance, my overly grumpy son shouted, "No!" to every rhetorical question posed by the performer on stage. The other parents laughed; I was mortified. A rundown on the rules of polite society would have helped.

- When the lights go down in the theater, it's time to whisper.

- When the show is finished, it's polite to clap.

- Inside a museum or theater, no shouting, running, or roughhousing with other children.

- Although children's museums are designed for abuse, be gentle when touching hands-on exhibits.

Museum	Don't Miss . . .
Brooklyn Children's Museum 145 Brooklyn Avenue Brooklyn, NY 11213 (718) 735-4402 www.bchildmus.org	Explore music from around the world and jam on stage at Music Mix; search for monsters in a giant bed in Ready, Set, Sleep!; or visit a greenhouse in Plants and People.
Chicago Children's Museum 700 E. Grand Avenue at Navy Pier Chicago, IL 60611-3428 (312) 527-1000 www.chichildrensmuseum.org	Artabounds Studio, an interactive art studio; Earth Balloon, a two-story replica of the earth; Info-Tech Arcade, a hands-on gallery filled with computers and wireless technology.
Lawrence Hall of Science University of California Berkeley, CA 94720 (510) 642-5132 www.lhs.berkeley.edu	Life-size model of the space shuttle *Challenger*; Surf City, a collection of computer terminals hooked up to the World Wide Web; Within the Human Brain, a look inside the brain with the help of computers.
The Children's Museum of Indianapolis 30th and Meridian Streets Indianapolis, IN 46206 (800) 208-KIDS www.childrensmuseum.org	Learn about physics while riding an Indianapolis 500-Mile Race Car; All Aboard!, a train with overhead trestle and Victorian railway depot; and SpaceQuest Planetarium.

I always make sure there's some end goal that I know that they will enjoy, whether it's stopping at the ice cream shop or picking up pizza for dinner. It keeps them motivated toward the end when I think they're going to melt!

With Lillie, we got her interested in art at home by working on various projects. Then she was interested in going to an art museum. It wasn't boring to her. Of course, we don't stay long, and we don't linger at one piece. We talk about the picture and move on quickly.

Museum	Don't Miss . . .
The Children's Museum of Boston Museum Wharf 300 Congress Street Boston, MA 02210 (617) 426-8855 www.bostonkids.org	Arthur's World, based on the popular PBS children's television series; Johnny's Workbench, a hands-on exhibit for young carpenters; Climbing Sculpture, a two-story playscape.
The Children's Museum of Denver 2121 Children's Museum Drive Denver, CO 80211 (303) 433-7444 www.cmdenver.org	Maze-eum, a 900-square-foot musical maze complete with instruments; Inventions, where kids can build a toy car or try their hands at woodworking; Community Market, a pint-size supermarket complete with deli and bakery counters.

CONSTRUCTION SITES

Bulldozers, cranes, cement mixers—if your kids are anything like mine, they could spend an hour watching these mighty machines at work. Not only are the noise and bustle of a construction site exciting for kids, they also get to see firsthand how a building is constructed.

Tip: if the kids have play construction hats and tools, have them bring them along so that they might "build" along with the pros.

FACTORIES

From Ben & Jerry's Ice Cream to The Original American Kazoo Company, more than 200 American factories offer a behind-the-scenes look at how their products are made. Many give away free samples, too.

Tip: always call to check if reservations are needed or if the factory has a minimum age requirement. Some factories will only offer tours to groups. If that's the case, gather up other stay-at-home parents in your neighborhood and create a group of your own.

FARMS

A visit to a country farm teaches kids that food doesn't grow in the supermarket but in the soil. Pick Your Own Fruit farms are especially fun on warm, sunny afternoons. Give each child a small pail and let her pick away.

Tip: time your visit around a holiday like Halloween or Christmas when farms are all decked out and many offer special events for the kids like hayrides or visiting reindeer.

FARMER'S MARKETS

These days, nearly every community hosts a farmer's market. Many now have petting zoos or pony rides for the kids.

Tip: save your produce shopping to do at the market, and enlist the kids' help by having them choose which fruit and vegetables to buy.

FIRE STATIONS/POLICE STATIONS

Many local fire and police stations are happy to show you and your kids around.

Tip: be sure to call ahead; don't just drop in.

INDOOR PLAY SPACE

From two-foot-deep ball pens to a vast maze of colorful tubes, indoor play spaces aren't just for birthday parties.

Tip: on your first visit, crawl along with your child to check out potential hazards or to point out areas that may be too advanced for him.

Grandparents have been a real blessing in our lives. My mother and father are very oriented toward the arts. While I get caught up in the daily grind, they're the ones who think of taking the kids out. A couple of weeks ago they took Jenna to see Beauty and the Beast. *Or they call and say there's a butterfly exhibit down in Grand Rapids, or let's go to the children's museum.*

LAKES/PONDS/OCEANS

Rent paddleboats or fishing rods; or, if at the beach, dig for clams or build sand castles.

Tip: being around the water provides the perfect opportunity to teach kids about water safety, but remember to cover the basics before your arrival.

LIBRARY STORY TIME

The beach is a great place for all of us. It's big enough for them to run around. There's enough to do to entertain four-year-old Lillie and eighteen-month-old Elliott. I can invite other mothers, and we can spend the whole day there without the kids getting tired.

The best free show in town, library story time involves more than just storytelling. There's singing, videos, and craft projects. Story time is also a great watering hole for local at-home parents to meet and mingle.

Tip: not all story times are created equal. If you don't like the one at your local library, try a different one. Usually, the bigger the library, the more elaborate the session.

PARKS

Another great no-cost field trip, parks are every kid's favorite. Grab a local map and note the plethora of parks within a five-mile radius of your home, then hit one park a week.

Tip: choose parks with age-appropriate equipment. (Some park equipment is too dangerous for toddlers.) Come prepared with a variety of outdoor gear: soccer balls, sand toys, and so forth.

RETAIL STORES

Pet stores, especially the large chains, are a great place to take the kids. It's a virtual minizoo. In our local pet store, my kids adore watching a twenty-foot Burmese python slither around his cage. Toy stores, gadget stores, and children's bookstores are other great choices.

Tip: in return for the free entertainment, patronize the stores you visit.

SHOPPING MALLS

The equivalent to the European public square, American shopping malls are a great place to let the kids run off some steam. Look for a mall that caters to kids. (A local mall here in Southern California has an authentic turn-of-the-century carousel.)

Tip: don't expect to get any shopping done—your main objective is to entertain the kids. Settle for a little window shopping instead.

SPORTING EVENTS

Root for the home team at a minor league baseball game. Tickets are usually less than $10, and there's plenty of excitement. (For information on schedules, visit the Minor League Baseball Association's website: www.minorleaguebaseball.com.) Or introduce your kids to a new sport by dropping by the roller- or ice-skating rink, tennis courts or basketball courts, or equestrian centers; and watch.

Tip: if you have toddlers, don't expect to stay for the whole game. An hour is usually all the kids can take.

ZOOS

What kid wouldn't love to mingle among some wild animals? A visit to a zoo is not only entertaining, but educational as the kids learn about various animals and their habitats.

Tip: go early in the morning when the animals and your kids are at their liveliest.

Top Zoos

Nearly every city has a zoo, but some are better than others. Here's a list of must-see zoos around the country.

Museum	Don't Miss . . .
Brookfield Zoo 3300 Golf Road Brookfield, IL 60513 (708) 485-0263 www.brookfieldzoo.org	The Living Coast, re-creating the western coast of South America; Tropical World with its three simulated rain forests and more than 100 primates; Habitat Africa, a five-acre savannah complete with giraffes, zebras, and African wild dogs.
San Diego Zoo Zoo Place and Park Boulevard San Diego, CA 92103 (619) 234-3153 www.sandiegozoo.com	Hippo Beach, a hippo-potamus habitat complete with underwater observation window; Gorilla Tropics, home to lowland gorilla; Ituri Forest, a central African rain forest with rare, exotic animals; Bai Yun and Shi Shi—resident pandas since 1996.
Bronx Zoo 185th Street and Southern Boulevard Bronx, NY 10460 (212) 367-1010 www.wcs.org	Bengali Express, a monorail excursion spotlighting tigers, rhinos, and elephants of Wild Asia; Jungle World, a one-acre indoor exhibit featuring three tropical rain forests; Himalayan Highlands Habitat, with Asian snow leopards and red pandas.

Museum	Don't Miss . . .
San Antonio Zoo 3903 North St. Mary's Street San Antonio, TX 78212 (512) 734-7184	Australian Walkabout, a trip Down Under with wallabies, emu, and redtree kangaroos; Komodo Dragons, the world's biggest lizards; Cat Grotto, highlighting a variety of leopards.
National Zoo 3001 Connecticut Avenue NW Washington, DC 20008 (202) 673-4821	American Bison Exhibit; Amazonian, a re-creation of the world's largest rain forest.

INVENT YOUR OWN JOURNEY

The list doesn't have to stop here. By investigating your own neighborhood you're sure to come up with an additional assortment of child-friendly destinations. Some other ideas include hiking in national or state parks, visiting the top of a tall building with an interesting view, taking a ferry ride, walking around a ship harbor or train station, or visiting a planetarium.

When choosing a destination, do what you enjoy. If you're excited, that makes the kids motivated and interested in it, too.

TRIP TIPS

Any trip can be fun, as long as you're prepared.

■ **Know your kids' limitations.** If you get tired after two hours of being on the go, your kids are probably doubly tired. Head for home before they have a meltdown. A two-hour field trip is usually the limit for preschoolers, an hour and a half for toddlers.

I always make sure I have a bag of sand toys, extra clothes, and her stroller in the car. If the opportunity arises, it's there. I try to repack my diaper bag with diapers, wipes, and snacks every night, so in the morning I can leave on a moment's notice.

■ **Know your kids' likes and dislikes.** Are they passionate about airplanes? If yes, a trip to the local airport might be exciting. Do they think marionettes are spooky? (I know I did.) If they do, you should probably skip the puppet theater until they're older.

■ **Read all about it.** Prepare your kids for their big adventure by reading stories relevant to your destination.

■ **Time your trips wisely.** Work around your kids' nap schedule. Go out when they have the most energy, usually in the morning. Don't postpone their naps just to see one more museum exhibit. Overly tired kids and field trips don't mix well.

■ **Call ahead.** Are you sure the place will be open? Better check. Will they let you use your stroller? Some museums (yes, even children's museums) won't allow them. And while you're at it, make sure you know how to get there. Will you have to pay for parking?

■ **Subscribe to local parenting magazines or newspapers.** National parenting publications may give you advice on potty training or persuading a finicky kid to eat, but local parenting magazines offer a wealth of information on special events in your area for kids, such as library story times, children's theater, and so on. If you don't know of any local publications, check the children's magazine section of your neighborhood library or bookstore.

■ **Save some money.** Many museums offer free admission one day a month. It pays to know which day that is and then cash in.

■ **Keep your diaper bag or backpack well stocked.** Because you never know how long you'll be gone from home, always be prepared with emergency supplies: extra diapers, a jacket, a change of clothes, and of course, plenty of juice and snacks.

■ **Prioritize.** The kids seem in a good mood now, but you never know what will happen in ten minutes. Saving the best for last doesn't make good sense when you're out with the kids. Start with the most-important exhibit and work toward the least-important.

■ **Be prepared with diversions.** Even kids can get bored at the zoo. Keep a variety of board books and small toys at the ready just in case one fidgety passenger needs something to keep him occupied.

■ **Talk about it.** Encourage them to talk about their experience. What did they see today? What did they like best? Would they like to do it again?

I try to take them out to restaurants. It teaches Max and Tessa about manners and how to behave out in public. Sometimes I take them out one-on-one, too, where I'll take one to a special lunch. I think it's really good for them.

Is Your Child Too Young for the Movies?

At two-and-a-half years old, my twins—Joseph and Michael—were ready to see their first G-rated, animated film on the big screen. Within five minutes, though, Joseph turned to me, crying, begging to go home. It was clear why he was upset. Within the first few minutes of the film, someone died, there was a violent battle scene, and the villain would have given Cruella De Vil nightmares. Minutes later, when we got outside (after I asked for a refund), Michael gave his critique, "Too big! Too noisy!" I had never considered that the size of the screen or the loud volume would be frightening to small kids. A friend had a similar experience when she took her five-year-old to another animated feature. Although she was shocked to see a bloody battle scene, she decided to stay, hoping to show her son that the story had a happy ending. Had she known of the film's content, she wouldn't have taken him. The moral of the story: just because it's rated G doesn't mean it's suitable for young children. Thoroughly investigate the contents of the movie you're planning on seeing.

Resources

Books

Doing Children's Museums: A Guide to 265 Hands-On Museums, by Joanne Cleaver; Charlotte, NC: Williamson Publishing, 1992.

Inside America: The Great American Industrial Tour Guide: 1,000 Free Industrial Tours Open to the Public Covering More Than 300 Different Industries, by Jack Berger and Eunice Berger; Peabody, MA: Heritage Publishing, 1997.

Little Museums: Over 1,000 Small (and Not-So-Small) American Showplaces, by Lynne Arany; New York: Henry Holt and Company, 1998.

Watch It Made in the U.S.A.: A Visitor's Guide to the Companies That Make Your Favorite Products, by Bruce Brumberg and Karen Axelrod; Santa Fe: John Muir Publications, 1997.

The Zoo Book: A Guide to America's Best, by Allen W. Nyhuis; Albany, CA: Carousel Press, 1994.

Hobbies

Developing Interests Outside of Parenthood

When you're a full-time parent, it's easy to put everyone else's needs ahead of your own. You are usually the first one up each morning and the last one to bed at night. When you're raising kids full time, there's little time for personal pursuits. Although caring for home and family is important, so is caring for yourself. Not only must the at-home parent take care of herself physically through regular exercise and diet, she must also nourish her spirit by getting involved in the things she loves.

All full-time parents need to take time away from the family to be with other friends and to pursue creative and intellectual passions purely for the love of it. Nurturing your own soul will help you better nurture the ones you care most about—your kids and your spouse.

Purely Personal

Recently, since my father's been sick, I've put myself to work after visiting him. I started painting—furniture, picture frames, all kinds of projects. I fixed up the garage into my workshop. Now I have a place to go. After dinner, I go there until eleven o'clock at night. It's very therapeutic, because while I'm creating, I'm thinking about all these ideas; I'm not thinking about the kids or my everyday life. I'm thinking about just myself for a few hours.

Just a few hours each week courting a hidden talent or developing a new one can mean the difference between intellectual starvation and personal fulfillment as a parent and as an adult. Even if you don't have a hobby, it's never too late to begin. For starters, check out adult education courses offered at many local high schools and community colleges. You might be surprised at what you find—ballroom dancing, wine tasting, film appreciation, travel writing, archery—you name it, and you'll probably find it.

- **Join a book club.** Many local bookstores offer monthly book club meetings, where members get together to discuss the latest in fiction.

- **Take up a new sport.** I love to ice skate; my California-native husband does not. So on occasion, a girlfriend and I have disappeared to the local rink for a few hours, dreaming of what could have been.

- **Learn to play a musical instrument.** Call your local university's music department for a list of qualified instructors. No need to buy your instrument, either; most music stores have inexpensive rentals available for beginners.

- **Try a craft.** A friend of mine found a group of elderly Mennonite women who meet every week to quilt (they auction off their exquisite wares every year with the proceeds going to charity). Try pottery, painting, sculpting, knitting, photography, sewing.

- **Take an academic class.** Art history? Contemporary literature? French? It's a lot more fun when you're older and not under enormous pressure to do well.

Passion Pursuit

Want to take time for yourself and nurture a hidden passion but don't know exactly what that passion is? Sit down and make a list of the ten things you want to accomplish before you die (macabre, perhaps, but remember it's just an exercise) or the career you'd pursue if given the chance. Get as way out as you want, and you might be surprised at what you write. Most will be out of reach, but getting in touch with what drives you will help to focus on what's important to you. Here are some of the surprising answers I got from other stay-at-home parents.

- **Screenplay writer.** "I have this great story in my head. I know it would never make it to Hollywood, but that's not the point. I just want to write it."

- **Travel planner.** "I love to travel or read anything about traveling. I'd love to plan some trips for other people."

- **Tennis player.** "It's too late to go to Wimbledon, but I can dream, can't I?"

- **Stand-up comic.** "Roseanne was a housewife when she made it big. I figure there's still time left for me."

- **Ballet dancer.** "I've recently begun taking lessons again. I was good as a teenager, and surprisingly, I'm still pretty good. It's great exercise, too."

- **Photographer.** "It's a great hobby, because I can easily involve the kids."

- **Bus driver.** "It always looked like fun."

I have this little dream of developing a website for new mothers.

Taking Time for Yourself

For many, it may be difficult to say, "I want some time each week for myself," but it's so important in keeping your mental wherewithal. Pursuing personal interests isn't selfish; it's a necessary element to personal growth and happiness.

Homeschooling

Here's a quiz: what do Thomas Jefferson, Thomas Edison, Daniel Webster, Queen Elizabeth II, and pop music group Hanson all have in common? Answer: each was schooled at home.

For true at-home pioneers, homeschooling just naturally evolves. As a family's young children reach school age, many full-time moms and dads opt to continue cultivating the close bond that at-home parenting has afforded them. Besides, homeschooling offers options that traditional public schools simply can't—individualized curriculum, one-on-one tutoring, and lots of flexibility. Its appeal is growing among many American families. Yet with all its positive attributes, the public-school system and many communities are still wary of home-based educators, citing that many parents aren't equipped to educate their children themselves and that home-schooled kids, isolated from their public-school peers, may not develop adequate social skills.

But if you ask Dr. Brian Ray, president of the National Home Education Research Institute, a nonprofit organization that acts as a clearinghouse for homeschool information, homeschooling methodology is right in line with a public-school teacher's utopia. He says most teachers would love just two, three, or four students in their classrooms, an opportunity to individualize each student's curriculum to match his or her interests, and lesson flexibility, so that when a blue jay lands on the windowsill, teachers could stop and talk about birds and ornithology.

"People have known for centuries that if you want to truly learn something, you hire a tutor," Ray explains. "You have a mentor. You work one-on-one." And that, he says, is what homeschooling is all about, and it shouldn't come as a surprise that its popularity is spreading.

I really believe that homeschooling is a very natural progression for mothers and fathers who have been home with their children. It may be a bit more difficult adjustment for parents who have not been at home full time, but like everything in life, where there is a will, there is a way.

In the Beginning

Homeschooling has gone through a number of reincarnations over the years, and once again, it is on the rise, making national headlines. During the '60s, homeschoolers were mostly left-wing counterculturalists who questioned the merits of institutional schooling. Realizing they couldn't reform the system, they chose to pull their kids out and educate them at home. Their numbers never added up to many, and the world viewed their movement as another hippie fad that would eventually go the way of bell-bottom pants.

Homeschooling caught a second wave during the '70s, when conservative Christians got into the act. They chose to homeschool to promote spiritual values, something that they saw was sorely lacking in the public-school system.

Today, home-based education has caught the attention of a new group—secular families disgusted with the academic decline of the nation's public-school system. Fed up with overcrowded classrooms, indifferent teachers, rising campus

I guess the biggest reason we homeschool is that I hate wasted time, and a lot of school is wasted time. Wait for everyone to sit down, wait for the papers to be collected, wait while the other kids finish. In a typical school day, about half the day is wasted time.

With a lot of pressure off his shoulders, my son has improved his behavior. Much of his anger has dissipated, and he is better able to concentrate on subjects that interest him with time to explore them. For my daughter, homeschooling means not being held back by the accomplishment level of her peers. She's completed all of the school work typical of grades five through eight in less than two years at home.

Dad is an astronomer and we live at an observatory. The ordinary school schedule would mean that our children and I couldn't stay up late observing with Dad, something we enjoy. With homeschooling, learning can occur anytime, anywhere.

crime, and drug use, parents feel that homeschooling offers an alternative to private or religious schools, which are often too expensive.

Once perceived as kooks, nuts, and fringe people, homeschoolers in the '90s are finally gaining respect. As more families investigate home-based education and talk to others who are involved in the forefront—and as more support services, state organizations, and entrepreneurial curriculum businesses arise—home-based education is slowly becoming a socially acceptable form of education. But is it right for your kids?

Why Homeschool?

Through his research at the institute, Ray comes into contact with thousands of homeschooled families across the country, and he lists five reasons why they choose this form of education, regardless of religion or race:

1. Parents want to pass something on to their children, whether it's a culture, tradition, or belief system. "Life is fast-paced, technological, cold," Ray says. "People want some human contact." As much as proponents talk about home-based education's high level of academics, the reason many want to homeschool is rather simple: parents want to reconnect with their children, and homeschooling offers them that luxury.

2. They want to provide strong academics for their children.

3. They want to develop close family relationships, whether it's sibling to sibling, or parent to child.

4. They want to provide guided social interaction for their kids. "Children who go off to institutional schools come under the influence of their peers," Ray notes. "Some children do fine, but others fall

prey to all of the forces at work." (Ray does admit that homeschooled children can also be wrongly swayed by their peers, but he says it's far less likely.)

5. They want to provide safety for their children.

And the Numbers Keep Rising

Today, homeschooling is legal in every state, although some states do regulate home-based education by requiring parents to follow approved curriculum. During the '80s, homeschoolers numbered a mere 15,000. Today, there are nearly two million homeschoolers, and Ray estimates that this number is growing by 15 percent per year, with no sign of peaking. Although rising in numbers, homeschoolers still represent only a small percentage of American families, less than 2 percent of all school-age children.

And what about their academic performance? In 1998, the average ACT score for a homeschooler was twenty-three (of thirty-six), compared to twenty-one for a traditionally schooled child. A study by the National Home Education Research Institute found that the national average on standardized tests for a public-schooled child is in the fiftieth percentile; the average for a homeschooled student ranks between the sixty-fifth and eightieth percentiles. Many credit the high scores to the individualized attention that the homeschooled student receives—parents are hugely devoted to their children in a way that public-school teachers could never be.

Homeschoolers are gaining entry into top universities, too. Known as homeschooling trailblazers, David and Micki Colfax, former educators and authors of *Homeschooling for Excellence*, taught all three of their sons at home during the '70s and then saw them graduate from Harvard. Today the husband-and-wife team speak throughout the country on the merits of homeschooling.

Enrichment in the public schools takes the form of an extra work sheet, letting the child read independently, or letting the child help a slower student. In the average classroom, less than half the children are well served—the pace is too fast for slower learners; the teacher often moves on before they have mastered the material. At home, the student can move at her own pace, as quickly or as slowly as she needs to go to master the material. A homeschooled student can be at several different grade levels in different subjects—all at the same time.

Do You Have the Right Stuff?

For me, the biggest challenge of home-schooling is the home part. Because we are home far more than people whose children attend public school, things tend to be hectic. I have a difficult time staying on top of house-work. I'd rather play in the mud! Like everything, there are good days and bad days, but I think most people who home-school would agree that after a while it isn't an educational choice, but rather a lifestyle; and it fits into the rest of your life, seamlessly.

Although the data present a strong argument in favor of home-based education, before you convert the basement to a classroom you should be aware of the many challenges facing homeschoolers. First, it takes an enormous commitment on the part of the parent who will be teaching the children. Many parents put in several hours a week preparing lessons, investigating prepackaged curriculum, and arranging field trips (this is in addition to the time it takes to conduct daily lessons). If you're a stay-at-home parent who feels there's little time for yourself, if you become a homeschooler, you'll have even less time to call your own.

Parents should also assess their own personalities before taking roll call. Are you patient with your kids? Well organized? Are you creative and resourceful? Although these traits are important, Ray stresses that anybody who chooses to be a homeschooler will do just fine. His institute has done statistical analysis among homeschoolers whom he advises on whether there's a relationship between a child's academic achievement and a parent's education level, family income, and race. None, he feels, has a significant statistical correlation with the child's learning. "It's not the function of demographics, or formal education that a parent receives," he says. "It's essentially the motivation of the parent. If a parent says, 'I care about my child, I want to do this,' he or she is probably going to make it."

Moreover, it's a financial sacrifice for many families because one parent needs to be home full time, thus eliminating that second paycheck. And there are out-of-pocket expenses, too. On average, homeschool families spend about $500 a year per child for things like prepackaged curriculum, books, equipment (microscopes, computers, etc.), and field trips. Finally, although homeschooling has received favorable press in the last decade, there's still social pressure against it from some in the community as well as family members.

The children must be taken into consideration, too. Will your kids look at a homeschool education as a positive experience or simply punishment for some infraction like poor school performance or out-of-control behavior? Will they respect and listen to you as a teacher? Finally, is it something that they also want?

Keeping the Kids Motivated

If your child complained of boredom while in school, you'll have to be twice as stimulating to keep him on his intellectual toes. Here's how.

- Choose subjects that interest your children, and have them help you develop yearly curriculum goals.

- Incorporate hands-on projects into daily lessons. For instance, creating a three-dimensional papier-mâché map of your home state is a great way to introduce geography.

- Don't forget the humanities. Lessons in music, drama, and art are not only important in developing a well-rounded student, but add a break to academics.

- Encourage sports. Teamwork, cooperation, sportsmanship—all are important qualities that organized sports add to a child's life.

- Take weekly excursions. Museums, farm and factory tours, zoos, theater performances—kids learn by being out in the world and observing life around them.

My children enjoy the flexibility that comes with homeschooling. On the first nice day in spring, they are out in the yard playing all morning, and schoolwork gets done later. Sometimes, we just take a day off and hop in the car and head to Chicago for a day or head to Grandma's in Kentucky for a week. The most important lesson I have learned is that everything is educational, and that children who are free to explore their own interests are the most eager learners of all.

And Now a Word from the Critics

Obviously, homeschooling isn't without its naysayers. The National Education Association (NEA), the country's leading public-school teachers' union, says, "Homeschooling programs cannot provide the student with a comprehensive education

The more I learned about homeschooling the more convinced I became that there was no way on earth I was going to teach my kids at home. I was scared. What about algebra? Jon reminded me that I'd have to teach the kids their ABCs before I could teach them to read, and that there was no reason to teach algebra in kindergarten. We decided to take it one year at a time.

It has made us closer as a family. We are together a lot and really know each other well. We have the time to grasp opportunities to love, live, and learn with and from each other.

experience" and suggests that homeschoolers be required to be licensed to teach by the appropriate state education licensing agency. The critics say many parents aren't qualified to teach their children. Ray counters this argument by saying that public school isn't the only place where a kid can learn and that a child's performance has little to do with the parent's level of education.

"That statement presupposes that children get everything that they need from public schools, that the only place a child can learn is in an institution," he says. "Yet the institutional public-school system has only been around for about 100 years. Many great and famous people of the first 150 years of America were homeschooled."

Another sticking point with the critics is that there are no national standards for homeschooled parents and children. Parents are free to choose the curriculum for their kids. Yet homeschoolers say that's the beauty of it—they're free to teach practical life skills, something that is lacking in the public schools. Many homeschoolers take everyday chores and turn them into a learning experience. A lesson in cooking, for instance, becomes an exercise in math and reading.

But when a homeschooled child needs advanced algebra to get accepted into an Ivy League college, and his or her parents aren't versed in the likes of $x^2 + y^2 = z$, they do have choices, Ray says. They can learn advanced algebra and stay one step ahead, or learn it with their child; they can call upon the local homeschool co-op and get another parent to come in and teach it; the child can take a correspondence course in algebra; or the child can go to the local community college and take the course.

The critics also question the issue of socialization—homeschooled kids spend more time with adults than with same-aged children; thus, they may not be as equipped to deal with their peers once they're out on their own. Yet many homeschoolers note the bad effect that same-aged peers can have on children. "Where is the research that suggests that age segregation for twelve years is the right way for a person to be mature by the time he's twenty-five?" Ray argues. "We're presupposing once again that public school provides kids with all the social interactions that they'll need to be socially, psychologically, and emotionally mature as adults."

He also notes that homeschooled kids aren't isolated at all, adding that the average homeschooled kid is heavily involved in outside activities, an average of five per week, including sports groups, church groups, field trips with other homeschooled children, music classes, and volunteer work.

Homeschool Start-Up Tips

Convinced that homeschooling is for your family? Ray offers the following advice on getting started.

- Find a local support group via a state homeschool organization, and attend the meetings.

- Investigate a national homeschool support group like the Home School Legal Defense Association (*see* sidebar on next page).

- Attend annual state or regional conference on home-based education.

- Subscribe to one or two homeschool magazines that generally match your philosophy on education and your life view.

- Realize that now you're going to learn a whole lot of things that you never learned in school. Get interested and excited, and start learning with your children.

OTHER START-UP TIPS

- **Know the state law.** Call your local board of education and ask what is expected of you. Are you required to submit your child's work on a yearly basis for review?

If socialization is the process through which children acquire the necessary skills to get along as responsible members of society, it seems foolish to limit their contact to those who were born within the same twelve-month period, who live in the same zip code, and who are similarly immature. The socialization that I witnessed in school (I taught in public school) consisted mainly of children learning to bend their opinions, tastes, behaviors, and wills to those who are the strongest and cruelest.

It wasn't difficult to start—overwhelming is more like it. There are so many materials out there that it is very difficult to decide what to use. At first I made some bad choices in materials; they were just a bad fit for my daughter. We eventually found material that was a good fit, and things are going smoothly now.

Homeschooling Support

Home School Legal Defense Association's (HSLDA) 50,000 members get free legal help if they encounter problems with the public-school system. Many homeschoolers feel their $100-a-year membership is like legal insurance and offers peace of mind if they should ever find themselves in court. HSLDA's attorneys are well versed in homeschool issues, something that other attorneys may not be. With membership, HSLDA will send a free copy of your local state law concerning home education.

To school at home was a difficult decision to make, but once we made it the transition was relatively easy. There are so many support groups out there willing to share information and offer help and advice, if one needs it.

- **Get help.** Don't homeschool in a vacuum. If you need help, ask.

- **Realize that every family (and every child) is different.** What works for one family may not work for yours. That's the beauty of homeschooling—you can tailor your curriculum to fit your kids.

- **Try out a curriculum before buying.** If you choose to buy a prepackaged curriculum, many suppliers specializing in homeschooling material will send you a sample of their curriculum so that you can "test-drive" it first.

- **Develop a relationship with your local public school.** If you choose to develop your own curriculum, talk with the teachers and administrators at your local public school, and get state board of education guidelines.

- **Take advantage of your local library.** Save money by searching for books in your local library. Pursue your child's interests by checking out books on subjects that interest him, then let him write a book report or create a science project. Teach him how to find the information that he needs.

- **Encourage your children to develop hobbies.** Promote participation in clubs such as 4-H and Girl/Boys Scouts; let the kids volunteer at the local hospital or animal shelter; foster their interests in stamp collecting, gardening, and so forth.

The Future

The numbers of homeschoolers, Ray predicts, will continue to rise, yet homeschooling will never become the norm "as long as state-run schools have the grip on taxes," he says. Ray also notes that there will be more attempts by public-school educators and unions and associations to make more restrictive laws and put more checks on homeschooling families. Yet, on the brighter side, he feels home-based education will become even more socially acceptable. With the technology via the Internet and computer software, and more people working from home, homeschooling will keep expanding and become easier for people.

RESOURCES

Books

Family Matters: Why Homeschooling Makes Sense, by David Guterson; New York: Harcourt, Brace, Jovanovich, 1992.

The Homeschooling Book of Answers, by Linda Dobson; Rocklin, CA: Prima Publishing, 1998.

Homeschooling for Excellence, by David Colfax and Micki Colfax; New York: Warner Books, 1988.

The Homeschooling Handbook, 2nd ed., by Mary Griffith; Rocklyn, CA: Prima Publishing, 1999.

Magazines and Newspapers

Home Education Magazine
P.O. Box 1587
Palmer, AK 99645
(907) 746-1336
www.home-ed-magazine.com

The Link
587 North Ventura Park Road
Newbury Park, CA 91320
www.homeschoolnewslink.com

National Homeschool Journal
6554 Winchester Road, Number 358
Memphis, TN 38115-4241

We've homeschooled for eleven years now. Our children have a different look about them—more innocent. We go on vacations whenever we wish. Our children can work with their dad sometimes. They don't hate school! I never hear any stories about "mean kids," or "cussing on the playground," or how much they hate riding the bus. I really know my children and have had the privilege of teaching them myself.

The Drinking Gourd: Multicultural Home-Education Magazine
P.O. Box 2557
Redmond, WA 98073
(206) 836-0336
Growing Without Schooling
Holt Association
2269 Massachusetts Avenue
Cambridge, MA 02140
(617) 864-3100

Organizations

Home School Legal Defense Association (HSLDA)
P.O. Box 5000
Purcellville, VA 20154
(540) 338-5600
www.hslda.org
National Home Education Research Institute
P.O. Box 13939
Salem, OR 97309
(503) 364-1490
www.nheri.org

Internet Site

School Is Dead—www.learninfreedom.org
With links to more than 1,000 homeschooling websites, parents can access magazine articles, research statistics, and much more.

Housework

Getting the Chores Done
with the Kids Underfoot

*"I hate housework! You make the beds, you do the dishes,
and six months later you have to start all over again."*
— Joan Rivers

*"Cleaning your house while the kids are still growing is like
shoveling the walk before it stops snowing."*
— Phyllis Diller

Ask any full-time parent today why he or she stays home and you'll get a variety of reasons, not one being, "I wanted a clean house." Today's mom doesn't see parenting and housekeeping (or even cooking, for that matter) as one and the same job, unlike stay-at-home moms of the '40s and '50s when women did all the housekeeping, cooking, and child rearing.

Today it's different. Men are helping out more with housework, cooking, and taking care of the kids. Perhaps not as much as some moms would like (read on), but certainly a lot more than dads did some thirty years ago. Plus, many of us have adopted a more laid-back attitude toward how clean and tidy our homes need to be. In fact, a national survey conducted during 1995–1996 by the University of Maryland Survey Research Center found that today's woman is just as satisfied with the cleanliness of her home as women of twenty

My favorite thing to do is to clean the bathroom when Olivia and Catherine are in the tub. I use a nontoxic cleaner; this way it's safe for them to be in there while I'm cleaning. If I'm rushed, I take an old, wet washcloth and just wipe down the surfaces.

We have a regimented routine. Our goal by the time Dan leaves for work at nine o'clock is to have the house vacuumed, the dishes done, and the laundry put in the washer. But some mornings we start out late, and it doesn't get done. Sometimes I put Francesca into the backpack and I do housework with her there. Yet sometimes I just have to let the housework go, as much as it pains me because I'm a neatnik. If I don't get to start out my day with everything in its place, though, the day seems off kilter. Then I'm catching up all day long.

Pop your baby in a child carrier or backpack and clean away! She'll love the constant motion (she may even fall asleep), and you'll love the workout. The extra weight offers resistance, a great calorie burner.

years prior, yet today's woman spends much less time cleaning (nearly ten hours less per week).

SOS: Getting a Reluctant Spouse to Pitch In

We may think we are enlightened, but statistics prove otherwise. According to recent research, women spend on average about fourteen hours more per week on household chores (child care not included) than men. If you're having trouble motivating your significant other into picking up a broom, here are some tips to help.

- **Set up an agreement.** Sit down with pen and paper and specifically divide up chores. Post your list on the refrigerator.
- **Give up control.** Accept his method of cleaning. He may not do it as well as you would like, but does it really matter if he doesn't vacuum under the bed?
- **Make specific requests.** Give up complaining; instead, ask for what you want: "Tom, would you do the dishes tonight? And while you're at it, throw the towels in the washing machine."
- **Do it together.** Choose one hour each week (but not during the weekend, and preferably after the kids have gone to bed) and make a mad dash around the house together.
- **Go on strike.** It may be a bit drastic, but it will sure make a point.

A Clean Style

When it comes to housework, there are three types of families. First are the "neat freaks"—everything in their home is always immaculately clean. They wash the dishes immediately following dinner and clean the coffeepot the moment it's empty. An earthquake could be happening and these people would insist on changing the bed linen.

Then there's the family that's totally at ease with their messiness. Dishes are always in the sink; a layer of dog hair and dust coat the floor. It doesn't matter, though. They don't even notice. In fact, they seem extremely comfortable with this way of life.

Finally, there's the "clean for company" group—the family that secretly lives in clutter. They rinse the dinner dishes and leave them for morning, and they get rid of yesterday's coffee grounds only when they're ready to make a fresh pot of joe. But when company comes to call, everyone gets into the act—feverishly vacuuming the rugs and scrubbing the bathroom tile.

For better or worse, that's my family.

I've never been an extreme housekeeper, but when the kids started showing up, what little cleaning I did do went along the way of the carpet sweeper. Fortunately, I'm not alone. Most full-time parents report doing as little housework as possible. Yet few of us are content to live in clutter. So how do we balance our need for a tidy home with our phobias of toilet brushes?

A clean house is possible even when the kids are small; just adopt a few housekeeping rules. First, prioritize chores: do what's most important, and leave the rest until you just can't stand to look at it anymore. For me that means before my husband leaves for work, I make the beds (it cleans up the look of a room tremendously), vacuum (I hate dirty carpets), and do the dishes. Yet I can let my kitchen floor go two weeks before I'll take a mop to it, I dust only after I can write my name across the tabletop, and I rarely clean the inside of my refrigerator or oven. (For those who are curious, my husband's morning responsibilities include getting the kids fed and dressed and himself ready for work.)

Next, develop a cleaning system that you can live with. For some, that might mean scouring the bathrooms every Sun-

Some families don't have a toy out, but that's not the way I live. I think it's hard for the kids to live like that, too. I let them play! When they're through for the day, some time after dinner, I usually say, "Can we get the twelve dolls off the couch? Let's try to put your toys away so that we can walk in the family room."

Cut down on vacuuming and carpet stains by adopting the Asian custom of removing your shoes when you first enter the house. Keep a variety of inexpensive slippers in the hall closet and offer a pair to guests, appliance-repair people, and family members.

Some days it bothers me that the house is not neat, and some days I think, I'm playing with them. I'm not going to worry about it. I'd rather be playing with the kids than cleaning the house.

day evening or dusting the den during an episode of *ER*; for others, it may mean hiring someone twice a month or having everyone pitch in early Saturday morning. Finally, clean as you go. That means washing a glass directly after using it (a lot easier than washing ten glasses at the end of the day) and never leaving a room empty-handed. Before you turn off the light, look around. What needs to be put back or returned to another room?

Get rid of excessive knickknacks. Not only are they notorious dust collectors, but you won't have to worry about the kids breaking them (and they will break them).

Mother's Little Helper

Next time your little one exclaims, "I want to help," let him. Although the task will take twice as long, allowing a child to help with the housework instills cooperation, teaches inde-

I'm great at multitasking, doing several different projects at once. Usually in the morning, while the kids are watching Barney, *I just kick into gear. I'm making phone calls, doing a load of laundry, sorting through old newspapers— I'm all over the place. I know I only have a half hour before the kids are under my feet, so you should see me go!*

Stupid Cleaning Tasks to Eliminate Forever
(Or at Least Until You Move!)

Stupid Task . . .	Instead, Try . . .
Cleaning the refrigerator	To prevent drips, use plates under packaged meats and place on lower shelves. Line vegetable bins with paper towels.
Cleaning the oven	Line the bottom of oven with aluminum foil; always cover food that's prone to splatter. Use a pumice stone for quick cleanups.
Cleaning cupboards	Put small plates under gooey condiments like honey and syrup.
Scrubbing bathroom tile	Keep a squeegee under the sink, and wipe off tile after each shower (it cuts down on mildew).

pendence and responsibility, and makes it easier for you to enlist his services when he's older and more capable. In time, your child will develop competence, which leads to higher self-esteem. Most importantly, helping out with the housework teaches a child that his contribution to family life is important.

Try to make housecleaning fun (yeah, right) by putting on some upbeat music. Give your toddler a small broom or mop and the two of you can clean side-by-side. The right-sized tool will help build his confidence and reduce frustration while performing certain tasks. Make cleaning a game like a competition to see who can pick up the most toys off the floor in a two-minute span. Set the timer, and go!

Clean in small, ten-minute increments. Set up a monthly calendar, and each day pencil in a short task, the ones that bug you but you never seem to have the time to accomplish. For instance, "Clean master bedroom ceiling fan," "Remove ashes from fireplace," or "Organize silverware drawer."

Pint-Size Chores for Pint-Size Kids

They may be short, but you'd be amazed at what two feet and twenty pounds can accomplish. Just remember, don't expect perfection.

- **Laundry.** Even young kids can sort laundry, or have them put the clothes in the washing machine as you sort and hand the clothes to them.

- **Yard work.** Kids can rake leaves, add garden trash to compost, or water the vegetable garden.

- **Dusting.** Hand her a small rag and watch her go!

- **Picking up toys.** Make cleaning up accessible by having low, open shelves or baskets.

- **Recycling.** Sort recyclables and put in appropriate bins.

- **Clearing the table.** Remind them to use two hands as they clear off plates and cups and take them to the sink.

- **Watering.** Give him a small watering can or plastic pitcher and let him water the houseplants.

- **Mail.** Hand her your stack of bills and let her put them in the postbox.

They like to help. I can see that it makes them proud to help. If I ask Rachel to fill up the napkin holder, for instance, she thinks that's the best job in the world. But it takes effort to find stuff that they know how to do and to remember to let them do it.

Control toy clutter by limiting which rooms your child's playthings are allowed in. For instance, no toys in the kitchen, bathroom, or hallways. And stop picking up the toys three times a day; once, right before the evening bath, is plenty. For the rest of the time, just kick them out of your way!

RESOURCES

Books

How to Avoid Housework: Tips, Hints, and Secrets on How to Have a Spotless Home, by Paula Jhung; New York: Simon & Schuster, 1995.

Talking Dirt: America's Speed Cleaning Expert Answers the 157 Most Asked Cleaning Questions, by Jeff Campbell; New York: Dell Books, 1997.

Too Busy to Clean? Over 500 Tips and Techniques to Make Housecleaning Easier, by Patti Barrett; Pownel, PA: Storey Books, 1998.

Illness

What to Do When You're the Patient

When the kids are sick, you're right by their bedsides to offer hugs and administer warm soup and fresh tissues. But what happens when you get sick? Who's going to fluff your pillows? The kids? Doubtful.

When you're a full-time parent, there's no such thing as a sick day. It's bad enough that your head feels like it's in a vise grip, but you also have three kids in the next room, all waiting for you to fix lunch. Although it's hardly a day you'll want to remember, there are a few things that you can do to lighten your load.

What's a Mom (or Dad) to Do?

- **Baby yourself.** Don't feel guilty about getting sick, as many parents do. Forget the martyr routine and get in bed.

- **Call in all favors**. Think of all possible baby-sitting candidates—in-laws, neighbors, friends, relatives, coworkers with lots of vacation time to burn—then start telephoning. Even if someone can drop by to take the kids to the park for only an hour, it's a help. At the very least, see if someone can drop off some lunch or dinner.

- **Order out**. If no one can help cook a meal, get out the phone book and order out.

- **Rearrange spouse's schedule**. Perhaps your spouse can leave for work late, come home early, work from home for the day, or even take the kids to the office for a while.

- **Stay together**. Rather than having the kids run wild throughout the house while you're holed up in the bedroom, choose one room (the living room or bedroom) where you can lie down and the kids can play.

- **Set up shop**. Set up your room with all the sick-day essentials: a pitcher of water, tissues, cordless telephone, magazines and books, TV remote, and so forth, so that you won't need to get out of bed often. And don't forget toys for the kids. Have plenty of books, puzzles, and "quiet" toys (ones *without* batteries) on hand.

- **Bend the rules**. You may be a "no television" family, but on days like these, there's nothing better than a few good children's videos to keep the kids quiet and entertained (so you can nap).

- **Secure the perimeter**. To protect your toddler from wandering outside while you're napping, make sure all doors are locked. Better yet, encourage her to nap, too.

What's a Kid to Do?

- **Let them play doctor.** Round up the play medical kit, and let your child give you a thorough exam. Not only is playing doctor fun, but the game empowers children, helping to ease their fears about Mom's illness.
- **Let them play masseuse.** Even children as young as three can give a comforting massage.
- **Let them go fetch.** Kids love to help. Let them go get an extra blanket, more water, another magazine.

Take Two Aspirin and Call Me in the Morning

Don't worry—you will get through this. If you're not prepared this time around, make sure you are for the next time by having frozen dinners on hand, a good supply of children's videos, and a few special "quiet" toys to dole out to the kids. And believe me, there will be a next time.

Internet

Staying Connected

Although the number of stay-at-home parents is on the rise, sometimes you may feel like you're the only one home on your block. Compound your isolation with bad weather, and you'll really be singing the blues. Fortunately, if you have a computer, you're only a click away from kvetching with other full-time parents from around the world.

Any Internet search engine will locate millions (yes, *millions*) of parenting sites, but I've checked out several hundred and have listed a few dozen that are worth visiting, encompassing a variety of tastes and lifestyles. Sites are listed alphabetically, not by preference.

■ **American Baby** (www.americanbaby.com). The official site of *American Baby* magazine, a how-to manual for new and expectant parents (pregnancy through the second year).

■ **Attachment Parenting** (www.gentleparenting.com). A great resource for those who want to learn more about *attachment parenting*, a nurturing lifestyle whereby mother/father and child connect through breastfeeding, wearing the baby in either a sling or a Snugli, and sharing sleep in the family bed.

■ **Black Parenting Website** (www.blackparenting.com). African-American parents get advice on building racial pride, heritage, and self-esteem during the first five years of their children's lives.

■ **The Blended Family Resource Guide** (www.blended family.com). For couples who bring children into their current relationship from previous relationships, this site gives advice on stepparenting, as well as other pertinent topics.

■ **Crayola Family Play** (www.familyplay.com). From the crayon giant, peruse a huge selection of craft ideas for the kids. Customize your search by your child's age, skill, and category (birthday, gift, etc.). Helpful parenting articles, too.

■ **CTW Family Workshop** (www.sesamestreet.com). Visit Elmo's World or the Golden Grover Awards, check out the Preschool Playground for the Parent's Activity Guide, or browse the Parent's Toolbox for tips on healthy living, safe Internet cruising, or raising good kids.

■ **Cybergrace Christian Network** (www.cybergrace.com). From family movie reviews to on-line Bible study, this site offers the Christian family numerous resources and Internet links.

■ **FamilyFun** (www.familyfun.com). The official site for *FamilyFun* magazine. Access a variety of suggestions for indoor and outdoor activities, themed party ideas, and contests.

■ **FamilyPC** (www.zdnet.com/familypc). Access *FamilyPC* magazine, where you can download articles on finding great travel bargains on the Internet, advice on what every parent should know about on-line chat rooms, and a discussion on buying name-brand computers versus brand-*X* computers.

■ **Healthy Kids** (www.healthykids.com). Home to *Healthy Kids* magazine, this site offers parental advice on healthy living, from recent medical news and vaccine updates to developmental problems like nail biting and self-esteem issues.

■ **Hip Mama** (www.hipmama.com). Nipple piercing and breastfeeding? Prenatal exposure to punk rock? This website is clearly not for the uptight.

■ **Jewish Family and Life** (www.jewishfamily.com). Stories sharing family traditions, a "Dear Rabbi" column, recipes for a vegetarian Seder and other holidays, a community bulletin board to share comments, and much more.

■ **Midlife Mommies** (www.midlifemommies.com). Information on midlife pregnancy, news that directly affects older women and families, personal essays, plus financial advice—funding your child's college, planning for retirement, and balancing home-based business with family life.

■ **Moms Online** (www.momsonline.com). A virtual smorgasbord of tips and advice, plus chat rooms, message boards, and recipes.

■ **Mothering** (www.mothering.com). The official site for *Mothering* magazine, advocates of a natural family lifestyle. Articles range from home births and homeopathy to organic foods and the vaccination debate.

■ **Mothers of Supertwins** (www.mostonline.org). Are you the parent of triplets or more? Then this site is for you. Get advice covering pregnancy through the school years. Shop their on-line store for special clothes and baby equipment designed just for families of supertwins.

■ **Multicultural Parenting** (www.familyculture.com). Geared toward Asian and multicultural families, articles on this site range from "Should We Raise Our Asian Adopted Daughter According to Our Non-Asian Heritage?" to "Asian Fathers on Fathering."

■ **Parents** (www.parents.com). Log on to the official site of *Parents* and *Child* magazines. E-mail their panel of parenting experts, check out the current issue, or scan the archives for past articles.

■ **Parents Helping Parents** (www.php.com). A resource for parents of special-needs children, this site offers information on support groups, weekly articles, and monthly events.

■ **Parents Place** (www.parentsplace.com). This site runs the gamut of parenting topics but also offers several different live chat groups, current parenting news, and an "Ask Our Experts" column.

■ **Parent Soup** (www.parentsoup.com). The granddaddy of on-line parenting sites, Parent Soup doles out advice from prepregnancy through the teenage years. Chat rooms, message boards, parenting experts, article archives . . . Need I go on?

■ **Parent Time** (www.parenttime.com). Home to *Parenting* and *Baby Talk* magazines. Parenting experts, celebrity parents, fun, and games—you name it, it's here. You can even customize the site according to your child's age.

■ **Sports Parents** (www.sportsparents.com). From the editors of *Sports Illustrated for Kids*, this site offers features on making sports fun, healthy, and accessible to kids. E-mail questions to resident experts—a pediatric sports physician and a sports psychologist.

■ **Twins** (www.twinsmagazine.com). Have twins? These days, who doesn't! Home to *Twins* magazine, you'll find parenting tips, book reviews, on-line shopping for twins equipment, support groups, and research notices.

Marriage

Keeping Your Relationship on Track

*"People are always asking couples whose marriage
has endured at least a quarter of a century for their secret
for success. Actually, it is no secret at all.
I am a forgiving woman. Long ago, I forgave my husband
for not being Paul Newman."*

—ERMA BOMBECK

*Children are an
amazing test
of a marriage.*

Any married couple can tell you: when kids come on board, everything changes.

"Kids bring a whole life and energy force of their own to a marriage," says Dr. Ellyn Bader, author of *In Quest of the Mythical Mate: A Developmental Approach to Diagnosis and Treatment in Couples Therapy* and codirector of The Couples Institute in Menlo Park, California. The experience can be bonding for many couples as they share in the joy of watching their children grow and develop. But for others, Bader explains, it's difficult managing the changes that they bring to a relationship. Unable to cope with the new stress that children add, some couples begin to compete and fight with one another. "I see many couples come in [to The Couples Institute] right after two years of marriage, usually right around the birth of the first child," she says. "They just don't succeed in being able to manage the major changes that a child brings about. Too many couples drift apart during those first two years, and some never resolve it."

From Full-Time Employee to Full-Time Parent

For most couples, children deepen their commitment to each other, but a couple's life, too, can suddenly go into a tailspin when one parent leaves his or her job to care for the kids full-time.

When a mother decides to stay home, there are all kinds of new emotional and psychological demands on her, and many husbands don't understand why their wives complain or aren't available to them. After all, they think, she has it easy because she's at home; she's not working. Now responsible for the day-to-day child rearing, a rewarding but sometimes difficult and often thankless job, the mother may be dealing with issues of loneliness and isolation as she struggles to find a new identity as a full-time mother. She may even be envious of her husband's freedom as he leaves for work each morning. Once a breadwinner herself, she now relies completely on him for financial support, something with which she may not be comfortable.

Some husbands rarely grasp these psychological, emotional, and physical strains of full-time motherhood during those first few chaotic years. Instead of being helpful, Bader observes, they become angry and withdrawn. Yet Dad, too, has plenty of new issues to deal with. He's now the sole supporter, an enormous responsibility. He may worry about money and how he'll stretch the family paycheck now that his wife is no longer working. Socially, he may feel like an outsider in his own family, not able to spend as much time with them as he would like. He may feel jealous of his wife

Our marriage didn't change as a result of my staying home full-time; it's just a result of us having a baby. I have to say that the marriage has almost totally gone down the toilet. I look at people without kids and I think, "Wow. Marriage is so easy when you don't have children." It's not like the kids are doing anything to make your marriage disruptive. My husband says, "I just want things to get back to normal." Yet I keep thinking, "Who are we kidding?" It will never be like before.

as she easily interacts with the kids, knowing their routines and likes and dislikes by heart. His wife may not understand the profound loss that her husband feels at not having as much one-on-one time with her.

"Each person can get narcissistically entrenched in his or her own situation and not see the other person," Bader says. It's this lack of understanding the other person's role, she says, that leads many couples to drift apart. All of these feelings are normal, and most successfully overcome them. Getting through the transition, Bader explains, involves slowing down the process. By actively communicating, parents can actually see what's going on with each other and try to resolve the negative feelings.

I was prepared for the way a child would make me feel, but I wasn't prepared for how differently it would make me feel about my husband. Before children, he was the center of my world, but now it has shifted so completely. His feelings were so important to me, but now at the end of the day I don't have any left over, and I don't care.

TIPS TO HELP COMMUNICATE

Learning how to listen as well as express yourself are keys to staying connected as a couple.

- **Take an interest in each other's lives.** Rather than saying, "How was your day?" ask specific questions, "Whom did you see at the park?" or "Did you discuss the April conference at your staff meeting today?" Simple questions such as these can open up dialogue and lead to more intimate conversation.

- **Try to empathize; get into the other person's world.** Learn to listen rather than criticize. Instead of getting angry when dinner is not on the table, husbands should say, "Tell me what it's like to cook dinner at five o'clock when you're also trying to feed the kids." Instead of becoming defensive, wives should ask, "What's it like to come home and see the kitchen a mess?"

- **Learn to praise.** Try using heartfelt compliments, and remember to say thank-you often.

- **Try humor.** Even during the ugliest of kid tantrumming, turn to your spouse and smile.

- **Hug, touch, kiss.** Don't just pass each other in the kitchen each morning. Take a moment to connect physically with a warm hug and tender kiss. It will jump-start your day.

- **Give a call.** Make it a point to call each other at least once a day (preferably when the kids are napping) just to say hello.

Great Expectations

When one parent leaves a full-time job to be a full-time parent, it's important for couples to be extremely clear about the expectations of each. "You're restructuring everything when someone decides to stay home," Bader notes. "Couples should literally list their expectations, making sure they're freely choosing them. It must be something that they want to do." Don't assume, for example, that because your spouse has chosen to stay home to care for the kids that dinner will be waiting on the table every evening when you get home from the office. Some parents feel that caring for the kids is a big enough job, and there is no time for cooking. "One woman I know chose to stay home and it was her expectation that she would simply take care of the kids," Bader explains. "That was her job. It didn't mean cooking, cleaning, or anything else. His idea was that there would always be dinner on the table and the house would be clean. Since it was never discussed beforehand, it led to huge fights."

The division of household chores should be hashed out at length before a spouse hangs up her briefcase in favor of the minivan. For instance: who's responsible for cooking dinner? Who will clean the house? Who's in charge of putting the kids to bed each night? Who will handle the finances (paying bills, making investments) now that there's only one income? Will these assignments change on the weekend?

We're adamant about a date night once a week. But it's getting harder to afford it. Baby-sitting for four kids is up to $15 per hour in our neighborhood. It's absurd. A friend of mine told me that she and her husband can't afford nights out, but she knows the importance of it. So she and her husband give one weekend night to the kids—they rent a family movie or play family games—the other weekend night she puts the kids to bed early; then, she and husband make a good dinner with wine, candlelight, the whole thing. She swears by it.

When we decided I would stay home, many household responsibilities shifted. Now when my husband walks through the door at 6:15, he's on evening kid patrol. Burned out on crayons, juice cups, and *Barney*, I see the kids only intermittently in the evening. Kevin, on the other hand, plays games with them, bathes them, and reads bedtime stories to our sons. The hour-and-a-half break gives me time to do any number of things, from relaxing with a magazine to cooking dinner (which is now my responsibility). The kids do see me one last time before they drift off to sleep—I sing them songs. This arrangement has rarely changed in more than three years and works well for us. I get some downtime, and my husband gets a chance to do some father-son bonding.

Even after the household schedule and division of duties have been agreed upon, Bader suggests that couples "check in" regularly with one another to make sure the transition is running smoothly. In the beginning she advises weekly chat sessions where a husband and wife reassess their new responsibilities and make sure each person is happy with his or her new role. There needs to be clarity and understanding of what each person is providing, Bader says. If there aren't any major stumbling blocks, move the talk to once a month.

John and I try to pick a day out of the week where we can connect, sit down in the evening, and talk. It's not like we have an in-depth conversation, but at least we sit down or lay together or watch a movie together.

Making Time for Yourself

Married couples with kids are always trying to balance their family relationships—parent to child; parent to parent. What should come first? The relationship or the children? Neither, according to Bader. A mother who puts all her emphasis on her kids, for instance, will soon be depleted. Instead the focus should be on nurturing herself, she suggests. "A parent should actually put herself/himself first," she says. "Not in a selfish way, but in a real way." A mom, she explains, should organize her week by thinking of ways to keep herself in top emo-

tional and physical health so that she can be a happy and ful-
filled mother, wife, partner. These might include arranging
to sleep in some morning, hiring someone to do a couple
hours of housekeeping, getting a massage, or making time for
friends.

There is a downside, Bader warns. "It steps over into
selfishness when the wants and needs of other people involved
are not seriously taken into account, and are made light of,"
she says. Their requirements, however big or small, must be
integrated into the plan.

Making Time for Each Other

It's easy for married couples to drift apart physically once the
kids enter the picture. Yet it's important to keep intimacy alive
in a marriage. But how? Evenings are usually the only time
for busy couples to reconnect, and often they're too tired from
a hectic day.

"Part of keeping the intimacy alive is having a business
or organizational type of meeting once a week," Bader suggests. "You need to make sure that the practical stuff is getting handled so that there is energy left over." Bader advises
couples to discuss everything from "How's the baby-sitting
hunt going?" to "Who's coming to bid on painting the house?"
Putting it off or assuming the other person will take care of
it only leads to resentment and arguments. "It's all that daily-
grind stuff. It needs to be managed well with enough support
systems. With many couples I have to push them to get it handled so there is enough energy left over for just each other."

HOW TO MANAGE THE DAILY GRIND

- Keep a list of projects, then sit down and divide the
  work.

Mark and I have been trying to go see a movie together for a month. But things have been so insane at home that when we leave the house we say to ourselves, "If we go to a movie right now, we'll sit there and not talk to each other and then go home." So we haven't been doing it. We've been going to get a bite to eat together instead. We sit and talk and have a glass of wine. We're away from the house, focused on each other, so that we start to create a dialogue together. Eventually, if we talk long enough, we get involved in other subjects. We walk away feeling much better, saying, "Oh, yeah, I remember you!"

- Assign one chore per day per adult. For instance, "Today I'll make dental appointments for every family member while my husband is taking the car into the mechanic's." Cutting the work down into smaller chunks makes it more palatable.

- Pitch in by offering suggestions and ways to help. For example, put up a notice at work advertising for a baby-sitter; or ask colleagues for their recommendations for a roofer. By making an effort, however small, the other spouse won't feel like she's the only one keeping the household running.

A Weekend Away

It was hard because we used to go out all the time before the kids were born, but when they were little we hardly went out to dinner. You have to find ways to make things entertaining and romantic. We used to put them to bed and then have a candlelight dinner. Or we'd rent a movie that everybody else was talking about. After Zach and Hannah went to bed, it was just Andy and me.

These days, my idea of romance is a home-delivered pizza and a video on a Friday night. I've forgotten the days B.K. (before kids) when my husband and I slept in on Sunday mornings, actually *read* the paper, or traveled to Europe untethered. And although I love being part of a family, like most couples, Kevin and I need a quick getaway—alone. (The last time I spent a night away from my kids was when I was in the hospital giving birth to my son Matthew. I have to admit, the peace and quiet of a hospital room seemed like a vacation.)

It takes planning and commitment to go away for even a night without the kids, but the payback is stunning. A romantic weekend for two is a chance to evaluate marital roles and renew intimacy.

COUNTDOWN TO ROMANCE

Planning and preparing for a weekend getaway well in advance helps keep anxiety at a minimum.

- Carry a notebook with you weeks before your departure, noting critical child-care information. Does your son need his special blanket to fall asleep, for instance? What are his after-school activities?

- Keep the children's schedule uninterrupted.

- Cook and freeze meals.

- Inform the children only a day or two before you leave, and show them how to mark off the calendar with stickers until you return.

Sometimes the craziness of your life with kids is bonding. Instead of taking everything to heart, if the two of you can just laugh at each other, and say, "Oh, my God, we're losing it!" If you can laugh at your own insaneness, that forms a connection to your husband.

Romantic Retreats

You've got the baby-sitter; now what? Choose one of these romantic spots for your second honeymoon. Be forewarned: romance has its price—some rooms listed below cost more than $200 per night.

Hotel Del Coronado Coronado, California (619) 435-3101	An historic Victorian retreat, the setting for the film classic, *Some Like It Hot*, the Del is situated right on the beach. Ask for the bed-and-breakfast package (use of the spa or tennis courts, and bicycle rental).
L'Auberge Du Soleil Napa Valley, California (800) 348-5406	Pure wine-country charm: rooms have fireplaces, terracotta tile, and porches overlooking the vineyards. First-class restaurant, spa, pool, tennis courts.

Petite Auberge San Francisco, California (800) 365-3004	A French country inn centered around a courtyard right in the heart of San Francisco's Knob Hill. Some rooms have fireplaces. Afternoon tea. Wine and hors d'oeuvres in the evening.
L'Auberge De Sedona Sedona, Arizona (800) 272-6777	A French inn in Arizona's "Red Rock" country. Romantic hillside cottages with a babbling brook right outside your door. Rooms have porches, fireplaces, and no TV.
Little Palm Island Little Torch Key, Florida (800) 343-8567	Just three miles off the main keys, but miles away in tranquility. Thatched-room villas with mosquito-net beds and outdoor showers. Great restaurant with French Caribbean cuisine.
Maison De Ville New Orleans, Louisiana (800) 634-1600	A brick courtyard centers this historic hotel. Pure New Orleans charm with antiques and wrought-iron balconies. Small rooms. Intimate bistro.
Mirror Lake Inn Lake Placid, New York (518) 523-2544	A 1924 white clapboard hotel situated on seven acres. Go in winter when you can skate on the lake, then come inside for an indoor swim. Afternoon tea. Lively pub. Leisurely stroll to downtown.

Le Parker Meridien New York, New York (800) 543-4300	In the heart of midtown Manhattan, this French-owned hotel has beautifully decorated rooms, many overlooking Central Park. Take a swim in their rooftop, glass-enclosed pool.
Mills House Hotel Charleston, South Carolina (800) 874-9600	Antebellum charm near Charleston's historic district, this hotel shines with antiques and southern service. Rooftop pool offers a welcome retreat.
Cliffside Inn Newport, Rhode Island (800) 845-1811	An elegant 1880 Victorian lady, one block from the historic cliff walk. Rooms are elegant, many with fireplaces.

When the kids are small and you're just buddies and business partners with your spouse, it's just part of the transition of married life. If marriage were solely based on physical attraction, then you wouldn't survive children. The romance does comes back, and when it does, it's just wonderful. You're with your best friend. You do have to have a mission together, and recognize that it's a joint venture. And you will survive it.

Till Death Do Us Part

It's important to remember that you're in this together. Change is never easy, but if both parties are committed to making full-time parenting successful, it can make your relationship and your family stronger.

RESOURCES

Books

The Complete Idiot's Guide to the Perfect Marriage, by Hillary Rich; New York: Macmillan General Reference, 1997.

15 Minutes to Build a Stronger Marriage: Weekly Togetherness for Busy Couples, by Bobbi Yagel and Myron Yagel; Carol Stream, IL: Tyndale House Publishers, 1995.

In Quest of the Mythical Mate: A Developmental Approach to Diagnosis and Treatment in Couples Therapy, by Ellyn Bader, Ph.D.; New York: Brunner/Mazel, 1988.

100 Hints: How to Stay Married for Life, by Bill Morelan; Tulsa: Honor Books, 1996.

1,008 Secrets of a Happy Marriage, by Andrew Williams and Andy Zubko; Arbuckle, CA: Radiant Summit, 1997.

Mealtime

- -

By the end of the day, most parents and their kids are tired, hungry, and cranky—not exactly a recipe for stress-free dining. If Mom or Dad gets a late start on dinner, for example, or just can't think of what to make, by the time the food reaches the table, the carrots may fly.

Families who successfully live through the dinner hour may approach it differently from one another, but one thing remains the same: they all have consistent nightly rituals. In our family, for instance, dinnertime is *usually* a peaceful affair. I try to make things fun by letting the kids pick out some music (at the moment their favorite is the cast album to the old Broadway musical, *Damn Yankees*); I give them colorful plates and utensils and straws for drinking; and when dinner is all done, I let them look through books while my husband and I linger. It works for us.

Mealtime can be fun. I don't get weird about what they can have for dinner. Like tonight, Max and Tessa each had a bagel and lox. They asked for it, and I said OK. It's easy for me; it's healthy.

MEALTIME TIPS

■ **Plan ahead.** Don't wait until the kids are starving before you start to cook. Take a preemptive strike and fix the meal before stomachs start to growl. And so you won't be left wondering what to cook, decide in the morning what you'll prepare that evening, pulling out food to defrost from the freezer if need be. Before going grocery shopping for the week, some highly efficient parents even plan a weekly menu, getting input from their children. (I'm not that organized.)

There are days when I put one twin in a Snugli and one in a backpack and make dinner. I don't always have to do this, but when they're both crying, it's grating on my nerves. Somehow, the physical endurance is easier than the mental endurance of the crying, especially at that time when I've got Sam doing homework and Abigail crawling up my leg. I'll probably pay for it someday in back pain, but for now it's working OK.

■ **Keep plenty of kid staples on hand.** Stock lots of tomato sauce (fresh or bottled), frozen vegetables (including french fries), organic turkey dogs (available in health-food stores), their favorite cheese, and fruit. I even keep a container filled with steamed rice and use it for all sorts of quick dinner ideas like peas, rice, and tomato sauce topped with grated cheese. The kids love it, and it takes less than five minutes to make and heat in the microwave.

■ **Get a microwave.** I held out for years; now I can't imagine cooking for kids without one. When they can't wait another minute to eat, a microwave can quickly heat up leftovers (not to mention defrost the turkey dog that you forgot to pull from the freezer).

■ **Have an emergency plan.** A great day at the park, but freeway traffic delays you well past the dinner hour. Have a few frozen pizzas on hand for just such a day.

■ **Create a kid-friendly atmosphere.** Let the kids help create the mood. Eat outside if the weather permits. Let them choose their favorite music to play. Let them set the table using whatever utensils they'd like. Let them create place cards and choose where each member of the family will sit.

■ **Serve small portions.** Adult-sized portions are intimidating to kids. Less is better.

■ **Serve what they like.** Sure, broccoli is good for them, but if they won't eat it, try something else. After a few weeks, try introducing broccoli again. Who knows? Maybe this time they'll try it. And if your kids flatly refuse to eat *all* vegetables, load up on fruit.

■ **Take them grocery shopping.** Show your kids where food comes from, and encourage them to ask questions. Tell them what you're buying and why. Let them choose the melons or which loaf of bread to buy. The greater the stake kids have in food, the more likely they'll eat it.

■ **Relax.** Remember, it's just food. Kids will develop better eating habits if you take a laid-back approach. Dinnertime should be a relaxing end to the day.

I never did caffeine in the afternoons, but now I do. I save it until four o'clock, and I swear that helps me through dinner. You almost feel naughty, like you're taking a drug that you shouldn't. I get such a great buzz from it!

Into the Kitchen

Kids still refusing to eat? Is dinnertime always a soap opera ending with someone in tears, and you ready to do battle with your spouse when he arrives home? The answer may be as simple as having your kids put on aprons and letting them help you in the kitchen while you cook.

The experts agree: when children help prepare a meal, they're more likely to eat it (well, at least *try* it). "I've never seen a child not excited about cooking," says Elaine Magee, registered dietitian and author of *Someone's in the Kitchen with Mommy* and *Alphabet Cooking*. "Kids are dying to cook. It doesn't matter what their gender or age is. It's a natural medium for kids. They can see it, they can smell it, they can touch it."

Magee stresses that cooking together has several benefits, the most important being that kids who help prepare healthful foods tend to eat healthful foods. But cooking with your children can also teach them practical cooking skills. It's a better alternative than watching television or playing video

I bring the portable stereo into the kitchen, and I put on some dancing music. Lillie loves to dance and so does Elliot. The kids just want to be around me when I'm cooking, so instead of trying to get rid of them, we're all together dancing. I'm still able to work and continue making dinner. I'm able to get dinner on the table and entertain them at the same time.

games, and it gives parents an opportunity to spend some quality time with their kids. "Why not bring them into the kitchen with you, and spend time together doing things you have to do anyway?" she asks.

Although the idea will sound appealing to many, Magee warns that it will take some time and patience on the part of the head chef (a.k.a. the parent), though the payoff will be worth it. Not only will it build confidence in your kids, but you get genuine help in meal preparation. No more whining from your little food critics demanding to know when dinner will be ready. Instead, they'll be right by your side actively taking part in tossing the salad and peeling the potatoes.

You can start your chefs-in-training as young as eighteen months, and have them participate in as much, or as little, as you feel comfortable. "Kids want to do anything," Magee notes. "If you just want them to do one thing, that's fine. It's a good place to start." But she suggests that the maximum time for small children helping out shouldn't exceed twenty to twenty-five minutes. Or, if you prefer, break it up into two short session. "If you're making something like tortillas, for example, you might need to let the dough take a rest. You can all take a break and go outside, throw the ball, then come back and pat the tortillas into shape and fry them up."

I started cooking early with my boys simply because I couldn't enter the kitchen without the two of them climbing up on their kitchen step stools (a must for little people in the kitchen), chiming, "I want to help." I also wanted to instill a love for cooking in my sons the same way that I acquired mine—from my mother. She always encouraged me to join her in the kitchen. Although she was not famous for her patience, my mom seemed so composed as she taught me the culinary basics.

But how do you know how much control to have over a cooking situation? "There's a fine line between challenging your children and wanting them to be successful," stresses Magee. "The bottom line is that they have to feel good about the cooking project at hand." Setting up the work space so that the mess (and there will be one) is self-contained is one way to allow your child full exploration. Put a cookie sheet under the mixing bowl so that if something spills, you can simply pour it back. And try to approach the experience with a sense of humor and a "that's OK" attitude. "Have them crack an egg," she explains. "What's the worst thing that could happen? So what if you're picking shell from the batter. Recipes should be forgiving."

Age-Appropriate Kitchen Tasks

Depending on your child's age, he or she can accomplish a number of helpful chores in the kitchen. Magee offers these tips to get you started.

Two-Year-Olds	• **Tearing:** hand your toddler a bowl and some freshly washed lettuce and watch him go to town.
	• **Stirring:** by far the easiest task and a great place to start.
	• **Pounding:** need some chicken fillets flattened? Cover the chicken with plastic wrap, give your child a plastic or wooden kitchen hammer, and let her loose.
	• **Snapping/breaking:** carrots, celery, green beans.
Three-Year-Olds	• **Wrapping:** allow them to wrap dough around vegetables or meat.
	• **Pouring:** you will still need to measure, but they can certainly take it from there.
	• **Shaking:** always a fun activity; just be sure to use resealable bags.
	• **Spreading:** batter or frosting; just be sure to use a plastic knife.

Children are more interested in what you have to eat than what you make for them. The first time I ever got the kids to eat stir-fried vegetables, I just made a big bowl of it and put it in the middle of the table and started picking at it with my fingers. At first they said, "We're not eating that." And I said, "Don't eat it. It's for me." And I kept picking at it, saying, "Mmmmmm. This looks good." So of course, they started picking at it with their fingers. Max found things in there that he liked, because I didn't just serve one vegetable. Stir-fry has so many vegetables that they could pick out what they wanted.

Four-Year-Olds	• **Rolling:** kids can flatten dough with their hands; or, with a little patience, they can learn to use a rolling pin. • **Peeling:** oranges, bananas, hard-boiled eggs; you name it. • **Juicing:** great for learning twisting and turning.
Five-Year-Olds	• **Measuring:** before they could simply pour what you had already measured out; now let them try it on their own. • **Cutting:** using a sawing motion, teach your child to cut soft foods such as cheese. For safety, don't forget to use a plastic knife. • **Grating:** large graters work best.

Dinner's Ready

Dinnertime doesn't have to be the most stressful time of the day. In fact, with a little planning, and a bit of patience, it may well turn out to be the most favorite.

RESOURCES

Books

Alphabet Cooking, by Elaine Magee; Chicago: Contemporary Books, 1997.

The Baby Cookbook: Tasty and Nutritious Meals for the Whole Family That Babies and Toddlers Will Also Love, by Karin Knight; New York: William Morrow, 1992.

Food for Little Fingers, by Victoria Jenest; New York: St. Martin's Mass Market Paper, 1997.

Jennifer Lang Cooks for Kids: 153 Recipes and Ideas for Good Food that Kids Love to Eat, by Jennifer Lang; New York: Crown Publishing, 1993.

Someone's in the Kitchen with Mommy, by Elaine Magee; Chicago: Contemporary Books, 1998.

365 Foods Kids Love to Eat, by Sheila Ellison and Judith Gray; Naperville, IL: Sourcebooks Trade, 1995.

Nap Time

I have to admit, my favorite time of the day is when my kids go in for their naps. After a busy morning of trucks, volleyballs, tricycles, and noise often escalating to epic proportions, the quiet that suddenly settles over my house is almost spiritual. For two (sometimes three) glorious hours I calmly putter about in my office, bask in the sun out on the front porch, or collapse from exhaustion on the living room couch. Fortunately, my sons have been devoted nappers since the day they were born, and, as an added bonus, they nap at the exact same time. I'm lucky, and I know it.

For the full-time parent, nap time can either bring a needed breather or, if the little ones refuse to cooperate, cause enormous stress and irritability (and that's just for the parent). Some parents have reported that their children will put up such a fuss when the hour comes that the kids will destroy the contents of their room as a show of protest.

If you've found yourself in a similar situation, fear not. Help is on the way.

Who Needs to Nap?

Talk with any parent about their kids' napping schedule and you'll get a wide range of answers. My sister's kids napped every afternoon until they were five years old, while a girl-friend swears her daughter never took a daytime snooze during her entire toddlerhood. Still, most kids under the age of three need one nap a day. How long she'll sleep, however, is another story.

From about eighteen months to three years, a time of rapid emotional, developmental, and physical growth, children's sleep patterns are constantly changing; and parents need to change along with them. Just because a kid is a marathon napper at the age of one doesn't mean he'll continue with the routine up until he leaves for kindergarten. As a child matures, his needs change. For better or worse, that includes his sleep, too. Altering your expectations about how much he needs, therefore, is the first step in ending the nap-time battles.

HOW MUCH DO THEY NEED?

How much sleep does your child need? Check out the nap chart to see, but remember, these are only averages. Your child may sleep more, or less.

Right around their second birthday, most children consolidate their sleep by giving up a nap, usually the one in the morning. On average, toddlers need about twelve hours of sleep total, so if they're getting that at night—say, going to bed at 8 P.M. and waking up at 8 A.M.—they won't need to make up any snoozing during the day. Yet, if your child goes to bed at 8 P.M., but wakes up at 6 A.M., she'll probably need

NEWBORN

6-MONTH-OLD

18-MONTH-OLD

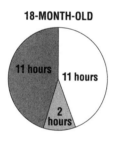

■ Night
▨ Nap
□ Awake

Nap chart showing
how much the average
child sleeps in a twenty-
four-hour period

a two-hour afternoon snooze to get her through the rest of her day, even if she thinks otherwise.

Beware, transitioning from two naps to one can be a stressful time—one day your little one functions fine on one nap, the next day she's cranky. Bear with her, though; most settle into their new routine after a month or two.

Lullabies to Live By

Music soothes the savage beast and, often, a fussy child. If you have trouble getting your little one to settle down, try a little bedtime music to help her relax.

Mozart	Eine Kleine Nachtmusik, Wind Serenade no. 4
Beethoven	*Moonlight* Sonata, *Pathetique* Sonata, Romance for Violin and Orchestra
Debussy	Children's Corner Suite, "Clair De Lune"

Why Doesn't She Nap?

Sleep begets sleep. If one day you're on the run from store to store, hoping your toddler will catch a few winks in the car between stops, you're setting yourself up for problems. When you tinker with a child's internal sleep schedule, it's harder for her to fall back in line. Experts say that a child's circadian rhythms cause her body temperature to drop a bit, naturally signalling nap time. If you're not attuned to when that happens, you'll miss the opportunity to put her to sleep. Unlike adults, who stay sleepy, kids will bounce back, often by being hyperactive. The key? As inconvenient as it may seem, try to work around your child's sleep schedule. Run your errands or make your play dates before or after her nap.

I learned that lesson the hard way.

As most parents do with second children, I loosened the scheduling reins with Matthew (technically, he's the third child, but the result of my second pregnancy), and I tried to make him adapt to the busy schedule I had with my other two sons. It rarely worked out well. For instance, we always attended library story time smack in the middle of Matthew's morning nap. It wasn't fair to him as I tried feverishly to rock him to sleep in his stroller, and it wasn't fair to Michael and Joseph because I couldn't actively participate with them. Matthew would ultimately fall asleep in the car on the way home, disrupting his afternoon nap, which disrupted his bedtime. Not pretty. We now attend a different story time (go shopping, run errands, whatever) after he wakes up. Matthew gets his nap; my boys get my full attention. Problem solved.

As toddlers develop and begin to assert their independence, many refuse to nap. A two-year-old will naturally say no to whatever Mom or Dad has on the agenda, even an opportunity to snuggle in a warm bed. (Oh, what a thought to this sleep-deprived mom.) And just like a teen who doesn't want to leave the party by ten o'clock because he might miss something, a toddler feels the same way about leaving his exciting backyard kingdom in order to catch a few *Z*'s.

What's a Cranky Parent to Do?

Although curling up with your child in bed may seem like a solution, it rarely solves the problem, as your child may then become dependent on you to help him fall asleep, including at night. Other pitfalls to avoid include driving him around in the car until he dozes off or spending an hour on a prenap ritual of reasoning, singing, and snuggling.

Make the prenap routine short but sweet. Encourage him to attach to a transitional object like a teddy bear or blanket, and keep the routine consistent—lunchtime, one story, one song, bed.

But what if you already have an elaborate routine? What if your prenap ritual has you singing the entire soundtrack to *Mary Poppins*? Should you cease and desist in just one day? Even if you're more than ready to give it up, your child may have other ideas. Make it easy on everyone, and gradually eliminate all the hoopla over the course of a week. Calmly but firmly explain to your child that the nap-time routine is changing, and then continue with your new plans by cutting back every day.

The End Is Near

Sooner or later, all kids ultimately give up napping. (Say it isn't so!) You can usually tell it's time when she's consistently alert and happy during her usual nap time or if she's still raring to go well past her bedtime. Once again, though, transitioning from one nap to none will be hard on everyone, as your preschooler may become a Jekyll and Hyde: a beast one day, her lovable old self the next. To be sure, giving up nap time altogether is probably hardest on the parent at home. To help ease the stress of a kid-filled, no-nap day, designate a "quiet time." Encourage your child to play quietly by reading or listening to soft music in her room by herself for a half hour. This downtime, although not nearly as serene as a full nap, will help to reinvigorate everyone, especially Mom.

As with all parenting strategies, consistency is the key.

RESOURCES

Books

Helping Your Child Sleep Through the Night, by Joanne Cuthbertson; New York: Doubleday, 1985.

Nighttime Parenting: How to Get Your Baby and Child to Sleep, by William Sears; New York: Plume, 1995.

The Self-Calmed Baby, by William Sammons and T. Berry Brazelton; New York: St. Martin's Mass Market Paper, 1991.

Solve Your Child's Sleep Problems, by Richard Ferber, M.D.; New York: Fireside, 1986.

Winning Bedtime Battles: Getting Your Children Ages Two to Ten to Sleep, by Charles Schaefer, Ph.D.; New York: Citadel Press, 1992.

Free Brochure

"Sleep Problems in Children"; send an SASE to American Academy of Pediatrics, Department C—Sleep Problems in Children, P.O. Box 927, Elk Grove Village, IL 60009-0927.

Playgroups

One of the strongest links in a stay-at-home parent's support system is the playgroup. These informal get-togethers, where parents and kids meet for an afternoon either at a park or in someone's home, are extremely beneficial for everyone involved: children get a chance to mingle with other same-age kids while parents have an opportunity to socialize and talk shop with other parents.

Why Join a Playgroup?

Gone are the days of the extended family, where in-laws and other family members all lived within a few mile radius of each other and were available to lend a helping hand in child rearing. Today, a close-knit playgroup acts as a surrogate family, offering members a sense of community and belonging.

With a network of adults all at or near the same station in life with young children, members often build secure relationships, developing close, deep friendships. They feel safe about opening up with their parenting concerns, they solve problems together, and they develop self-esteem as they see that they are not alone. Moreover, as you see other parents interacting with their children you may learn a parenting tip or two. A big plus to meeting regularly is that it helps combat the loneliness that many at-home parents feel. Finally, attending a playgroup is a great opportunity to learn more about your child and develop a closer relationship as you interact through play.

Children benefit from joining playgroups, too. Kids learn by playing, and playgroups let them explore at their own pace, free of rigid preschool restrictions. Often a playgroup is a child's first introduction to group socialization, and children, too, have the opportunity to develop close friendships, some that will last a lifetime. It provides a secure environment where they can learn to trust others. Through team play, the group teaches sharing and cooperation. It builds confidence.

Different Playgroup Styles

Before you join a playgroup, check to see if the group's parenting style is in sync with yours. Each group has its own personality and structure, and one may be more comfortable for you than another. For instance, some groups are highly organized, complete with monthly newsletter and dues; others are less structured, where parents and kids simply make a promise to meet on a certain day, at a certain time, at a certain locale. Some playgroups have all the parents participate, while others have one or two parents host the group on a rotating basis. (This can be a bonus, giving you a few hours to yourself.)

Let the Playgroup Begin

Finding a playgroup in your area may take a little investigating. Most don't advertise, so you'll have to ask around to locate

With Sam and Abigail I started a cooperative playgroup with another woman who had some early childhood education background. It was very structured. We had six mothers, and we would meet two days a week in the mornings. We had an itinerary but our focus was mostly socialization. Two adults would be on duty, and we would rotate homes. It was one of the best things I could have done for my kids. They learned to trust adults and separate from me, and they gained the concept of structure. It was easier to drop them off at preschool in later years. They were confident they would have a good, trusting relationship with their teacher.

one. Start with other parents in your neighborhood or ones you come into contact with at library story time or mommy-and-me classes. If finding one is proving to be an impossible task, starting your own is easy.

Locating other interested parents with same-age kids is often as simple as asking. Don't be afraid to approach other parents with your idea; most are looking for creative ways to spend time with their kids and would welcome an opportunity to form a group. Advertise in your church or synagogue bulletin, ask neighbors (or friends of neighbors), approach parents in the park or even at the supermarket (chances are they live nearby, too), ask your spouse's coworkers (maybe they have a full-time parent at home), ask your pediatrician, or post a message on an Internet chat room.

Once you've formed a group of eager participants, it's wise to hold a meeting to discuss playgroup policy and structure. Some questions to discuss follow.

- How often and when will you meet? At someone's home, or at a park? Must all parents accompany their children, or will the group have rotating leaders?

- Will the day be structured with specific times for games, reading, and free play, or will the kids simply gather and let the day dictate the events?

- How will you handle discipline problems like biting, hitting, and kicking?

- Do you want to structure extra activities like group field trips or a monthly night out for the parents?

- Who will provide the snacks and juice?

- How sick is too sick to attend the playgroup?

Playgroup Tips

- **Limit your size to a maximum of five or six kids.** Too many children create chaos and defeats the purpose of the playgroup—a chance for children to play and socialize in an intimate setting.

- **Limit your time.** Two hours of play should be the maximum for toddler groups, but preschoolers can socialize a bit longer. And don't forget to schedule your dates around toddler nap time.

- **Limit your age span.** Children far apart in age often cause behavioral problems. Older children may try to dominate the younger ones, or younger kids may interrupt the structured play of older counterparts.

- **Carefully choose your location.** Can your apartment hold five kids and their parents comfortably? If not, you may want to rent a space or meet at a park.

- **Have adequate home-owner's insurance.** If you meet at someone's home regularly, make sure that person has enough liability insurance.

- **Be prepared for emergencies.** If parents run the group on a rotating basis, have an emergency card on file for each child, telling whom to contact in case of emergency. Also list height and weight of the child (in case of accidental poisoning warranting a call to poison control center).

Playgroup Politics

It's the first meeting of your newly formed playgroup and the kids are all standing around, too timid to interact. What went wrong? Probably nothing. Don't expect young children to greet each other with open arms (at least right away); kids need time to develop relationships. You can help with the transition by following a few basic playgroup steps.

- **Create a "kid-friendly" environment.** Childproof the play area, and place all toys within reach.

- **Have duplicate toys.** One tricycle for three kids won't cut it; try to have more than one of any popular toy.

All together, the group involves about one hundred people, but not everybody gets together at the same time. Usually when we would get together at someone's home, there would be anywhere from four to ten mothers. We'd all give ideas about the playgroup's weekly itinerary. There were officers—president, treasurer—and a monthly newsletter. Occasionally, we'd take field trips to the zoo or beach.

It's as informal as you can get. We have three moms and one dad. The kids range in age from eighteen months to four years. We meet twice a month either at someone's home or at the park, depending on the weather. Occasionally, we'll do a structured activity or game, but mostly we just let them play.

- **Start with a structured group activity.** A good ice-breaker is doing a game, song, or story together.
- **Provide lots of healthy snacks and juice.** After two hours of play, kids need to refuel. Eating together builds a sense of community.
- **Have some quiet-time activity.** Whether group or individual reading, or any other calming project, kids need some downtime, too.
- **Encourage kids to cooperate in cleaning up.** At the end of the playgroup, encourage children to help each other clean up toys.

A Playful Group

Structured or carefree, large or small, whatever group you join, playgroups are a wonderful way to introduce your child to new social situations and a chance for you to develop important friendships with other like-minded parents.

RESOURCES

Books

How to Start Your Own Preschool Playgroup, by Harriet Watts; New York: Universe Books, 1973 (out of print; check your local library).

Playgroups, by Sheila Wolper and Beth Levine; New York: Pocket Books, 1988.

Preschool Playgroups: A Handbook, by Ann Henderson, Lucas Henderson, and Joyce Henderson; New York: Unwin Hyman, 1983.

Preschool

When Is It Time?

Whether or not you should send your little one off to preschool is a very personal decision. Some parents feel that their three-year-old would benefit from the exposure to other same-age children and the daily structure of a school day, while others feel that they can more than adequately fulfill their child's needs both emotionally and socially until it's time to enroll him or her in kindergarten.

If you're facing a similar situation, you should base your decision on a number of factors, including your child's readiness, your needs, and the financial consequences.

Does My Child Really Need Preschool?

"Preschool is as important as it isn't important," says Doris Herman, a preschool teacher for more than twenty-five years and author of *Doris Herman's Preschool Primer for Parents*. Studies have

With Jenna it was obvious that she was ready. Being the first child, she was very precocious. But with Peter we probably sent him before he was ready, based on the fact that we didn't have many kids in the neighborhood. He needed friends, and he needed to learn to separate from me a little bit. It was for company more than anything.

Montessori School

- - - - - - - - - - - - -

The Montessori philosophy believes that when in the right environment, kids are completely motivated on their own to learn. The classroom is set up to stimulate inner development by teaching certain self-help tasks like pouring, slicing, buttoning, tracing, ironing. *Work*, as it's called, is more valued than *play*; therefore, no special art project or planned imaginary play is included in most Montessori schools. Children make their own decisions about what they want to do, when they want to do it. In Montessori, older children are mixed with younger ones. (Younger children learn by watching the older ones, and the older children's self-esteem is bolstered by helping the younger ones.)

shown that children who haven't attended preschool do just as well scholastically once they reach kindergarten as their preschooled peers. Yet, some experts argue, children who didn't attend preschool lag behind socially. Still, is that reason enough to send your child to preschool? Not necessarily, according to Herman. "If a child does not attend preschool, and the parent has made sure that the child is well socialized by joining playgroups, interacting with siblings, playing with the kids in the neighborhood, and he knows all the social rules, then he will have an easy time of going to kindergarten," she says.

With that said, preschool still offers many advantages to young children. "There are so many wonderful preschool programs all across the country," Herman notes. "Once a parent goes and observes a preschool, she will automatically fall in love with it for her child." (Preschool, however, should not be confused with day care, whose main objective is to provide custodial care for children of working parents.)

In preschool, children learn to sit and pay attention to a story or a task, an important precursor to kindergarten. Preschool builds children's self-confidence and self-esteem while teaching them how to share and take turns. Preschool aids in language development, introduces kids to the world around them, and (if the program succeeds) sets the stage for a lifelong love of learning. If there should be a neurological, behavioral, or developmental problem, preschool teachers are educated to pick up on the signs, something that first-time parents often miss, facilitating early intervention.

"Most of the time the parent doesn't realize there's a problem even if the child is wild, tearing things up or not paying attention," Herman says. They often dismiss it as overactivity and may not seek help right away, which can translate to trouble once the child does hit kindergarten.

Beyond that, most older toddlers simply like preschool and all the social stimulation—story time, arts and crafts, an abundance of educational toys, physical activity, and same-age friends—that goes along with it.

When Is It Time?

Take a look at your child: is she bored with her daily routine at home? Is she asking to play with other children or wanting to take more family field trips? Does she enjoy her time away from you, whether it's visiting the baby-sitter or Grandma's house? If so, according to Herman, your three-year-old may be developmentally and socially ready to separate from you and join a preschool.

Choosing the Best School

The place to start searching for the right school for your child is right in your own backyard: ask neighbors and friends of preschool children, members of your church, and former coworkers for recommendations. Look through the education directory in your local parenting publication, or obtain a list of accredited schools in your area from the National Association for the Education of Young Children (NAEYC). Once you've made a list of several that pique your interest, and have narrowed it down through phone interviews during which you ask about cost, availability, and location, it's time to pay the remaining few a visit.

Remember, too, that although most preschool programs may look the same from the outside, they may embrace different philosophies when it comes to children's learning. The most common methodologies that you'll come across are Montessori (based on the work of Maria Montessori), cognitive-based (based on the work of theorist Jean Piaget), religious institutions, and play-based or academic-based programs. How you decide on which program to choose will strongly depend on your personal beliefs about child rearing in general and specifically how you think your child should spend his day.

Montessori impressed us because they were doing the things that we were doing at home, allowing Olivia to be engaged in what we did. She had the freedom to choose what she wanted to do, not have restrictions or a time schedule. I like the idea that a child's interests could be pursued.

Piaget-style preschool just made sense to us. It taught the kids based on how they learn, yet they didn't drill them in academics. Both Robert and Scott flourished in the program.

SAFETY COMES FIRST

What should you first look for when assessing a school? "Safety. Capital letters. Safety," stresses Herman. "I don't care how magnificent the facility or fantastic the teacher, if that school isn't safe no one should send a child there." One way to tell if your particular school has met minimum health and safety standards is whether it's licensed by the state. If it's not, Herman warns, look elsewhere. Another advantage is if the school has been accredited by the NAEYC, a volunteer process that meticulously evaluates the school's program and staff. Although finding a NAEYC-accredited school is a definite plus, it shouldn't be the only guiding factor in choosing a school.

You may want to address other safety concerns during a prearranged meeting with a school administrator.

- What is the student-to-teacher ratio? The recommended ratio is as follows—one adult for every six two-year-olds; one adult for every eight three-year-olds; one adult for every ten four-year-olds.
- What's the school's policy on keeping sick children home?
- How are diaper changes handled? Are staff members required to wear disposable gloves?
- Is the playground equipment safe? Does it meet the U.S. Consumer Product Safety Commission's standards?
- What are the school's security procedures concerning dropping off and picking up children?
- Are teachers and staff certified in infant and child CPR?
- What's the school's policy on disciplining children?

TRUST YOUR INSTINCTS AND TAKE A GOOD LOOK

What else should you consider when evaluating a school? "I think parents do a lot of reading and a lot of studying," Her-

Cognitive-Based School

Based on Swiss psychologist Jean Piaget's theories of child development, cognitive-based preschools focus on the process of learning through developing a child's symbolic functioning. Like traditional nursery schools, cognitive-based schools arrange their classrooms with activity centers, yet the teacher has specific goals for each area. Using everyday nursery-school activities, four cognitive concepts are introduced—*classification* (understanding that certain things go together, such as fruit, shapes, or colors); *seriation* (activities that encourage size or quantity relationships); *temporal relations* (exercises that stress duration of time); and *spatial relations* (concept of space—direction and position).

man observes. "But I think something that's really undervalued is a mother's or father's own gut feeling about a particular school." When you visit a school for the first time, take a good look around. How does the place look and feel? Bright and cheery, or dark and depressing? Ask to sit in on a class or two in progress. Do the children and staff seem happy, alive with laughter? Finally, is this someplace that you would feel comfortable sending your child?

Additional questions to ask or signs to watch for:

- **Teachers.** Don't focus on the student-to-teacher ratio as much as the quality of the teaching staff. What's the teacher turnover rate? The longer the tenure of a teacher, the better. How about their educational backgrounds? Most of the teachers should have bachelor's or associate's degrees in early childhood education. Ask to see a list of teacher bios. How do the teachers interact with their students?

- **The classroom.** Is it large, appealing, and functional? What about artwork? Is it displayed proudly around the room? Are there a variety of interesting toys and designated play and learning areas (block-building area, arts-and-crafts area, dress-up area, a book corner)?

- **The children.** Are they respectful (as much as kids can be) of each other? Or are they yelling and ignoring the pleas of the teacher? Are the children involved mostly in active rather than passive tasks?

Preparing for the First Day

Once you've selected a school that you feel would be a perfect match for your child, it's time to gently prepare her or him for the first day.

"Make the idea of going to school exciting and good without overdoing it," Herman warns. "Children are so per-

Religion-Based School

Religious-based preschools can be enrichment or academic programs depending on the school, but all offer some degree of age-appropriate religious instruction through singing, storytelling, and drawing based on the church's philosophy.

I knew they would get an introduction to the Jewish religion in a fun way through puppetry, cooking, singing. The girls really enjoyed it, and they got a lot out of it, more than I would have given them at this age by myself. By getting religious training now, I think it will stay with them, it will be more important to them. It's more a part of them from the beginning.

Play-Based School

Called *enrichment orientation*, or *traditional nursery school*, a play-based preschool allows the child to explore and learn at will with the teacher somewhat in the background guiding rather than directing. Proponents say young children learn and develop naturally through active play. Therefore, the classroom is designed around *activity* areas—an art corner, a block-building section, a music and book area—and children are free to roam from one to the next. Usually, a teacher is stationed at each with a planned activity. The day is balanced between free time and organized time, when the class as a whole will participate in a group story time or music exercise.

ceptive, they pick up the parent's anxiety so quickly." She advises parents to dig deep and examine their own feelings about sending their children off for the first time. "Even though a parent is happy that her child is going to have a good time, every parent has ambivalent feelings," she says.

If a parent had an unpleasant first school experience, he or she needs to work it out before putting it on his or her child. "I have heard parents say, 'Don't worry, don't worry. Mommy's coming back.' Well, why would you introduce the word *worry*?" she asks. "It's not necessary. The child picks up on it and thinks, 'Is there something I should worry about?'"

For some parents, the difficulty in letting go of the control of their children, allowing someone else to be such a strong force in their children's lives, can come across negatively as well. "You're going to be sharing some of the goodies with the teacher," Herman notes. "The affection that your child has had for you 100 percent might now be shared with the teacher as the child transfers his trust."

TIPS TO PREPARE YOUR CHILD FOR THE FIRST DAY

- **Begin early.** Don't wait until the week before; rather, begin to introduce the idea of preschool several months in advance.

- **Talk about it.** Take notice of other children playing in the school yard and find other subtle opportunities to talk about school every day with your child.

- **Go for a visit.** After getting permission, stop by the school you have chosen for a short visit with your child. Ask if it's possible to return again.

And when it comes time to kiss your child good-bye on that first day and leave the classroom, never quietly disappear in hope that your child won't notice. "Never sneak away," Herman urges. "Always prepare the child beforehand by going through the schedule." Let her know when you'll be returning, and always exit with a big smile on your face. "It's better to deal with your child clinging and crying to you for a moment and let the teacher come and help you depart than to sneak away and leave your child feeling abandoned," she says.

Occasionally, some children don't adjust well to preschool. If your child comes home week after week upset, and puts up a fuss in the morning when it's time to get ready for school, you should try to assess the problem. Perhaps by week two a phone call to the teacher might shed some light on the problem. Herman suggests sitting in the classroom with your child for a longer period of time; arrive a little later than the others, when the teacher has the time to give your child her full attention; or simply remove your child and try again in a few months. "If you have really done your homework and have researched a good school with a loving and nurturing staff, and your child is still not happy week after week, it's entirely possible that your child is not yet developmentally or emotionally ready to separate from you," Herman says. "Take that child home and let her be with you. There's nothing wrong with your child. You didn't do anything wrong. Some children just need more mothering or parenting at home."

Academic-Based School

Structured around short sessions of reading, language, and math, along with unstructured activities like free play and quiet indoor play, most academic-based schools feel that mere enrichment (a.k.a. play-time) alone is not sufficient for a child's total development. Understanding that a child's first school experience is important in developing his or her feeling toward school in the future, teachers are pivotal and offer plenty of encouragement and structured activities.

School's Out

Cognitive-based, academic-based, or play-based programs? Religious or Montesorri? When it comes to choosing a preschool, ultimately the decision will be based on your own level of comfort and child-rearing philosophy. Trust yourself.

W*e chose a play-based preschool because I didn't want them to be pushed. I wanted them to learn basic things like waiting their turn, reciting the alphabet, and memorizing colors and shapes, not how to read. When kids are developmentally ready, they'll learn.*

I *give my children so much developmental, hugging, kissing, nurturing, do-the-craft-project stuff at home, so why would I need to pay a preschool to do that? I want somebody to reinforce the academic aspect of their lives. It's basically prepping them for kindergarten. These days, kids going into kindergarten know so much. You have to keep up with the times and make sure your children are competitive.*

RESOURCES

Books

Doris Herman's Preschool Primer for Parents: A Question-and-Answer Guide to Your Child's First School Experience, by Doris Herman; New York: J. P. Tarcher/Putnam, 1998.

Preschool for Parents: What Every Parent Needs to Know About Preschool, by Diane Trister Dodge; New York: Sourcebook Trade, 1998.

Smart Start: The Parents' Complete Guide to Preschool Education, by Marian Edelman Borden; New York: Facts on File, 1997.

Organizations

National Academy of Early Childhood Programs
    1834 Connecticut Avenue NW
    Washington, DC 20009
    (202) 328-2601

National Association for the Education of Young Children (NAEYC)
    1509 16th Street NW
    Washington, DC 20036-1426
    (800) 424-2460; in DC: (202) 232-8777

Separation Anxiety

I t's a heart-wrenching problem that troubles every parent at some point: when it's time to leave your child with a sitter or at preschool, she or he cries and begs you not to go. You need to leave, but it tears you apart to watch your child in such distress. So why is your outgoing toddler suddenly becoming clingy and needy? She's merely exhibiting the classic signs of *separation anxiety*, a normal stage in cognitive development that nearly every baby or toddler goes through.

Separation anxiety is actually healthy. It means that your child has formed a close, healthy bond to you. The cause, experts say, could be that a baby's instincts tell him that he could not survive without his mother; therefore, he cries when she leaves. Yet others speculate that children become more fearful at a time when they are becoming more independent, developing a greater sense of themselves. A true toddler paradox—the more she pushes you away, the more she wants you.

When Mom or Dad Feels Separation Anxiety

The first time parents leave their children is always difficult. Not only are they trusting someone else (often a new sitter) to care for their most valued possession, but they're relinquishing their primary role to someone else. Separating may also bring up unsettling childhood memories; perhaps your mom or dad would sneak out and leave you with a baby-sitter or leave you at preschool without saying good-bye. Helping your own child deal effectively with separating is a good way to help you heal, too.

During the first few months of life, infants haven't yet developed separation anxiety. Actually, separation is much harder on parents than it is on the infant herself. As long as your two-month-old is held and cared for, she's usually content. Yet by six months, most children can discriminate among faces and usually prefer those that they know. By nine months babies become wary of strangers and most show some degree of discomfort when a stranger approaches. Separation anxiety peaks between twelve to eighteen months as children become independent, curious toddlers. It lasts for several weeks then usually disappears as quickly as it appeared. For some, separation anxiety will reemerge around their second birthday, a time when they understand the implication of Mom or Dad leaving. Rest assured, though, that this second bout will wane as your child grasps the concept that a parent who leaves will return.

Many preschoolers, too, feel the pangs of separation anxiety. Being left all day in a new environment away from Mom or Dad can be frightening to many children. If you're enrolling your child in a preschool, be sure to prepare her well in advance by visiting the school together on several different occasions before her first day. Let her get used to her surroundings and the other children, and introduce her to her teacher. When you do leave her for the first time, reassure her that you'll return soon.

Tips on Saying Good-bye

- **Be sensitive to how your child reacts to new situations.** Some kids are slow to separate from their parents, requiring a little more attention and diplomacy when saying good-bye.

- **Don't show how upset you are when you leave.** Although you may be feeling pangs of separation anxiety, too, be upbeat about going out. Babies, especially nine to twelve months old, look to their parents to gauge their own emotions.

- **When you do leave, never just disappear.** Leaving without saying good-bye frightens children and violates the trust they have for you. Offer plenty of reassurance that you will return and offer a time frame. But instead of giving a time, a concept that he can't grasp at age two, tell him you'll return home "when it's time for dinner" or "at bath time."

- **Don't comment negatively on his clinginess.** Remember, separation anxiety is a normal phase of development. Show patience and give your child lots of reassurance when you're together.

- **Introduce your child to lots of different social situations.** A variety of social experiences will help your child feel more comfortable with others, but if your child is having trouble separating, keep your play dates to a single, familiar child.

- **Have your baby-sitter arrive early.** Never rush out the door as soon as the sitter arrives. Instead, have her come over while you're preparing to leave, allowing the kids to transition to a new situation.

RESOURCES

Books

Bear Hugs for Saying Goodbye: Positive Activities That Ease Separation Anxiety, by Patty Claycomb; Everett, WA: Warren Publishing House, 1994.

Mommy, Don't Go, by Elizabeth Crary; Seattle: Parenting Press, 1996.

Separation: Strategies for Helping Two to Four Year Olds, Kathe Jervis, editor; Washington, DC: National Association for the Education of Young Children, 1989.

Shopping

Since the day they were born, I've taken my kids shopping. Although two shopping carts, each carrying one child, and an infant secured in a baby carrier have drawn lots of attention, I've gotten used to it. My logic is simple: kids need to get out of the house and see the world around them and learn how to function in society. In addition, it teaches them manners as they watch me politely interact with others. Besides, there's no way that I'm going to waste precious baby-sitting time by going grocery shopping or running errands.

Yet, as my twins have gotten older and have demanded more independence by walking instead of riding in the stroller, shopping carts, and so forth, shopping isn't always a pleasant experience. These days our excursions are often a mixed bag of "Wow! Wasn't that fun?" with many instances of "If you touch that again, we'll have to leave!" thrown in.

Still, I keep taking my three sons out nearly every day. I've even gone so far as to take all three to a department store to shop for postpregnancy clothes. Now *that* was interesting, although I don't think the other women in the adjoining dressing rooms thought so.

It's All How You Look at It

To get my kids excited about running errands, I explain that we're about to go on an adventure, and then I promise an enormous amount of ice cream at the end of our trip.

Every few weeks I take them to downtown Pasadena, park the car, and strap the baby in the stroller. We walk to

I have to be conscious of the time of day. I realize with her that after 4 P.M., I have no business being in a store.

To Shop or Not to Shop?

Stores Kids Love . . .	Stores Kids Hate . . .
Dry cleaner "Lots of steam, and it's fun to watch the clothes go round."	Video store "I can't touch anything."
Post office "They give me special-delivery stickers that I put on my shirt."	Fabric store "It's boring."
Grocery store/ delicatessen "I always get a piece of cheese or turkey."	Hardware store "It's big. It's loud. Nothing to hold."
Pet store "I like to look at the rats and mice."	Beauty parlor/barbershop "It smells funny. I don't want to get my hair cut."

various businesses—the bank, the post office, Target—exploring our surroundings along the way. We count buses and trucks as we stroll from place to place, we stop for the much-anticipated ice cream, and we ride the big glass elevator in Target at least four times. I always end our trip with a stop at the local bookstore. The children's section there offers a variety of toys, the main attraction a wooden train set. As my kids play, I sit and peruse books that I had either waiting for me at will call (I would phone ahead that morning and have the clerk pull certain titles aside for me) or picked up off the shelf as we entered the store. After a half hour, we take off for home. I got my errands done and a bit of exercise. They got some ice cream, a few exciting rides in a glass elevator, their fill of the big wooden train set, and of course, some quality time with Mom.

I think it's fun and stimulating for the little ones to go grocery shopping.

Handling a Midstore Meltdown

Something just set your three-year-old off. Maybe he didn't get a long enough nap, or maybe the salesclerk looked at him funny. Whatever it was, he's now on a roll. What should you do?

- **Ignore it.** It's the hardest thing to do, but according to parenting experts, ignoring it is the best strategy for tantrumming.

- **Leave.** Put down your basket, pick up your child, and leave. Initially, it will make him scream louder, but it also teaches him that you mean business—when he misbehaves, we leave.

- **Find the humor.** Sometimes *it is funny* when your child is flailing his body around the floor. Start to laugh, give him a tickle, and maybe he'll laugh, too.

- **Distract him.** "Wow! Look at that! Balloons!" Sometimes that's all it takes to put an end to the hysterics.

SHOPPING TIPS

With three small boys in tow, I've learned a thing or two about shopping successfully.

- **Go early in the morning.** A grocery store or department store is relatively quiet at 10 A.M., and no one is apt to mind a brood of kids tearing up the place. Not true at 5 P.M., when all of working America (including you) is tired, hungry, and in a rush to get home.

- **Call ahead.** If you're going out to pick up something specific, for example, the latest *Three Tenors* CD, be sure to call ahead to see if it's available. Before I go to the video store, I call ahead and ask them to pull my selected video off the shelf and hold it at the counter. I'm in and out of the store so fast, my kids hardly have time to pull more than a dozen videos off the shelves!

- **Pay attention to them when you shop.** Get them involved. Ask them questions about what they see. Ask them to help you look for something. Ask them for their opinions: "Should we buy the red towels or the blue ones?"

- **Give them some latitude.** As long as they're not breaking anything or screaming, relax the etiquette rules and let them explore and have some fun.

I try not to take them shopping. It just prolongs the task. I don't mind getting a sitter to watch them while I shop. Shopping is like an escape for me. It's therapy for me to do my errands by myself. I'm sorry to say that it's my only time alone and that I'd rather be doing something else. But if I get it done quickly, then I do have time to do something else.

A Good Goodie Bag

Lengthy visits to any store can be agonizing for young kids. Be prepared with an emergency goodie bag, and dole out the treats one at a time. Change the contents of the bag on a regular basis. Recently, while driving through the neighborhood house hunting, I relied heavily on the contents of that magical bag to keep my boys occupied. I couldn't have done it successfully without it. Consider the following goodies.

- **Kitchen gadgets.** Pastry brushes, tea strainers, timers, measuring spoons. They're all interesting to young kids.
- **Small boxes with lids.** Tuck a treat inside.
- **Pipe cleaners.** Encourage them to make interesting shapes.
- **TV remote.** Preferably an old, outdated one.
- **Small board books.** Have them count the trees, animals, etc.
- **Magnet.** Fun, and a science lesson to boot.
- **Calculator.** A large, inexpensive model.
- **Pad and pencil.** A reliable standby.

May I Help You?

Many parents opt to leave their kids at home when they shop. Yes, it's easier and quicker, but your kids learn by watching you. Teach them to be responsible consumers and take them along.

Simplify

Getting Back to Basics

We have exactly three closets in my turn-of-the-century bungalow, hardly enough space for a family of five. Although we often can't pass from one room to the next without tripping over small piles of oddments waiting for a home, somehow we manage. Let's face it, back when my house was built, families didn't have much stuff—a couple pairs of work pants and a suit for Sunday, and that's it. They didn't have videos, CDs, computer equipment, ten-speed bikes, shoes for every mood, and all the other accoutrements that we take for granted. They simply had no need for walk-in closets.

Yet here we are, a mere ninety years later, a nation renting storage lockers by the millions just to find a place for stuff we'll probably never use again. Is all this clutter making our lives any easier? Probably not. Admittedly, some things do make life more enjoyable and do free up time—like E-mail and microwaves—but the majority of modern conveniences accomplish just the opposite by complicating our lives—call waiting and cable, to name two. Whether you're a stay-at-home parent or a full-time working parent, we could all use a lesson in simplifying our lives.

Is Less More?

"There are tremendous benefits to cutting back," explains Elaine St. James. The guru of simplification, she's written five books on the subject, including *Simplify Your Life with Kids*. "There are people out there reaping the benefits of cutting back and they're realizing that we don't have to do everything, that we don't have to have everything, and we don't have to go every place."

Simplifying—reducing or trimming back on areas of your life that are complicated—frees up a tremendous amount of time. "You can slow down the pace of your life so that you can enjoy it," St. James says. "You now have the time to spend with your kids and your friends." There's a hidden bonus, too. When you eliminate the mental and physical clutter that once enslaved you, you now have the freedom and wherewithal to evaluate other aspects of your life that caused you unhappiness. "If we free up one area of our lives, then it's possible to see there are other options, other choices," she notes. "We don't have to commit our entire lives to a career that we don't like, for example."

Who can benefit the most from simplifying? St. James says without a doubt it's couples with kids. They're the ones who lead the most complicated lives and need to step back and evaluate the madness. "If you've got kids, you almost have to simplify if you want to stay in touch with why you had them in the first place," she laughs. "If you're so busy that you can't enjoy them, what's the point?" The problem, she says, is our do-or-die culture and parents' insatiable need to give their children the best of everything. Yet how can kids get in touch with their creativity if they're off to various activities every day? "We don't have time to be together, or on our own. When we're kept that busy, we can't be in touch with who we really are," St. James says.

Sign Me Up

Contrary to what many believe, simplifying doesn't mean your life will suddenly become boring or that you have to live frugally. "Many people think by simplifying they're going to miss out on something, or that the next-door-neighbor's kids are going to be better, smarter, or more exposed to things out there," St. James says. In fact, the opposite is true. "What people are finding out is that they're missing out on life by being so involved in too many activities." When they simplify, they open up many more possibilities for adventure.

The degree to which you should simplify also varies from family to family. *Simplification* means different things to different people. Your first step is to take a look at what's complicating your life. Are you involved in too many after-school activities and weekend birthday parties? Start setting boundaries by limiting the number you and the kids will attend each year. Is it all the clutter in your home? The endless stream of electronic toys, latest fall fashions, and state-of-the-art gym shoes that take over the closet? Do a major spring cleaning and follow the two-year rule—if it hasn't been used in the past two years, donate it to charity and vow not to buy anything to replace it.

For me, obstacles escalate at dinnertime, that hour before my husband walks through the door when my eight-month-old is fussing, my two preschoolers are bouncing off the walls refusing to eat their broccoli, and I'm trying to do the dishes, start dinner, and return a few phone calls. St. James's advice?

Take a little more time to make mealtime fun. I get my kids excited by letting them help. So now I have them set the table while I get their dinner. They love to participate. It keeps them focused and out of my hair. And, oh yeah: I now return phone calls in the morning when everyone is more refreshed (and quiet). As for my cranky baby . . .

For all those popular muddled areas, St. James suggests the following to help streamline your routine.

- **Mornings.** Organize as much as you can the night before—set the breakfast table, iron spouse's work clothes, make lunches and put them in the refrigerator.

- **Bedtime/nap time.** Set a reasonable time and be consistent. Eventually the kids will naturally become accustomed to it, and they will willingly accept the sandman.

- **Housekeeping.** Start at an early age to teach your children how to put their own toys away, and make cleanup easy and accessible by storing toys and books on low shelves. Show them how to hang their clothes and put them in the hamper.

- **Holidays.** Cut back on the number of gifts you give the kids. One family St. James knows gives only two gifts—one material, the other time. The child can request a day at the zoo with Mom or Dad, for instance.

- **Birthday parties.** Keep it small and be selective. Invite one guest per year of age—three years old, three guests. Conversely, allow the child to choose a certain number of parties that he can attend during the year.

Are You a Superparent?

Are you one of those parents who does it all, much to the amazement of family and friends? You host grand Halloween parties for the neighborhood, your kids are always dressed like walking ads for Baby Gap, you can and pickle homegrown vegetables. Yet you feel tired, stressed, and overworked. It's time to give up the Superparent role. Here's how.

- **Prioritize.** Decide what's important in your life, and forget the rest.

- **Learn to say no.** Never wanting to disappoint, the Superparent always says yes even if she wants to say no. Memorize catchall phrases like "I'm sorry; now's just not a good time" or "I'm afraid we're busy." Be selective when you volunteer your time. You have the freedom to use your time in ways that you see fit.

- **Ask for help.** From your spouse, your neighbors, your family.

- **Insist on time alone.** Whether for an hour to read a book or a monthly dinner and a movie with a friend, you need time away from family to refuel.

Organizing Orgy

Do you need to organize to simplify? Although organizing a chaotic household does have its merits, St. James warns that the two are different and should not be confused. "People hear *simplify* and they think they have to get organized," she says. "But if you're simplifying, like drawing names at Christmas time and buying only one gift instead of twenty-five, you're doing less, which means you have less to organize."

But for those of us who haven't opened the hall closet in five years for fear that we might get caught under an avalanche of sporting gear, get cracking! Tackle a drawer, closet, or room each week. Get rid of broken apparatus, items that haven't been used since the Ice Age, or clothes that the family has outgrown. Make three piles—charity, storage, garbage—then organize what's remaining.

The girls just produce so much stuff. They keep bringing projects home from school. I just make a pile and eventually weed through it. I save the cute stuff in a box and put the rest in the recycling bin, hoping they won't notice, but every once in a while Rachel sees it and gets upset.

CLOSETS

- Simplify your wardrobe by building it around one or two neutral colors.

- Hang like items together, and put off-season clothes toward the back or store under the bed in boxes.

- Install extra shelving, Peg-Board (for hats, belts, and scarves), and hooks.

- Install wire baskets on the back of the door for frequently used items.

> People say that the closet is the number-one clutter catcher.

KIDS' BEDROOMS

- Rethink dressers because drawers can be frustrating for small children. Instead, opt for clear plastic crates with cutout pictures of pants, socks, and T-shirts pasted to the front to help them easily locate what they need.

- Forget the toy box, a cavernous mess, and categorize toys in small laundry baskets or crates.

- Install a large shelving unit to organize toys (bolt it to the wall to prevent it from tumbling over) and small shelving (like spice racks) to organize tiny or breakable toys.

- Use resealable plastic bags for things like art supplies, puzzle pieces, marbles.

- Tall plastic hampers are great for storing an array of sporting equipment like tennis rackets, hockey sticks, and baseball bats.

KITCHEN

- Weed out old cookbooks and keep your favorites accessible.

- Use plastic utensil trays in all drawers to organize kitchen tools, silverware, and small household gadgets.

- Keep countertops clutter free by storing small appliances that you don't use every day.
- Use tiered shelves in cabinets to help quickly locate items.

BATHROOMS

- Organize the medicine cabinet by grouping like items together.
- Allocate each bathroom its own supply of cleaning supplies and rubber gloves for quick cleanups (but be sure to keep hazardous cleaners out of children's reach).
- Rolling towels saves space and makes them easier to grab in a hurry.
- Place a basket next to the toilet to store extra bathroom tissue and magazines.

Garage-Sale Savvy

Periodically clearing out the clutter for a garage sale not only means less junk to organize, but when done correctly, a single sale can rack up hundreds of dollars. Here are a few tips to make yours a success.

- **Advertise.** Put an ad in your local paper highlighting items of interest—baby furniture, bicycles, televisions. On the day of the sale, be sure to post well-marked signs within a mile radius of your home using simple directions like arrows.
- **Have enough merchandise.** You need at least 100 items to make a sale interesting. If you don't have enough goodies, team up with neighbors or friends for a group sale.
- **Clean items.** Take the time to clean each item for sale. No one will want to buy a high chair with dried-on pasta.
- **Display items.** Use folding tables to get the stuff off the ground. Hang clothes from a line or fence. Run an extension cord to the site so that people may test electrical appliances.

- **Set realistic prices and tag each piece.** Remember, your goal is to sell the stuff. If you turn down an offer, you are, in essence, buying it back. Shoppers like a bargain. For general merchandise, tag it 20 percent of its original price. Less for clothes—no more than one dollar.

- **Be prepared.** Get out there early—shoppers often show up before the advertised time. Have plenty of change on hand—lots of singles, fives, tens, and coins. Enlist the help of a family member or friend—you'll need the extra help. Be courteous—willingly answer any questions.

OTHER SIMPLIFYING TIPS AND TECHNIQUES

- **Cancel the paper.** Do you really read it? Or have it delivered only on Sundays.

- **Cancel cable.** You hardly ever find anything worth watching. Besides, you'll save a bundle.

- **Get rid of the gadgets.** Exercise bike, bread machine, satellite dish, video games, call waiting. (Don't worry; I'll call back.)

- **Don't always answer the phone.** Let the machine get it.

- **Pay bills automatically from checking account.** End the monthly bill-paying madness by having them paid directly from your checking account.

- **Cancel memberships.** Do you really go to the gym? Do you really read the monthly newsletter from the Society of Seashell Collectors?

- **Remove your name from junk-mail lists.** Send an SASE to Mail Preference Service, Direct Mail Marketing Association, P.O. Box 9008, Farmingdale, NY 11735-9008.

- **Hold weekly family meetings.** Discuss upcoming appointments and events.

- **Wait.** Before making any major purchase, wait at least three months and then reassess whether you truly need it.

It's So Simple

Simplifying sounds enticing, but you're afraid to give it a try? Remember, there's no need to go cold turkey and give up *every* gadget or social engagement. Start small; get your feet wet by eliminating one item of madness from your life. The rewards are rich in so many ways.

RESOURCES

Books

The Circle of Simplicity, by Cecile Andrews; New York: HarperCollins, 1997.

Confessions of an Organized Homemaker: The Secrets of Uncluttering Your Home and Taking Control of Your Life, by Deniece Schofield; Cincinnati: Betterway Publishing, 1994.

500 Terrific Ideas for Organizing Everything, by Sheree Bykofsky; New York: Budget Book Service, 1997.

The Garage Sale Handbook, by Peggy Hitchcock; Greenport, NY: Pilot Books, 1998. (To order, call (800) 797-4568.)

Lighten Up! Free Yourself from Clutter, by Michelle Passoff; New York: HarperCollins, 1998.

More Time for Sex: The Organizing Guide for Busy Couples, by Harriet Schechter and Vicki T. Gibbs; New York: Dutton, 1995.

Organize Your Home! Simple Routines for Managing Your Household, by Ronni Eisenberg and Kate Kelly; New York: Hyperion, 1999.

Organizing from the Inside Out, by Julie Morgenstern; New York: Henry Holt, 1998.

Simplify Your Life with Kids, by Elaine St. James; Kansas City: Andrews and McMeel Publishing, 1997.

Taming the Paper Tiger at Home, by Barbara Hemphill; Washington, DC: Kiplinger Books, 1998.

Voluntary Simplicity: Toward a Way of Life That Is Outwardly Simple, Inwardly Rich, by Duane Elgin; New York: Quill, 1993.

Internet Sites

www.tgon.com—The Get Organized! News
   Electronic monthly newsletter devoted to time management and clutter control.

www.web-oats.com/clutterbug—Has the Clutter Bug Got You? A professional organizer offers tips for every room in the house.

www.123sortit.com—1,2,3, Sort It
   A pair of professional organizers helps clutter bugs simplify business and home. Find useful organizing books and gadgets.

Stress

Learning the Art of Relaxation

H ere's a recent scenario: my morning is a disaster; nothing goes as it usually does. Matthew just isn't ready for his morning nap, so he lies in his crib and cries. When I finally pull him out to nurse him yet another time, my twins, Joseph and Michael, get into it outside. From my bedroom I hear Michael screaming my name, pleading for help as Joseph incessantly rams his trike into his brother's. I hastily put Matthew back in his crib and hurry outside to negotiate a peace settlement. Matthew cries louder. Giving up, I put him and his brothers in the car and head to the supermarket. Chasing each other down the grocery aisles, the two older boys are out of control, knocking into one another and falling on the floor laughing. I'm mortified as I pull them off the ground. Matthew still won't nap in the store. I somehow manage to get the shopping done between threats and

There are days when I look in the mirror and I don't know whether to cry or be so proud of myself.

215

For me, it's stressful getting the kids ready for school. There's so much screaming that goes on in the morning. You're running around the house yelling, "Get dressed! Hurry up! Quit messing around!" Then you get everyone in the car and drive them to school, and you turn around and say, "Bye, honey. Have a nice day at school." Suddenly, you're trying to be nice, but yet all you've done for the past two hours is scream.

My husband travels a lot for his job. When he's gone for days at a time, those are my worst days. In the beginning I think all is fine, but toward the end—when you're feeding them three meals a day for four days by yourself, and putting them to bed every night by yourself—it's exhausting.

clenched teeth. On the way home, Matthew falls asleep. Even a ten-minute snooze in the car will ruin his afternoon nap.

Back home, while I'm putting the groceries away, Michael and Joseph start another skirmish—this time over a building block! Their anger turns toward me, and I'm forced to give each one a time-out. I make the mistake of putting Michael on the front porch to serve his time, but he screams so wildly that I'm forced to pull him back inside for fear that the neighbors will call the cops. Time-out's over, but peace doesn't prevail. Matthew falls face first out of his bouncy seat and whacks his head on the hardwood floor. My fault, really; I should have retired the infant-only contraption a month ago. Oh, did I mention that I burned my hand on the stove *three times* that day? And although I had given up wine for Lent, I poured myself a large glass that evening. God will understand; He's got kids.

Before we continue, I'd like to stress that that day was *atypical*. Normally, Matthew sleeps soundly in the morning, the boys play reasonably well together, shopping can be pleasant, and Matthew *never* falls face first onto the floor, but no matter how well behaved my kids, I'm bound to feel frazzled by the end of the day.

We can all relate to stress. Everyday life with kids, no matter how peaceful, can sometimes get to us. And although periodic stress isn't life threatening, constant stress can lead to medical problems like nausea, dizziness, and chronic headaches. We all need to learn how to better manage the stress in our lives.

STRESS-REDUCING TIPS

■ **Stop stress before it starts.** Easier said than done, but it is possible. Take notice of when you feel stress—for instance, right before dinner—then, try to head it off by starting dinner sooner or feeding the baby first so she won't fuss when you're trying to cook. If morning is the time when you feel your blood pressure starting to rise, prepare as much as you can the night before by setting the breakfast table, laying out clothes, even showering.

■ **Concentrate on breathing.** Long, deep breaths throughout the day give your body more oxygen and, therefore, more energy. You'll be able to better concentrate and solve problems.

■ **Call a friend.** Only one who's composed and cool. Checking in with someone in the adult world helps bring your stress level way down.

■ **Pay attention to your body.** Your energy rises and falls throughout the day. For instance, most of us have higher levels of concentration during the mornings. Schedule stressful or important tasks—like calling the bank to dispute a service charge—during the time when you're most alert and energized.

■ **Eliminate unneeded chaos.** Turn off the TV (the 6 P.M. news only heightens anxiety), don't answer the phone when you're trying to cook dinner or deal with the kids, learn to say no to unwanted projects or social commitments.

■ **Set the mood.** Studies indicate that playing calming music—whether Gregorian chants, Mozart, or Native American flute music—can lower blood pressure and reduce heart rates.

■ **Project calm.** Stress is contagious, and so is laughter. When you concentrate on bringing peace into your life, your kids will learn from your example and learn to take things in stride.

Ten Relaxing Ways to Spend Ten Minutes

• **Nurse.** When you breast-feed, your body produces the hormone prolactin, a natural sedative.

I'm a screamer. I just let the air out, "Ahhhhhhhhhhhh!" When I'm about to blow, I let out a good one. Somehow it helps. It makes me feel like it's OK to get a breath, then I can continue. But lately the kids told me that my screaming freaks them out. Even my husband has said, "Sounds like it's freaking them out." So now I have to find another way. In terms of maintaining everyday stress, I use these words to the kids: "I am feeling overwhelmed." They know by the time I say that they'd better just go find their spots. They know they have to change what's going on or they're going to hear the scream.

I'm not saying we're not crazy around here sometimes, but I have the luxury—if that's what you want to call it—of making my own schedule. It doesn't have to revolve around anyone else's. I think that reduces the stress. If the kids are sick, I'm here to stay home with them. I don't have to worry about what I'm going to do. I don't have to think which grandparent is available to take care of them.

I always feel better when I'm exercising.

- **Sit in the sun.** Turn your face toward the sky and stretch out.

- **Cut and arrange flowers.** Every home owner has some kind of colorful plant life growing on her property. Take a moment and wander your yard and find a few sprigs of spring. Or, pick up a few colorful stems at your local market. Back inside, slowly arrange them in that vase you got as a wedding gift but never seem to use.

- **Have a minimassage.** Okay, so maybe you gave Sven, the twenty-one-year-old Swedish masseur, the week off, but you can still give yourself a massage. Start with a few neck rolls, then relax your shoulders. Next, try some waist twists, and end your session with a large, yawnlike stretch, all the while concentrating on taking slow, deep breaths.

- **Weed.** Head out to the garden and dig your hands in the damp, cool earth. A slow, hypnotic task, weeding is rewarding, especially as you look back at your progress. If you live in an apartment, head to your patio or terrace and pick through your terra-cotta pots.

- **Make yourself some tea.** Forget the coffee, and opt for herbal tea. Chamomile's relaxing aroma and therapeutic properties have been used for centuries as a natural sedative.

- **Take a steamy, hot shower.** The shower is the one and only place for true privacy. Turn on the faucet and get the bathroom warm and steamy before you venture in. Light a candle if you can.

- **Exercise.** Even moderate exercise releases endorphins, a natural relaxant. Try a miniworkout: ten sit-ups, ten push-ups, and ten bicep curls.

- **Take a short nap.** Short, sporadic naps refresh and recharge the soul, and sleep experts say that they are more efficient than long naps.

- **Pray.** Like meditation, praying clears your mind.

Stopping the Stress

Life is more complicated today. By staying home with the kids you may have reduced much of the day-to-day tension in your life, but let's face it, being home with preschoolers on a daily basis brings a different kind of stress. When the kids have gotten on your last nerve, just remember that this, too, shall pass. Take a deep breath and give them a hug.

RESOURCES

Books

Five-Minute Massage: Quick and Simple Exercises to Reduce Tension and Stress, by Robert The; New York: Sterling Publishing, 1995.

Instant Calm: Over 100 Easy-to-Use Techniques for Relaxing Mind and Body, by Paul Wilson; New York: Plume, 1999.

60 Second Stress Management: The Quickest Way to Relax and Ease Anxiety, by Andrew Goliszek; Far Hills, NJ: New Horizon Press, 1992.

60 Ways to Relieve Stress in 60 Seconds, by Manning Rubin; New York: Workman Publishing Company, 1993.

Any time between 4:30 P.M. and 6:30 P.M., when her father comes home, that's really trying. Francesca doesn't want me to be cooking, she doesn't want me to be on the phone.

At times I'd go into the bathroom, lock the door, turn on the fan, and read for fifteen minutes. I only did it when they were old enough not to kill themselves out alone in the living room. They'd bang on the door, pry their fingers under the door. I don't know if it was relaxation, but sometimes you just need to leave the room.

Support System

Building a Network of Allies

H aving a group of understanding allies—friends, family, and former colleagues—helps enormously in adjusting to life without the time clock. Whether it's a friend offering a sympathetic ear after a tough day, someone coming over and helping out with the kids, or just having other parents with whom you share the same child-rearing philosophy, every at-home parent needs to build and nurture some kind of support system.

I get a ton of support from Matt. He helps around the house; he's much more neat and organized than me. He's the one who always cleans the 800 piles of junk sitting on the bed. If he's home, he'll clean up after dinner and then bathe the girls.

Support Is Where You Find It

Once a month I leave my husband and kids and head out the door for dinner and conversation with three other women with whom I used to work and now consider to be some of my closest girlfriends. These women and I couldn't be more different—we're all at different stages in our lives and hold such different life philosophies—but that's what makes our evenings and conversations so interesting and enjoyable. We rarely talk about kids. (I get my fill of parenting advice by meeting regularly with other moms.)

Yet my support system doesn't end there. My mother-in-law stops by every week to spend the day with my kids and me. Not only is she building a strong relationship with her grandsons, but she helps me tremendously by doing my dishes and other household chores. My husband is extremely supportive, too. Because he works only minutes from our home, he comes home for lunch every day and helps out by putting the boys in for their nap. Often he stays home long enough for me to disappear for a midday breather.

All these relationships are special and important in my life and the lives of my kids. They help to keep me focused and centered on why I stayed home in the first place—to participate and be a positive influence in the lives of my kids.

Let's Get Organized

Although you can never have too many friends or family willing to offer a hand, joining a group is an important link in the support chain. Finding an organization where the members speak with the same philosophical voice and can laugh with you as you sometimes stumble through parenting is extremely therapeutic.

"With so many mothers working, it can feel like you're the only one out there," says Katherine Rogers, president of Formerly Employed Mothers at the Leading Edge (FEMALE), a national organization geared toward sequencing women. "When you look up and down your street and you see other families dropping their kids off at day care in the morning and you're not doing that, you can feel isolated when in fact

When I first had Francesca, whenever I'd see someone walking by my house with a stroller, I'd go out and introduce myself. I still do it. I now know every mom within two blocks of me. We meet all the time at a park close to my house. I'll just pick up the phone and say, "Going to the park. Want to come?" or "Going to the drugstore. Want to come?" And people now stop by all the time. They just drop in, and I love it. That breaks up the day. We all have an informal agreement to go visiting, especially if we hear another mom is having a hard day. We'll just go and visit her.

I tend to surround myself with people who are so sensitive to mothering and kids that I rarely hear anything negative about full-time parenting.

FEMALE

With more than 166 chapters serving 6,300 members, Formerly Employed Mothers at the Leading Edge (FEMALE) serves an important niche by helping full-time career women successfully transition to full-time mothers. The group was formed in recognition of the fact that these women have a need to socialize and develop friendships with other like-minded women. FEMALE tries to nurture the whole person, not just the mother, by focusing bimonthly meetings on general interest topics or women's issues rather than straight parenting themes. The organization also sponsors family functions, playgroups, and moms' night out.

there are others like you in the community. It's just a matter of finding them."

During the '50s and '60s when full-time moms were the norm, support could be found by simply opening up the back door and calling to your neighbor across the fence. Today we don't have that luxury, and women need to reach out to organizations to find the female comradeship that they crave. "You have to make a virtual neighborhood where you aren't necessarily geographically close, but philosophically you're on the same page," notes Rogers, a former television journalist and producer in the Seattle area before she became a full-time mom.

"You network at your job. You've got to do the same at home in order to stay current and to keep abreast in doing the right thing for your child," says Margie Johnson, public relations assistant for Mothers at Home, the nation's oldest and largest support group for women who choose to stay home to raise their children. "You need resources in your job, and you need resources to raise a good child."

While homemaking is the largest occupational group in the United States, Johnson says women who stay home full-time are clearly underrepresented. "There are many women's organizations but they don't speak for women who want to stay home and raise their children. Stay-at-home mothers are a wonderful group, and much larger than the media would portray us being, but they need a voice."

When Nothing Seems to Fit

Shortly after my twins were born, I joined a mothers-of-twins support group. Although I consider myself an outgoing person and someone who enjoys the company of women, I never felt comfortable in the group. The women had all been together for years, and most didn't seem receptive to new members. Yet, I kept going to the monthly meetings and functions, hoping that I would click with some of the mothers. It never happened. Finally, after seven months I gave up and withdrew my membership.

At first I felt upset and confused by the whole experience. Why hadn't I been able to fit in? Was it me? Eventually, I realized that not every group is for every person. Rogers agrees. "I tried out a couple of groups," she says. "I went to one mother's group and felt completely out of place. But when I walked into the first FEMALE meeting, it was really clear to me that was where I belonged. I fit in."

Finding the right group will take time and persistence, but the payback in finding the right one will be worth the effort. There are hundreds of organizations out there, each with a unique message to offer women, and each with its own distinct energy. It's up to you to find the perfect match.

TIPS ON FINDING THE RIGHT GROUP

Hundreds of groups are out there just waiting for your participation. But how do you find the one that's right for you?

- You don't have to limit yourself to mothers' groups. Decide what's important to you and try to match a group to your interests.

- Before deciding if you want to become a dues-paying member, take advantage of a prospective group's trial period during which you can participate for several meetings before making a financial commitment.

- If you know another full-time mom, join a group together. It's sometimes easier to become assimilated into a group where you already know someone else.

- Choose a supportive group where you feel comfortable with the other members and where you feel a great deal of commonality with the members.

Mothers at Home

Committed to women who have decided to stay home to nurture their children, Mothers at Home communicates with full-time moms through *Welcome Home*, a nonprofit monthly journal filled with personal essays, informative articles, problem-solving tips, and poems. With more than 28,000 subscribers from more than thirty countries, the organization also lobbies to change public policy toward at-home mothering and acts as a media watchdog.

- The Internet is a great place to start looking for a group. Try keywords: women's support groups; full-time parents support groups.

- Pick up your local parenting magazine and look in the back for listings of new groups forming or monthly meeting announcements.

- Call your local Chamber of Commerce for a list of organizations in your town.

Organizations Made to Order

It's very important to me that I'm around other people with a parenting philosophy similar to mine. It supports what I'm doing and makes me feel like I'm not alone, because my ideas are not always mainstream.

If you can't find a group in your area, or you simply don't like the ones that you have found, start your own. There are no rules; let your imagination guide you. Support can be found in just about anything that you find important or interesting.

If you're a big tennis fan, for instance, why not start a group for tennis lovers whose children are around the same age as yours? Advertise at the local tennis club or public courts, even in your church bulletin. Decide how often the group will meet and where, either at the city courts or a private tennis club. Collect dues to pay for court fees and arrange to have one or more baby-sitters on hand to take care of the kids while the adults play. When the game is over, everyone (kids included) can sit down to a potluck lunch. This same idea could work for golf, hiking, or any number of other sports. Just think about what interests you and build a group around that.

Enrolling in baby classes is another way to meet and gain support from other parents. Investigate Mommy-and-me-type classes offered by Gymboree, Music Together, and Kinder-musick International; classes offered at your local YMCA or Red Cross; or classes at your local recreation department.

Support Comes in All Forms

An organization where all members speak the same philosophical language is important for the stay-at-home mom, but women can find support from a variety of peer groups and even family members. With all your support systems in place, offering many different levels of friendship, staying home full time will become an enriching experience for you and your kids.

When I take Rachel to gymnastics on Thursday, the other moms and I sit around and talk. We're not watching what our kids are doing in gymnastics, but that's our time to have some social interaction.

Resources

Book

Creating Community Anywhere: Finding Support and Connection in a Fragmented World, by Carolyn Shaffer; New York: Perigee, 1993.

Organizations

Formerly Employed Mothers at the Leading Edge (FEMALE)
P.O. Box 31
Elmhurst, IL 60126
(630) 941-3553
www.femalehome.org

Mothers at Home (publishers of *Welcome Home*; $18 yearly subscription)
8310A Old Courthouse Road
Vienna, VA 22182
(703) 827-5903
www.mah.org
E-mail: mah@mah.org

Mothers of Preschoolers (MOPS)
1311 S. Clarkson St.
Denver, CO 80210
(303) 733-5353
www.gospelcom.net/mops

La Leche League International, Inc.
  P.O. Box 1209
  Franklin Park, IL 60131-8209
  (630) 455-7730
  www.lalecheleague.org
National Organization of Mothers of Twins Clubs
  P.O. Box 23188
  Albuquerque, NM 87192
  (505) 275-0955
  www.nomotc.org

Mommy-and-Me Classes

Gymboree
  (800) 520-PLAY
Music Together
  (800) 728-2692
Kindermusik International
  (800) 628-5687
YMCA of the USA
  (800) 872-YMCA
  www.ymca.net

Television

The other day I saw a bumper sticker that read "Kill your television."

"Kill it?" I thought to myself. "I'd rather canonize it." Yes, I'm one of those mothers who not only lets her children watch television, but I *encourage* it. Television has rescued me during some rough times as a stay-at-home mom. In the mornings, it helps me get organized. While the kids watch *Barney*, I get my dishes washed, phone calls made. At times it calms my sparring boys when no amount of my mediating works, and TV has even allowed me to grab a catnap every now and then (especially helpful when I was pregnant with my third son). Besides, I think my kids learn something from the likes of Elmo and Mr. Rogers.

But television isn't for every family. If you're a parent who chooses to live without it, I have great respect for you. I, too, know the dangers of too much television, and I question my motives every time I pick up the remote. I try to be consistent in my TV-viewing rules, limiting the time my sons get to watch. But for better or worse, television is a part of our lives.

The Good News

There are so many good shows on PBS. *I never have to worry about them flipping to the cartoon channel. They just don't like violent shows like* Power Rangers. *Rachel won't even go and see a movie with a scary character in it.*

With the average household owning two television sets, unless you choose to get rid of your boob tube altogether, it's almost impossible to totally eliminate it from your kids' daily diet. Yet a few studies say that some exposure to TV can be good for young children and may actually help to educate them. The trick is for parents to use the medium wisely. Letting the little ones view only quality programming (PBS is a good place to start) and in moderation are the keys, say the experts.

One virtue: television helps to break down ethnic and social stereotypes. In a single episode of *Sesame Street*, for instance, children are introduced to more than four ethnic groups, as well as children with disabilities. Kids of all races see themselves and identify with the people on the screen. *Sesame Street* also builds vocabulary in young children and helps them learn to count and recite the alphabet. In other PBS programming and some quality cable shows, too, children are exposed to new ideas and introduced to science, nature, and faraway cultures, places, and creatures that they may never have discovered on their own. From African-American astronauts to Mexican-American political leaders, educational television provides positive role models, too.

Of course, instructional television isn't the only place where a child can learn all these things. Clearly, parents who are highly involved in their children's lives can introduce their sons and daughters to new ideas, but watching quality shows is just one way to teach children how to be tolerant, feeling citizens.

Using TV as a Learning Tool

Like it or not, television is a major part of our culture. Parents can make the most of it by tapping into TV's positive potential. Use your set as one of many learning tools in your children's lives by following these tips.

- **Preview the show.** To make sure the content is age appropriate, view the show with your kids. They'll learn more if the show is intended for their specific age group.

- **Monitor the show's content.** You don't have to like the big purple dinosaur, but do you value the message that he and his little buddies are conveying? Will your child learn something from the program?

- **Is there a variety of cultures represented?** Educational television shows offer a variety of genders, races, and classes of characters, all of which help to break down stereotypes.

- **Try follow-up activities.** Once the program has ended, read a *Barney, Arthur, Sesame Street,* or other show-related book together, which helps to reinforce the show's positive goals. Or, if the program was about nature, take a walk outside and look for some!

- **Have teaching aids near the TV.** For nature shows, keep handy an atlas, globe, or any book with lots of animals; for shows like *Sesame Street*, keep toys that reinforce the alphabet or counting nearby.

- **Choose videos wisely.** When children's programming isn't airing, keep a collection of educational videos on hand that they can view on their own.

I think it's important that I give them a limit to how much they can watch, but I also feel that I need to be flexible about it. There are times that Olivia, for some reason, needs more veg-out time. We've been lucky that she eventually goes back to not wanting to watch TV. In fact, sometimes she doesn't want to watch it at all.

The Bad News

Although your toddlers and preschoolers probably won't be adversely affected by television because the majority of them are tuned into educational television, parents should worry

I'm a TV person, so it's hard for me to put constraints on them. I just like to have it on. Even when they're just playing Barbies, it will be on. It's just background noise.

more about television's negative influences on older children—grade-schoolers and teenagers, who spend the majority of their TV time watching network and commercial television. Public television caters to toddlers and preschoolers, encouraging creative play and imagination building. Commercial television, on the other hand, is a whole different beast. It's specifically targeted to school-age children, a very influential lot indeed.

Problem number one: cartoons and sitcoms often portray an unrealistic view of the world. Violent programs, whether cop shows or fast-paced cartoons, desensitize children to violence to the point where they may use violence to solve problems. At the very least, children who view violent programs have less empathy toward victims in real life. And research has shown that there is a strong correlation between TV-viewing habits and a child's level of aggression.

Network Rating System

What exactly are those little white boxes that appear in the upper-left corner of our sets at the start of each show? It's the networks' program-rating system, designed to inform parents of a show's content. To many parents, however, the system is confusing because many shows have more than one symbol. A recent episode of NYPD *Blue*, for instance, posted a TV14-L symbol, and *In Living Color* slated a TVPG-DL. See if you can break the code.

TVY	Appropriate for all children
TVY7	Geared toward older children
TVG	Appropriate for all audiences
TVPG	Parental guidance suggested
TV14	Parents strongly cautioned
TVMA	Mature audiences only

D	Suggestive dialogue
L	Coarse language
S	Sex
V	Violence

Next, because television is a passive pastime, it also interferes with such intellectual activities as reading or communicating with family. It competes with relationships, and its mind-numbing effect inhibits creative thinking. Children who watch too much commercial TV often don't engage in imaginary play where they are in complete control of a made-up world, an important developmental step.

Because TV watching is a sedentary activity, some speculate that too much TV can lead to obesity. In the results of the Third National Health and Nutrition Examination Survey, published in the *Journal of the American Medical Association* on March 25, 1998, researchers found that children who watch more than four hours of television per day are more likely to be physically inactive and have a higher body weight and more body fat than those children who watched less television. Yet the researchers conceded that more study is needed to determine conclusively if television viewing is tied to obesity in children.

And finally, children are more receptive to advertisers' ploys and often become brand loyal, evident when they insist on one type of breakfast cereal or a certain brand of gym shoes.

Parenting experts agree that to keep the peace, balance TV with plenty of hands-on experiences like reading, painting, and physical activity. The Academy of Pediatrics recommends no more than one to two hours of viewing per day, and none for children younger than two. And no long bouts in front of the set—only a half-hour show at a time.

I definitely use it as a calming-down tool. When the energy is getting too big and I can't manage it, I encourage TV time. And the kids refer to it as "TV Time." Somehow that makes me feel good, that they know that it's a designated amount of time and it's limited.

But wouldn't it be better to throw the set away altogether? Some experts say that trying to eliminate TV completely may have the opposite effect on older children—the set becomes even more of a temptation, and denying television viewing won't teach children self-control. Instead, they say, TV should be considered an occasional treat.

Terrifying TV Tidbits

- The average American family has the TV on for nearly seven hours each day.

- The average American child watches four to five hours of TV per day.

- By the time the average child leaves high school, he'll have seen more than 350,000 commercials and 18,000 (simulated) murders.

Tv Taboos

Television is here to stay, but make the most of it by avoiding these TV taboos.

- **Having more than two sets in your household and allowing a child to have a set in his or her bedroom.** Keep the TV in a room where you can monitor the programs your kids are watching.

- **Allowing your kids to watch more than two hours of television per day.** Make it less for toddlers.

- **Allowing your child to choose the program without your first knowing its content.** Never assume the program's content is harmless; always preview a program with your child.

- **Being a TV hypocrite.** If you watch a lot of television but tell your child not to, she won't listen. Instead, maybe you should try a TV diet yourself.

- **Allowing your children to watch the six o'clock news.** Although the murder rate in the United States is significantly down in recent years, you'd never know it watching the local news. The content in local news programs can be very disturbing to children.

- **Assuming "dinner hour" shows are family shows.** These days, adult shows in syndication air from 6 to 8 P.M., and many of them are inappropriate for young children.

Has Anyone Seen the Remote?

Television habits are set at a very young age. So beware, prepare, take an active role in your child's TV diet, and don't hog the remote.

RESOURCES

Books

Critical Viewing of Television: A Book for Parents and Teachers, by Ibrahim M. Hafzallah; Lanham, MD: University Press of America, 1987.

Remote Control: A Sensible Approach to Kids, TV and the New Electronic Media, by Leonard A. Jason and Libby Kennedy Hanaway; Sarasota, FL: Professional Resource Exchange, 1997.

See No Evil: A Guide to Protecting Our Children from Media Violence, by Madeline Levine; San Francisco: Jossey-Bass Publishers, 1998.

TV-Proof Your Kids: A Parent's Guide to Safe and Healthy Viewing, by Lauryn Axelrod; New York: Carol Publishing Group, 1997.

Time Management

Keeping the Household Running Smoothly

*"I'm having trouble managing the mansion.
What I need is a wife."*
—FORMER GOVERNOR OF CONNECTICUT,
ELLA GRASSO

In my house, I wear many hats. Not only am I the primary caregiver, but I'm also the chef, head of housekeeping, personal shopper, family physician, financial planner, social secretary. And, oh yeah, I'm a mother and a wife, too.

There's comfort in having a schedule. Monday we go to the market, Tuesday is playgroup, Wednesday is carwash day. It makes every day special, as banal as that sounds.

There's one thing that I've learned about simultaneously taking care of the kids and taking care of the house—the kids rule. No matter how important the phone call or bill to be paid, if the kids want you, they're going to have you. Yet dinner needs to be made; the clothes need to be washed. How do I do it? I'm a master at organizing my time.

Schedules Rule

With three kids within two and a half years of each other, a husband, a busy household, and a freelance writing career, the

234

only way I can survive my day is by sticking to a schedule. Not only do kids thrive on routine, but it helps keep the family focused and cuts down on stress and confusion. Scheduling a planned activity for each day also helps to keep the blues at bay.

I Want to Be Alone

When you're a full-time parent, time alone is a rarity. Part of the problem is that when your spouse walks through the door at the end of the day, you want to spend time with him or her, too, once again pushing your time alone onto the back burner. Schedule time for just yourself by following one of these tips.

- **Get up early.** Just a half hour before everyone gets up each day can be rejuvenating. Take a brisk walk, read the paper with a cup of coffee out on the patio, or simply watch the sun rise.

- **Rely on your spouse.** Drop the kids off at the office for an hour on Friday afternoons, or take an hour off when he or she gets home from work.

- **Join forces with a friend.** Find another at-home parent and offer to take her kids for a few hours one day if she'll take yours for a few hours the next.

- **Run an errand.** Take off on Saturday morning and get a few things done. Just getting out of the house, even if it's business related, feels refreshing.

For us, Monday mornings mean library story time. Tuesdays we hit the supermarket and take care of such errands as mailing packages, picking up dry cleaning, going to the bank, and so on. Wednesday mornings my beloved baby-sitter comes to call (soon to be replaced by preschool), followed by an afternoon visit by Grandma. The baby-sitter comes again on Thursday mornings, and in the afternoon, we head out to the park for a play date with friend Nathaniel. Friday is an open

I take care of household business between ten and eleven in the morning, when Sesame Street *is on. I couldn't get the kids' attention then even if I wanted to.*

Even when you're wrapped up in some project that just can't wait, when the kids cry out for attention, give it to them or they'll become more demanding of your time and nothing will ever get done. Take ten minutes and focus solely on them by doing something they want to do like read, color, or dance.

day, usually reserved for field trips or additional play dates. When we're home, the kids eat, take their naps, and go to bed at night at roughly the same time each day. This routine rarely changes.

Sound a bit rigid? Perhaps. But it works for us. The kids know what to expect and when, and I know when I'll have free, uninterrupted blocks of time to schedule things like phone calling, bill paying, cooking, or writing.

Scheduling is comforting to Elliott and Lillie. They know what's going to happen ahead of time, and they're able to look forward to something. When we were out of town when my father was sick, the kids were out of their routine for more than a week, and it was difficult for them. It threw them off.

Central Command Post

Listen up, troops: whether it's a small desk in the corner of the kitchen or a private home office, every family needs to have a central command post, an area where family members can easily go to when they have a question concerning the inner workings of domestic life. When you're on the phone with the bank or your mortgage company, you don't have time to fumble through a mishmash of files to find the appropriate documents. With a command post, all household information is always at your fingertips (albeit fingertips smeared with peanut butter).

I run our command post, and although it may appear to be a mess to an outsider, I can quickly locate even last year's gas bill. When mail comes in I immediately sort through it and discard the junk, open bills, check them for accuracy, write the due date on the envelope, and then file them according to which needs to be paid first.

My command post is close to the phone and is amply supplied with paper and pens and a message board. It's well stocked with a stapler, tape, paper clips, and other basic office supplies. There's a dictionary close by, a calculator, too; and tucked underneath the desk, there is a small filing cabinet. The most important member under my command? The family calendar.

Eight Days a Week

At the beginning of each January, I perform an important ritual—the signing in of the new calendar. With last year's by my side, I transcribe birthdays, anniversaries, and even paydays onto the new calendar. To cut down on confusion, I write those dates in one color ink. For appointments and social engagements, I assign each member of the family a different color. If Matthew has a pediatrician appointment, for instance, I mark it in red. If Kevin has a dental appointment, I write it in green. You get the idea.

    I'm particular about what type of calendar gets the place of honor—it has to have large-enough blocks on each day to accommodate several appointments. The bigger the better. No half-inch squares for this house.

Keep a List—Check It Twice

Another technique to organize your time is to keep copious to-do lists. Not only does scratching off a completed task give me a sense of accomplishment (yes, buying stamps is an accomplishment when you're a full-time parent), but these days I simply can't remember anything unless I write it down.

    Be specific when making your list. "Clean the bathroom" is too general, and with small children underfoot, it's probably impractical. Instead, write down small, precise tasks for each day, things that can be accomplished in a short span of time such as "clean out medicine cabinet" or "scour tub."

    I created a master to-do list on the computer with four categories—phone calls, E-mail and letters, projects, and errands—and I print a fresh one each week. You can make your list on the back of a grocery bag or create something more elaborate, with grids for each day of the week. You can

Color Coded Cool

Got a large family and want to cut down on confusion? Color code them. It's simple: assign each member a different color and use it for everything: toothbrushes, sippy cups, pacifiers, sneakers, bicycle helmets, appointments and dates notated on the family calendar, and even file folders containing important documents and medical records. It's especially helpful if you're a family with multiples, like us, where our twins wear roughly the same size and are at the same developmental stage. When both boys drop their sippy cups, I immediately know whose cup is whose.

If there's any consistency to my day it tends to be a ten o'clock nap for the twins. I make my calls; I pay my bills; I rearrange a drawer of clothing for seasons, ages, or sizes.

prioritize your list from most important to least, or write it down according to amount of time each task will take.

Are the kids glued in front of *Barney*? Grab the list and find a ten-minute task. However you choose to do it, making a daily to-do list is an enormous time-saver.

Telephone Tantrums

It happens to all of us: as soon as you get on the phone, the kids think it's time to show you how loudly they can whine. There are a few tricks (alas, not many) that can help you get through a five-minute call without frantically waving your arms.

- **Do it early.** Make business-related calls early in the day, when your kids are more likely to be otherwise engaged.

- **Explain the situation.** Older toddlers usually grasp the concept that you need to use the phone for a few minutes and rise to the occasion by giving you the peace you need.

- **Engage them.** Set them up with a craft project (pull out the play office supplies).

- **Let the machine get it.** When the phone rings right when your daughter decides it's time to have a meltdown, don't feel compelled to answer it. They'll call back.

We had such a bad day last week. I was talking on the phone with the bank to clear something up and Francesca was screaming, "Off, Mommy. Off." I had to shut her out of the den. She was hurling herself at the door, and I felt terrible, but I had to have two minutes of grown-up time.

Gotta Have Gadgets

Although I'm a true believer in cutting down on clutter and staying away from needless electronics and doohickeys, there are some tools that are actually big time-savers to full-time parents.

- **Cordless phone.** Follow the kids inside and out while you RSVP for their next birthday party. Better yet, why not get a hands-free phone (available at most electronic stores). You clip the receiver on your pants and wear a headset. Now you have two free hands.

- **Backpack or child carrier sack.** With a new baby in the house and preschoolers who insist on dinner at 6 P.M., the Snugli sack has saved my sanity. Babies love it because they get to be close to Mom. My son has fallen asleep in his on many occasions.

- **Wagon.** What kid can resist a ride in a wagon? Do your grocery shopping or any other errand while your kids sit back and enjoy the scenery.

- **Microwave.** It's *fast* and cheaper to use than turning on the oven. When you get in late, dinner can be ready in a matter of minutes.

When I need to make a call, I put John in his younger sister's crib with her and a few toys. He gets a kick out of playing he's the baby. He's safe, and occupied, so I can leave the room for a little peace.

OTHER TIME-SAVING TIPS

- **Cook and freeze.** Take one night and cook for the entire week. Not only will you save hours later by just reheating your meals, it saves energy and money, too.

- **Shop the Internet.** You can buy just about anything on-line and usually at substantial savings. The best part is, you can shop anytime.

- **Use a printed grocery list.** Type up all the items that you usually buy—from vegetables to shampoo—and arrange the list in the order in which these items are found in the store. Print one out on your computer each week and check off what you need.

- **Cut down on after-school activities.** Does your son need to take karate, tennis, and soccer? Decide what's truly important and discard the rest.

- **Carpool.** If your kids are in school, find a classmate who lives in the neighborhood and suggest to her parent that you carpool.

- **Have the kids pitch in.** From cooking to gardening, housekeeping to shopping, teach your kids how to help. They'll love being independent, and you'll love the help.

- **Watch the clock.** Ironically, the best way to save time is to watch it. Assign a specific amount of time per task, and when the moment approaches, stop doing whatever it is.

Time Is on Your Side

It's important to get that job done, but be careful. It's OK to just hang out with your kids and let everything else go. In fact, my kids can't think of a better way of spending an afternoon than on a blanket staring up at the sky, singing every song we know. It's important to just spend time with the kids doing absolutely nothing. They need to see that time can be enjoyed, not just used as a means to an end.

RESOURCES

Books

Busy Woman's Organizer, by Susan Tatsui-D'Arcy; Englewood Cliffs, NJ: Prentice Hall Trade, 1998.

The Family Manager's Everyday Survival Guide, by Kathy Peel; New York: Ballantine Books, 1998.

Get More Done in Less Time—And Get on with the Good Stuff, by Donna Otto; Eugene, OR: Harvest House Publishers, 1995.

MOM Central: The Ultimate Family Organizer, by Stacy Debroff and Marsha Feinberg; New York: Kodansha International, 1998.

Volunteering

W hether it's devoting a few hours per week to the local hospital, serving Thanksgiving dinner at a homeless shelter, or teaching adults how to read, volunteering keeps full-time parents tuned into the world around them.

Not only does altruism have an enormous impact on those in need, but it has a marvelous healing effect on those who give of themselves. Volunteering helps you to get outside yourself by focusing on others, allowing you to truly appreciate your life; and in the process, you become a better parent. When you put in your time as a volunteer, knowing that you made a difference in someone's life is enormously gratifying.

Recording for the Blind and Dyslexic provides books on tape and CDs. Do you have a good voice? Perhaps this organization is for you.

20 Roszel Road
Princeton, NJ 08540
(800) 803-7201

I was at my parent's house, and I read in the local paper how the people of the town built a Playscape, a community-built, community-funded playground built with volunteer effort. The article said how unifying it was to the community, an exhilarating experience to have people from all walks of life come together working toward a common goal. I thought I wanted to try to do this in Big Rapids. One thing we desperately needed was a playground. We live in a town where the only playgrounds were at the elementary schools. I went to my neighbor down the street, and he said he'd do it with me. So we called the city, and they gave us park space. Then we assembled a core committee of twenty people, which my neighbor, Pat, and I cochaired. We put the word out through the elementary school. From start to finish, it took thirteen months. It was a

Junior Achievement helps students understand the world of business and economics.

(800) THENEWJA

www.ja.org

League of Women Voters' more than 1,000 national chapters work on such community issues as affordable housing, child care, and, of course, voter registration.

1730 M Street NW

Washington, DC 20036

(202) 429-1965

www.lwv.org

Disabled Sports USA offers physically challenged individuals the chance to engage in a number of sports, including skiing.

451 Hungerford Drive, Suite 100

Rockville, MD 20850

(301) 217-0960

www.dsusa.org/~dsusa.html

National Trust for Historic Preservation needs volunteers to help with its more than nineteen museums.

1785 Massachusetts Avenue NW

Washington, DC 20036

(800) 944-NTHP, ext. 6120

www.nationaltrust.org

Girl Scouts of the USA needs volunteers for their annual cookie drive and parents to serve on regional council boards.

(800) GSUSA4U

www.girlscouts.org

Habitat for Humanity International provides affordable shelter for families. Volunteers with or without construction experience are needed.

121 Habitat Street
Americus, GA 31709
(912) 924-6935
www.habitat.org

National Center for Missing and Exploited Children has found more than 40,000 missing children since 1984. Volunteers are needed to staff phones and distribute fliers.

2101 Wilson Boulevard, Suite 550
Arlington, VA 22201
(800) 843-5678
www.missingkids.com

The American Cancer Society helps educate the public on cancer prevention but also provides a number of services to patients and their families.

(800) 227-2345
www.cancer.org

lot of work. But it was well worth it. I formed and still maintain a lot of friendships from the project, something I didn't have before.

The Good and the Bad

The number one reason to become a volunteer is to help make the world a little better for all, but there are perks for the former professional, too. If you plan to return to work sometime in the future and give your time to an organization that's linked to your former career, you have the opportunity to make networking contacts, keep abreast on what's new in your field, and perhaps advance your career. Even if you're thinking of changing careers, volunteering gives you the opportunity to test-drive other vocations that have always interested you. You get to learn new job skills, obtain hands-on experience, and help others in the process.

If you've volunteered your time in the past, however, you know that good intentions alone won't make the experience pleasurable or even helpful to others, for that matter. Groups that are disorganized, have no leadership, or staff the wrong people for the job are usually a waste of everyone's valuable time. Before you commit to a worthy cause, do your homework.

Making the Right Choice

Although you won't be paid for your time, try to be selective about which group you join. To help you decide, follow these guidelines.

■ **What are your skills? Interests?** Try to find a group that matches your skills or interests. Are you a whiz at numbers? Volunteer to help low-income families prepare their taxes. Do you love to cook? Why not help prepare meals for elderly shut-ins? Yet this type of strategy doesn't work for everyone. Perhaps you'd be happier working where you are most needed in your community.

■ **Know your personality.** Think about if you'd like to work independently or with a group. Are you outgoing and a master at soliciting funds, or rather shy and prefer to put your skills to work in other areas?

■ **How much time are you willing to give?** It's best to start out with a small commitment of just a few hours a week or month; then, gradually add time as your interest peaks or your schedule permits.

■ **Talk with others in the group.** Speak with other volunteers and ask them about their experiences with the group. How long have they been there? What's great about the organization? What's not so great?

To try and keep in touch with the Dietetic Association, I volunteered to organize the Food and Fitness 5K Run. But I was stupid. I was trying to manage too much stuff from my home. I took on the whole thing. I was in charge of it. One time I was talking on the phone to the head of some company and here my child had just taken something out of the refrigerator and dumped it on the floor, and the phone cord is too short to reach him. Meanwhile, you're trying to sound professional over the phone. If I had to do it over again, I would have only taken on a small segment. Instead, I kept saying, "Oh, I can do that."

■ **Don't assume you know everything about the group.** Ask to see a mission statement to clearly understand the organization's goals.

■ **Look for a well-run outfit.** Do they offer training or seminars to prospective volunteers? Does the agency regularly meet with mentors to discuss problems and complaints? Are there any expenses involved?

■ **Don't be pushed into something you really don't want to do.** If you hate fund-raising and would prefer another job, say so.

School Involvement

With so many schools experiencing budget cuts and concern with the quality of academics, now more than ever a parent's help is needed in the classroom. Unfortunately, with busy family schedules, few moms and dads have the time to volunteer in their children's classrooms. Parent-Teacher Association (PTA) membership is dwindling, too, to half of what it was back in the '60s when there were even fewer students in our nation's schools.

Most teachers and school administrators would welcome parental aid on any level. In fact, successful schools, those whose students have continually performed well on achievement tests, attribute their accomplishments to parental involvement. Research from the U.S. Department of Education states that when parents participate in their children's education, their kids are more likely to bring home better grades and have an overall positive attitude toward school.

You don't have to have a degree in early childhood education to make a difference. Parents of all backgrounds can have a huge impact in improving the quality of their kids'

I volunteer at our church's thrift store every Saturday. I really love it because I'm out in the world, I'm doing something that I feel good about, and I'm doing something for the community. Those few hours just energize me, helping me to regroup. And it gives Francesca some alone time with Daddy.

I like volunteering, but I always like to do things that I can include my kids.

education by simply giving their time. Even as little as an hour a week or a day a year is helpful.

Volunteer in the classroom by grading tests, checking homework, reading to a small group of students, photocopying tests, or lending a hand during a class field trip. If your child is older and at the age where he'll be embarrassed by having his mom in the classroom, help out in the front office, school library, or even the lunchroom.

If you're strapped for time during the week, lend a hand on weekends. Make it a family day by planting a vegetable garden for the science class, planting flowers to beautify school property, or adding color to hallways by helping to paint a mural. And even if you can't spare a weekend, there's still plenty that you can do over the phone—organize fund-raisers, help write a grant proposal for new equipment, update mailing lists or phone chains, set up a class website so that parents and teachers can exchange important information, or gather other professionals in the area to set up a special assembly like Career Day.

The U.S. Department of Education's website offers a vast collection of free publications, including The Partnership for Family Involvement in Education, a series of titles focusing on ways to improve the quality of schools and student achievement.

U.S. Department of
   Education
400 Maryland Avenue
   SW
Washington, DC 20202-
   0498
(800) USA-LEARN
www.ed.gov

School's in Session

Not only does volunteering help out the school, but parents benefit as well by getting better acquainted with the school. Parent volunteers can join committees where they help to determine school policies and budget. And it's an excellent way to check on a child's progress.

It means a lot to Lillie when I volunteer at her school. She's so proud. Marty volunteers, too. He reads stories to the kids in the morning before he goes to work.

RESOURCES

Books

The Fundraising Planner: A Working Model for Raising the Money You Need, by Terry Schaff and Doug Schaff; San Francisco: Jossey-Bass, 1999.

The Halo Effect: How Volunteering Can Lead to a More Fulfilling Life and a Better Career, by John Raynolds; New York: Golden Books Publishing, 1998.

Volunteering: 101 Ways You Can Improve the World and Your Life, by Douglas M. Lawson; La Jolla, CA: Alti Publishing, 1998.

Organizations

The following organizations act as clearinghouses, matching volunteers with local groups.

Points of Light Foundation
    1400 I Street NW, Suite 800
    Washington, DC 20005
    (800) 59-LIGHT
    www.pointsoflight.org

America's Promise—The Alliance for Youth
    909 North Washington Street
    Alexandria, VA 22314
    (888) 55-YOUTH
    www.americaspromise.org

ABC's Children First
    (800) 914-2212

Internet Sites

www.servenet.org—SERVEnet
    Type in your zip code to find a volunteer organization in your community.

www.idealist.org—Action Without Borders
    Choose among 17,000 volunteer organizations, or search for a charity event or job internship.

I volunteer at Rachel's kindergarten class. You get to see what goes on, how the kids interact, how they're learning. I really enjoy being there.

To encourage parents to get involved in their children's education, The Parent Institute publishes a collection of booklets, brochures, videos, and the newsletter *Parents Make the Difference!*, available for downloading from their website.
P.O. Box 7474
Fairfax Station, VA
    22039-7474
(703) 323-9170
www.parent-institute.com

Work

Going Back Full Time

Sooner or later, most full-time parents decide to return to their former careers. But many, after having taken a five- or six-year sabbatical, worry that they will have to start climbing the corporate ladder all over again or won't be able to pick up where they left off. Although these are legitimate concerns because a person with recent job experience is usually more desirable than someone who hasn't worked in a few years, successfully returning to your former profession is possible.

The key to getting back on track, according to Betsy Sheldon, coauthor of *The Smart Woman's Guide to Résumés and Job Hunting* and *The Smart Woman's Guide to Networking*, is to position yourself in a powerful and positive light. "You need to positively communicate what you've been doing during your absence with regard to the skills and experiences you've had and translate that into value to a potential employer."

Your First Step:
Keeping Up-to-Date

Even though you may be out of the workforce, staying active and up-to-date with your industry now will help when you do decide to return. The biggest problem in finding work, according to Sheldon, is that most full-time parents drop out of the loop. "They may not be aware of the opportunities out there since most jobs aren't advertised but are found by word of mouth," she explains. "They may not have the networking contacts as someone who is in the workforce." But these challenges are surmountable. Sheldon suggests doing the following while at home to help in your eventual job search.

- **Stay connected.** You may be knee-deep in diapers and laundry, but keep memberships to associations and professional organizations current. Don't let industry licenses lapse; renew regularly. Read trade periodicals, and cruise the Internet for current information in your field.
- **Update your computer knowledge.** Stay abreast of the latest software used in your industry.
- **Create your own networking group.** Stay in touch with former coworkers by meeting with them regularly.
- **Freelance.** Depending on how involved you are at home, make yourself available to do some contract work with your former employer, or be available to substitute on a project. "Continue to produce," Sheldon stresses. "Show off your skills. It just doesn't have to be on a nine-to-five basis."

Volunteers of America

Even mothers who have never held a job outside the home but want a taste of corporate life now that the kids are in school often have the skills that translate into highly productive employees. "Homemakers, or people who have never been in the workforce, absolutely have skills that can be transferred into value for the employer," notes Sheldon. "Some of the most confident people I've ever met are homemakers involved in the volunteer world, people responsible for fundraising and organizing major events." The skills that they gain through these functions, Sheldon explains, especially when working with a group of other volunteers, are vital in the corporate world. "They're working with a staff of unpaid people. Imagine how tough that is," she stresses.

The biggest drawback to this group is that most of them don't know their worth. "Most come into an interview apologetic for their volunteer work, or many may not know to tell the employer about it," she says. "They think because it wasn't paid work, it isn't worth bringing up." Nothing could be further from the truth, says Sheldon. Volunteer work should not only be listed on your résumé, but proudly highlighted during the interviewing process.

Is It Time for a Change?

But what if you want to return to work—not as a research analyst, but as an escrow officer? Is it still possible? Absolutely. "Sabbaticals are a ripe time to do the groundwork for changing careers," Sheldon says. "You need some sort of transition. You couldn't hop from your position as an accountant to fiction writer. You need to do the legwork while home." In addition to updating your skills through adult education classes, Sheldon suggests looking to trade associations for help. "If you have time flexibility, do an internship," she adds. "By interning, you become a known entity so when a position comes up and you're ready for it, you're in a great position to be considered."

Your Second Step: The Résumé

A basic job-hunting tool, a résumé summarizes your professional skills, and if done correctly, it can show them off in a positive light. But make no mistake, a résumé, no matter how great, is merely a calling card and it alone won't land you a job. Sheldon suggests thinking about what you can do ahead of time to pave the way for your résumé by making a personal contact with the hiring person.

"Let's say you hear about a position from a friend in a company that you'd like to work for," she explains. "Rather than sending your résumé to the personnel department where it will immediately go into a stack, ask your friend if she knows who's doing the hiring, then make a tactful and diplomatic phone call to that person expressing your interest in the job." It may not go any further than the hiring person telling you to send in your résumé, but chances are you've gotten her attention. "The antenna is going to go up," Sheldon says. "She'll probably go to personnel and tell them to be on the lookout for your résumé."

Résumé Dos and Don'ts

There are as many styles of résumés as there are types of employees, but there are some hard-and-fast rules that you should follow when drafting a résumé.

- **Do** keep your résumé current. You never know when opportunity will knock, so it's best to be prepared. As soon as something professionally significant occurs, update your résumé.

- **Do** customize your résumé to meet the current job you're seeking. By editing your résumé to meet the needs of an employer, you're more apt to convince her that you're the one for the job.

- **Do** get to the point quickly. With the average employer spending a mere thirty seconds perusing your résumé, be concise in explaining your job skills.
- **Don't** use colored paper or a fancy, unreadable typeface to make your résumé stand out. Always make your résumé neat and professional looking with traditional type and layout, and let your credentials speak for themselves.
- **Don't** include photographs, personal stats, or profiles on your résumé.
- **Do** include any related skills such as computer expertise, volunteer work, and military service on your résumé.

A Word on Cover Letters

With all your energy and emphasis on creating a great résumé, another important marketing tool, the cover letter, often gets overlooked. Although Sheldon admits that some employers never read cover letters, they expect them, nonetheless. Cover letters are required protocol, and a résumé should never be faxed or mailed without one. Sometimes, a great cover letter, one that expands and explains an area of your résumé that pertains to the job you're applying for, can even clinch the prospect of an interview.

Cover Letter Dos and Don'ts

To properly introduce your résumé, follow these cover letter dos and don'ts.

- **Do** address your cover letter to a specific person, not just the general "To whom it may concern." To get the name of the hiring person, you may have to call the company.
- **Do** check and double-check for spelling and grammatical errors.

- **Do** highlight relevant experience from your résumé in the body of your letter.
- **Don't** forget to include a contact phone number and address in your letter (just in case it gets separated from your résumé).

Your Third Step: Networking

If your idea of networking is a well-dressed pest working a function by shoving business cards in everyone's hands, you're not alone. "Most people, women in particular, have a simplistic definition of networking," Sheldon explains. "They think it's asking someone they don't know very well for a favor from someone that they don't know at all. Of course that's inappropriate, and they should feel uncomfortable with it."

So what is networking and what's the correct way to do it? Simply stated: it's relationship building, the sharing of information with someone. Because most jobs aren't advertised, networking is the one way to come into contact with an employer seeking the exact qualifications that you have.

When you meet people with whom you've built a rapport, stay in touch with them on occasion through E-mail or corresponding. But don't expect to stay in touch with everybody, Sheldon warns. "You need to develop relationships with people who are good matches for you. Obviously, if you don't hit it off with someone, no matter how well connected they are, you shouldn't expect to make them a networking contact."

Stay-at-home parents are great networkers, and often they don't even know it, Sheldon explains. "They do it all the time when they ask friends and neighbors, 'What's a good day care? Where do you take your dry cleaning? When you go in there, tell them I sent you.' That's networking." It's the asking and giving of information.

Assuming that you've built up a strong list of networking contacts, notify them when you're ready to reenter the workplace. A simple E-mail or short letter to each explaining the type of position that you're seeking should be enough to get the ball rolling.

The Fourth Step: The Interview

Be on time. Don't smoke or chew gum. We all know these basic dos and don'ts, but there's a lot more to the fine art of interviewing, and savvy job seekers prepare for this make-or-break meeting as they would prepare for an exam.

So what's the biggest mistake prospective employees make during an interview? Setting too many limitations, according to Sheldon. Although being positive is important, sometimes job seekers focus too much on what they want instead of focusing on what the employer needs. "Rather than saying, 'I see what you need and I have what you want,' often people go into an interview with too many requirements," she says. "For example, you shouldn't go into an interview and say, 'I'm looking for a job with flexibility since I've just had a baby.'"

Job seekers should anticipate questions and prepare. When an employer asks the dreaded, "Why did you decide to take time off?" answer positively. Rather than saying, "I had to stay home with my kids," be decisive. A better answer would be: "My husband and I decided that staying home was best for our children. My long-term plan had always included my taking time off to be with my children. And now that they're in school, I want to return to work." Never apologize. Be confident and sure of yourself. "Any employer is going to look for someone who is confident of what they have to offer," Sheldon adds.

To help you prepare for your interview, Sheldon proposes some quick answers to some tough questions.

- **Why did you leave the workforce?** "I wanted to give my family as much attention and focus as I had given my work."

- **Will you have more children?** (This question may be discriminatory but it doesn't stop many from asking, say, at the end of an interview when you're making small talk.) "I sense that you have a concern that I might be leaving, but if I were not committed to this job I wouldn't be here today. You have my assurance that I would be committed to this job."

- **Why are you coming back to work now?** "It was part of my plan. I had intended to step out of the workforce to raise my family, and then when my children reached a certain age, I would get back in the workforce. This opportunity came along at the same time I was prepared to return to work."

Job seekers should think about questions to ask the employer as well. Sheldon says all too often prospective employees never ask a single question during the interview, and nothing shows a lack of interest more than someone who doesn't ask a question. When you ask questions, it shows the employer that you're a forward thinker.

What kind of questions? Sheldon recommends doing a bit of research on the company before the interview by going to the library in search of newspaper articles or simply phoning the human resources department and asking for an annual report or any other information that they might have on the company. Your research should bring up some ideas and aid in mentally preparing a few specific questions. For instance, ask if the position will change or evolve in the next few years. Or, what's a typical workday like? Ask with what other departments in the company you'll be working.

What kind of questions should you avoid? "How much vacation time do I get?" and "What kind of health benefits do you offer?" are always big no-nos. Salary questions should also be avoided for as long as possible, according to Sheldon.

"Avoid them until you've made them feel as though they can't live without you," she says.

Back to Work

Even though most parents who return to work do so after their kids reach school age, thus eliminating the need for full-time child care, there's still that block of time from 3 to 6 P.M. when the kids need after-school supervision. According to the National Institute on Out-of-School Time at Wellesley College, more than seventeen million working parents need some sort of after-school care for their kids. Though leaving the little ones alone in the house won't work, some other inexpensive child-care options exist.

One alternative is to hire a part-time baby-sitter, usually a local college student, who picks the kids up after school, takes them home, and remains with them until the parents arrival at the dinner hour. Duties vary from family to family and budget to budget. Some do light housekeeping (like vacuuming or the dishes), start dinner, or even help the kids with their homework. Parents like this arrangement because the kids get a jump on their schoolwork, there's no need to pick anyone up, and often household chores are taken care of. The cost varies from $6 to $15 an hour, depending on your location and number of children.

Another possibility are "extended" or "expanded" after-school programs. Part recreational, part educational, these school-based programs are designed to spur a child's creativity while enhancing her academic skills. Parents favor this type of care because the programs supplement the school day by offering classes that are not offered in their children's regular curriculum. In addition, parents who don't want to see their children spending their afternoons in front of the television set find that the programs help better prepare their children for the future.

Currently, there are three popular enrichment programs.

Voyager Expanded Learning Program

2200 Ross Avenue, Suite 3800
Dallas, TX 75201
(888) 399-1995
Cost: sliding scale, capping at $45 a week.

Partners with the Smithsonian Institute and The Discovery Channel, Voyager offers a wide range of hands-on classes such as Pre-med, where kids get an age-appropriate crash course in medicine in just four weeks, and NASA Space Camp. Classes last from 3 to 6 P.M., from one to seven weeks in length.

Sylvan Learning Systems

1000 Lancaster Street
Baltimore, MD 21202
(888) 356-3456
Cost: around $255 per month, or $5.50 per hour for part-
time participation.

Sylvan's Mindsurf program, developed in cooperation with the National Geographic Society, focuses on geography, art, current events, and history. Classes rely heavily on the use of computers (including use of the Internet) and video cameras.

Explore! Inc.

4900 Wetheredsville Road
Baltimore, MD 21207
(888) 41-EXPLORE
Cost: $225 per month, or $3 to $5 per hour for part-time
participation.

Explore! concentrates on teaching kids the value of community service by having young activists participate in park and stream cleanups or help homeless people by volunteering at a food bank.

All three of these programs may seem like a great solution to the after-school problem, but parents should carefully think before signing on the dotted line. First, decide what your child would like best. By the end of a long school day, some kids might do better with a purely recreational program rather than an academic one. Although after-school enrichment programs are catching fire across the country, some educators warn that a full six-hour school day may be enough for some children. These kids may not be able to sit for yet another two hours. They may need to burn up some pent-up energy instead.

Other things to consider:

- What are the qualifications of the instructors?
- What's the student-to-instructor ratio?
- Are the activities age appropriate?
- Are you welcome to observe the class at any time?

Back-to-Work Countdown

Just like the first weeks home with the kids, the first few weeks back at work can be a huge adjustment. To make the transition a little more bearable, follow these tips before your first day back.

Right Away	• Look into and then arrange after-school care (or day care).
	• Tell the kids of your plans to return to work.
Three Weeks Ahead	• Cook and freeze ready-to-heat-and-serve dinners.
	• Review your work wardrobe. Make alterations or shop for new work clothes.

Two Weeks Ahead	• Arrange a farewell play date with your toddler's friends and their parents, or plan a special after-school outing.
	• Make a hair appointment.
One Week Ahead	• Hold a meeting with spouse to discuss new schedule and division of household duties.
	• Fill out employment paperwork.
The Night Before	• Iron work clothes.
	• Bake something special for breakfast.
	• Go to bed early.
On the Big Day	• Get up early. Leave yourself plenty of extra time.
	• Don't expect smooth sailing; the first day back can be stressful as everyone adjusts.

The Daily Grind

Going back to work is a big step. Although it's exciting, it also can be stressful as you and your family adjust to a new schedule. Allow yourself the time to slowly ease back.

RESOURCES

Books

Best Answers to the 201 Most Frequently Asked Interview Questions, by Matthew J. Deluca; New York: McGraw-Hill, 1996.

The Damn Good Résumé Guide: A Crash Course in Résumé Writing, by Yana Parker; Berkeley: Ten Speed Press, 1996.

Job Hunting for Dummies, by Robert Half and Max Messmer; San Mateo, CA: IDG Books Worldwide, 1999.

Job-Hunting on the Internet, by Richard Nelson Bolles; Berkeley: Ten Speed Press, 1999.

The Smart Woman's Guide to Networking, by Joyce Hadley and Betsy Sheldon; Broomall, PA: Chelsea House Publishing, 1997.

The Smart Woman's Guide to Résumés and Job Hunting, by Julie Adair King and Betsy Sheldon; Broomall, PA: Chelsea House Publishing, 1997.

Working at Home

When people find out that I'm a full-time mother and a freelance writer, they always ask, "How do you find the time to write? You have twins and a new baby."

But it's precisely because I have three kids that I write. My writing has not only brought some extra cash flow to the family account, but working on various projects and focusing on something other than kids, husband, and running the household keep me sane, and help me stay in tune with my former livelihood. When my boys are having a bad day, or I just can't sing another round of "London Bridge," my mind drifts to my writing, and I begin to mentally organize what I need to do once I'm free to slip away to the privacy of my home office.

Shouldn't I be concentrating on my kids and their needs? Sure. And I do for more than ten hours per day, but if I didn't mentally escape to my work every now and then, or take a few hours each day to actually do some writing, I'd lose it. It's called *survival*. Parenting is just one facet of my life (albeit a very large facet), and although I love being a full-time mother, writing keeps me centered and helps me survive the sometimes tumultuous antics of stay-at-home parenting. Besides, I like it. I truly enjoy playing with words.

Home Is Where the Office Is

Think you'd benefit both financially and psychologically from working at home? You're not alone, according to Ellen Parlapiano and Patricia Cobe, coauthors of *Mompreneurs: A Mother's Practical Step-by-Step Guide to Work-at-Home Success*. They admit that the exact number of mothers working from home is hard to determine, but they estimate that nearly ten million moms have set up shop from home—from women who telecommute for major corporations to women who run either a full- or part-time business. And the numbers are growing daily.

"Many of the women we interviewed for our book were former corporate rising stars who wanted more control over their personal and professional lives," explains Parlapiano.

"Most of the mothers do it because they want more time with their children. They don't want to work ten-hour days then come home and be with their children for an hour before they put them to bed," Cobe adds. "If they start a business and they want to expand it, they can. If they want to pull back, they can, depending on the needs and ages of their children."

Women who work at home don't have to worry about the "corporate glass ceiling" or the threat of downsizing. "Being one's own boss provides an unequaled opportunity to call the shots," Parlapiano says. "She can set her own schedule, establish her own income goal, advance at her own pace, and never have to ask a boss for permission to attend a child's school play on work time."

Nearly all of the mothers that the authors interviewed worked part-time hours. "Most women were trying to find work that would allow them to work thirty hours or less a week," Cobe says. "That's something that they just couldn't get in the corporate world." And although some work-at-home moms work close to sixty-hour weeks, Cobe says they were the ones whose businesses took off, and they wanted to devote more time to their ventures. "A workaholic is always going to be a workaholic whether working for herself or working for a corporation," she laughs.

The Right Stuff

Many women may question if they have what it takes to start and succeed at a home-based business. Curious if you have the right stuff? Cobe suggests some questions to ponder.

- **Are you self-motivated?** Not only do you have to be a self-starter, but Cobe says you need to be a self-stopper, too. "You can't just let your workday go on and on. Even if you don't have an office door, you must mentally close the work door at the end of the day."

- **Can you work with distractions?** If it's not the kids, then it's the neighbors, or the plumber, or the gardener. Often, people don't think you have a "real job" when you work at home. "You have to put up a professional front and have the discipline to work around those distractions. Have the ability to say no."

- **Can you work in isolation?** For those women used to an office setting, working from home can be lonely. There's no one available to bounce ideas off of or simply to talk shop with.

When Sam was born nine years ago, I started working from home. I did a lot of freelance work in industrial design. It worked out great with one baby. I'd put him in my backpack and sit at my drawing table. If he'd get cranky and I had a deadline, I'd pass some crackers over my shoulder.

- **Can you quickly shift gears?** With kids in the house, you need to shift from the work mode to the mommy mode and back again—often.

- **Do you have a sense of humor?** A lot of funny things can happen when your kid picks up the office phone by accident.

Choosing the Right Business

It was difficult to juggle work and the kids, but the adrenaline and the excitement of the project would get me going so I would pull all-nighters. I'd work until two or three in the morning because I wouldn't start until I put the kids to bed at night. The projects were short-term, though, one to two weeks.

Most former corporate women who are now at home often turn the skills that they learned in the workplace into a home-based business. For instance, if you were once an office manager, a possible home business might be one offering secretarial support to local businesses. But the possibilities for potential at-home careers shouldn't stop with past experiences. Some women turn completely away from their former professions and start their fantasy businesses. Women who love to cook, for instance, often use their talents and start a catering business.

Service-based businesses are hottest these days, according to Parlapiano and Cobe, because they usually require less start-up money than product-based businesses. "But no matter what type of business you choose, *specialization* is the buzzword for the millennium," Parlapiano notes. She suggests targeting your business to a very specialized market to make it different from other businesses out there. "For example, instead of simply starting a home-meal delivery service, provide timesaving, delicious meals that are also low in fat, cholesterol, and calories." Or, she adds, if you want to be a personal trainer, specialize in exercises that help people with back problems.

But Parlapiano cautions that if you don't investigate your potential enterprise by doing market research, your business may not succeed. "Gather as much information as you can about your prospective service or product and about the business in general," she says. Before launching your home business, she suggests asking yourself the following questions.

■ **Is there a market?** Before you sell a product or service, there must be people who want it. "Look for a need that isn't being met in the marketplace." Then informally interview potential customers through questionnaires. Also, scope out the competition through small-business development centers (*see* the resources at the end of this chapter).

■ **Do you have enough money?** Unless you have a husband who can support you until your business is viable, you'll need to put aside the equivalent of six to twelve months' salary. Budget your start-up costs, your overhead (telephone, postage, office supplies), and if you're specifically leaving your corporate job to work at home, budget monthly living expenses, too (rent, food, insurance). Then Parlapiano suggests putting aside an extra three to six months' salary as a safety net for unexpected costs.

■ **Are you competitively priced?** Ask similar businesses what they charge. And review your market research to determine what potential customers are willing to pay.

■ **Have you researched the legalities?** Talk with an attorney; or check with local and state agencies to determine what permits, licenses, or insurance you'll need.

■ **Are your expectations realistic?** Don't expect to be a successful entrepreneur overnight. Most businesses take three to five years to take off.

Gathering Clients

Have a great idea? Now what? How do you get people to notice your business? Most women transfer a skill that they had mastered on the job into a home business (Cobe and Parlapiano estimate this happens about 70 percent of the time) enabling them to have a built-in client base. Cobe, for example, took some important steps before leaving her editing post at Scholastic Magazines for home. She went through her personal Rolodex (some companies, however, have strict policies against former employees contacting clients for a certain number of years) and sent a letter to everyone she had ever worked with, explaining her shift in gears. "I said that I was now freelancing, and that I'd like to stay on their press list," she says. "Now many people knew that I was working from home. I tested the waters that way, and the positive response that I got from that letter made me think that my idea was viable. I saw that I would get work from these people that I had known all along."

But clients come from many places. As a parent, you'll meet lots of contacts. By simply talking to other moms and dads, you'll encounter other potential clients every day. "You have to network wherever you go," Cobe explains. "It's very hard for most women to sell themselves. That's the hardest part of starting your own business. But it's something that you must do if you want to get work." She even made a contact at her son's soccer game. "On the sidelines, I met a lawyer who needed a brochure done. He gave me the job just by talking to him."

It's also a good idea to have some professional-looking marketing materials. Design a catchy logo for your business cards, and make matching stationery. It can be done on a desktop publishing program or done inexpensively at a print shop. Perhaps design a flyer explaining your new business, but shy away from pricey brochures until you actually have something to show in them.

Finally, talking with other people in the same business will give you lots of insight into your new venture. "People are surprisingly open," Cobe notes. "They won't give you their clients, of course, but you can call people, ask questions, and even say, 'If you find yourself overloaded, please feel free to send people my way.' Most businesspeople are amenable to that."

Business Boo-Boos

Before you hang up that shingle, though, make sure you're not doing one or more of the following boo-boos.

■ **Not putting up any separation between work and family.** According to Cobe, the lines between work and family can often become very blurry. Although it's tempting to work every waking minute, work-at-home parents must set a schedule and stick to it.

■ **Not getting your own business phone with separate phone number.** A separate line makes for a professional appearance, and you'll never have to worry that your child will pick up the line by accident.

■ **Investing too much money in fancy equipment and furniture.** When Cobe first started freelancing from home, she used a door perched on top of two filing cabinets as her desk. She says she did purchase a computer, but it wasn't top of the line. Although you may want to spring for an inexpensive desk, the lesson is still clear—don't waste precious money for status items. Many of the women who Cobe and Parlapiano interviewed for the book didn't even have a home office. Most used the kitchen table or a small space set up in the laundry room.

■ **Not being professional.** Cobe tells me how often she finds a child's voice on a home-business voice mail message. Although many of your clients are bound to have kids, it's important to keep up a professional image with clients. Save the cute-kid antics for home videos.

What About the Children?

The kids got a kick out of the fact that Mom worked at home. In fact, now that I'm no longer working from home, I'm continually reminding them that I did so that they have a sense that women work, too. When they see their dad leaving for work, I say, "Mommy used to work, too, just like Daddy does."

Although you want to keep your kids away from clients and client phone calls, working from home overall serves as a great role model for your children. They can actually see you working. "A lot of kids never know what their parents are really doing in the office. But when your office is right in your house, they have a greater understanding," Cobe says. "Even though they interfere sometimes, they really see what work is about."

Parlapiano agrees. "Mompreneurs™ instill kids with entrepreneurial spirit. When you work at home, every day is Take Your Daughter (or Son) to Work Day. Kids see what it takes to build a business firsthand."

Although most mothers choose to work part-time while their kids are napping or sleeping, others try to incorporate their children to some extent by setting up a corner in Mom's office with a toy phone, paper, and markers. But children need to learn from the beginning that if your door is closed, they have to respect your work time. "It's hard for you because you hear them on the other side of the door and it's difficult to focus," Cobe admits. But she says older kids can actually help Mom by learning and executing small chores: filing, faxing, and stuffing envelopes. "But in the end, you want a chunk of time when they're not going to be in the office with you."

There are some moms who can run a home-based business without child care—they have supportive husbands who sometimes have flexible schedules, or they don't mind working late into the night when the kids are asleep—but Parlapiano and Cole feel that the absence of child care is a big mistake for moms who work from home. They insist that you must have some form of coverage, even if it's just for a few hours a day, whether it's taking your child to preschool or hiring a part-time baby-sitter. This way, they say, you know that you can devote a certain amount of time each day to making phone calls and getting work done without being distracted.

The Real Reality

You may dream of being the next Mrs. Fields or Lillian Vernon (founder of the highly successful Lillian Vernon catalog), but the reality is that most women never reach those heights. Instead, millions of women find contentment generating a small income from home all the while being able to spend more time with their children. To them, they have it all. But for those whose fantasies run grand, they need to understand the realities of starting a business from home.

First, expect that the business is not going to take off right away. It takes time to build a network and a substantial clientele. Women who recently left the corporate world to work from home should expect a cut in pay, too. For the first few years, you many not be making what you made at your last job. You'll have sporadic paychecks, and your cash flow is rarely consistent.

Finally, Cobe says not to get disillusioned if the business doesn't take off in the first year. "If you've been doing it for two years and you still haven't made much progress, then you should reconsider who your market is, or try to target the business somewhere else," she advises. Another alternative is to partner up with someone else. "That's a big trend right now," she notes. Join forces with someone whose skills you can use and who also needs your skills. If you're in desktop publishing, for example, team up with a graphic designer. "Together you can get a lot more client base."

The kids were so tuned in to my anxiety or excitement about a project that they acted up every time. They knew my focus was on something else other than them. Even when I would sit with them during lunch, they were so aware that my mind was somewhere else that they reacted to that and became so much more needy. So if you don't have help, which I didn't, the best way to handle it is to arrange play dates outside of the home, call in friends to lend a hand, or enforce an early bedtime for the duration of the project.

What About Telecommuting?

Establishing your own home-based business isn't the only way to spend more time at home while producing an income. Today, more than fifteen million people telecommute, that is, do most or part of their corporate jobs from home. With the increase in technology services like the Internet, many employees can work from home. These days, big-name companies like Merrill Lynch, Unisys, and AT&T (to name a few) are offering telecommuting as a way of attracting (or keeping) employees, and as a way to save on overhead costs such as office space.

A successful telecommuter possesses many of the same attributes as a successful entrepreneur: someone who manages her time well, is a self-starter, someone who isn't bothered by working in isolation, is self-disciplined, a person who's able to meet deadlines. Yet the biggest problem a telecommuter may face is convincing her boss that it's mutually beneficial.

If you think telecommuting is for you but you need some help in persuading your employer, start by writing a proposal detailing what you want to do, and how often (the average telecommuter works two days a week from home). Don't forget to stress the benefits to the company—less overhead costs and an increase in employee productivity. Cite examples of other successful telecommuters within the company, or within competing companies. If your boss is still hesitant, suggest a trial period of one day a week for six weeks. Even that small amount of time should be enough to get the go-ahead.

Now, Go Get 'Em!

So many opportunities, so many possibilities. If you think that an at-home business is for you, let your mind wander and create your perfect niche. "Building a business is a lot like raising a child," Parlapiano muses. "You have to be patient and nurturing, organized and disciplined, flexible and able to juggle lots of tasks at once. Moms do that every day, which is why moms make such great entrepreneurs."

Resources

Books

How to Raise a Family and a Career Under One Roof: A Parent's Guide to Home Business, by Lisa Roberts; Moon Township, PA: Bookhaven Press, 1997.

Integrating Work and Family Life: The Home-Working Family, by Betty Beach; New York: State University of New York Press, 1989.

Mompreneurs: A Mother's Practical Step-by-Step Guide to Work-at-Home Success, by Ellen H. Parlapiano and Patricia Cobe; New York: Perigee Books, 1996.

Moneymaking Moms: How Work at Home Can Work for You, by Caroline Hull and Tanya Wallace; New York: Citadel Press, 1998.

101 Best Home-Based Businesses for Women, by Priscilla Y. Huff; Rocklin, CA: Prima Publishing, 1995.

121 Internet Businesses You Can Start from Home, by Ron E. Gielgun; New York: Actium, 1998.

The Stay-at-Home Mom's Guide to Making Money: How to Create the Business That's Right for You Using the Skills and Interests You Already Have, by Liz Folger; Rocklin, CA: Prima Publishing, 1997.

Working at Home While the Kids Are There, Too, by Loriann Hoff Oberlin; Franklin Lakes, NJ: Career Press, 1997.

Organizations

Small Business Development Centers
   Call (800) 8-ASKSBA for a business development center near you.
The National Foundation for Women Business Owners
   (NFWBO)
   Silver Spring, MD 20910
   (301) 495-4975

Internet Sites

www.gohome.com—Business@Home: Making a Life While
  Making a Living
    Huge site containing articles on E-commerce and tips
    on the law, finance, and business opportunities.
www.onlinewbc.org—The Small Business Administration's
  Online Women's Business Center
    Learn how to run a business by "asking the experts"
    or connecting with other entrepreneurs.
www.gilgordon.com
    Tips on how to start telecommuting.

Index